D0977539

America in Theory

AMERICA IN THEORY

Edited by

LESLIE BERLOWITZ
DENIS DONOGHUE
LOUIS MENAND

NEW YORK   OXFORD
OXFORD UNIVERSITY PRESS
1988

Oxford University Press

Oxford   New York   Toronto
Delhi   Bombay   Calcutta   Madras   Karachi
Petaling Jaya   Singapore   Hong Kong   Tokyo
Nairobi   Dar es Salaam   Cape Town
Melbourne   Auckland
and associated companies in
Berlin   Ibadan

Copyright © 1988 by Oxford University Press, Inc.

Published by Oxford University Press, Inc.
200 Madison Avenue, New York, New York 10016

Oxford is a registered trademark of Oxford University Press

All rights reserved. No part of this publication may be reproduced,
stored in a retrieval system, or transmitted, in any form or by any
means, electronic, mechanical, photocopying, recording, or otherwise,
without prior permission of Oxford University Press.

Library of Congress Cataloging-in-Publication Data
America in theory / edited by Leslie Berlowitz,
Denis Donoghue, and Louis Menand.
p.   cm.
ISBN 0-19-505396-6
1. United States—Politics and government. 2. United States—
Politics and government—Philosophy. 3. United States—
Constitutional history. 4. Civil rights—United States—History.
I. Berlowitz, Leslie. II. Donoghue, Denis.
III. Menand, Louis.
E183.A535 1988   973'.01—dc 19
88-10083 CIP

2 4 6 8 10 9 7 5 3 1

Printed in the United States of America
on acid-free paper

ᕙ Acknowledgments ᕙ

This book was conceived to mark the tenth anniversary of the Humanities Council of New York University, which has long been committed to the development of the humanities, the advancement of interdisciplinary learning, and the role of humanistic scholarship in the public realm. Our work on this volume could not have gone forward without the encouragement of John Brademas, President of New York University, and L. Jay Oliva, Chancellor, Executive Vice President for Academic Affairs, and Co-chair of the Humanities Council. Both Brademas and Oliva have greatly contributed to the growth of the humanities at New York University. Without their enlightened leadership, projects of this kind could not be carried to completion.

Since its inception, this project has received generous funding from the Exxon Education Foundation. We would like to thank Exxon for making it possible for humanists and social scientists to contribute to public discourse on politics and culture. Our thanks go especially to Robert Payton, former president of the Exxon Education Foundation, and to Arnold Shore, current president, both of whom saw the virtue of this project and supported it.

The editors of this volume are grateful to their colleagues at New York University, including Thomas Bender, Eliot Friedson, Bert Hansen, David Richards, Richard Sennett, and Bayly Winder, as well as for the advice and counsel of Jay Kaplan and Catharine Stimpson of the New York Council for the Humanities. Some of these scholars ultimately wrote essays for *America in Theory*, while all of them helped define the problems and issues that gave rise to this volume. We are especially indebted to William Sisler, our editor at Oxford University Press, for his advice and confidence. We are grateful as well to Mary Anne Shea and William Leach for their editorial assistance.

On behalf of the Humanities Council, we want to express our gratitude to the Andrew W. Mellon Foundation, whose continued support has helped to promote interdisciplinary scholarship and learning. We are grateful as well to the Pew Memorial Trust, the Ford Foundation, the Rockefeller Foundation, and the National Endowment for the Humanities for their contributions to Council projects.

~ Contents ~

ॐ Introduction ॐ

When Federal Appeals Court Judge Robert H. Bork was nominated by Ronald Reagan in 1987 to sit on the United States Supreme Court, a volatile and engrossing public debate ensued. The debate concerned "the jurisprudence of original intent"—the doctrine, long championed by Judge Bork, that interpretations of the Constitution should be strictly guided by the specific intentions of the framers. The debate was crucial because it turned, as political debates rarely do, on hermeneutic questions, questions about intention and interpretation, meaning and understanding. The debate centered implicitly on who has the right to lay claim to the guiding myths and icons and to a true "theory of America."

Since the nineteenth century the struggle over identity and origins has distinguished the political and cultural life of all major nations. This potentially dangerous struggle has been especially problematic for Americans, who fear that they have had no past, no patriarchal traditions or customs in the European sense, no feelings of permanent rootedness and stability. Americans have often responded to this "fear" of pastlessness by making rigid assertions about the founding myths and symbols and by insisting upon the constancy of certain values which, they have argued, constitute the moral core of America. Adept leaders, from Lincoln to Reagan, have recognized this tendency and exploited it for social and political purposes.

It was in light of this quest for unifying values and myths, and their recent exploitations, that we decided to press for a scholarly reexamination of the way competing factions have used or abused the Constitution. It seemed to us that, of all American icons, the Constitution had suffered most at the hands of the simplifiers and ideologues who sought to protect it from changing interpretations and to stamp it with a divine destiny.

In the late seventies and through the eighties, the zealous simplifiers managed to get the upper hand; they dominated popular discourse on American institutions and ideas and gained positions of intellectual power and authority. In the academy, many scholars, deeply upset by these circumstances and by cutbacks in federal support of education, were on the defensive or were overtaken by feelings of disengagement. Other scholars, often in the humanities, were drawn to the study of texts, rather than of "contexts," thus reinforcing the conservative climate of the times. Fascinated by small gardens, these intellectuals neglected the larger landscape, the more pressing general concerns, the work of larger cultural and historical explication.

By organizing this volume it was our intention to view the Constitution not as an intractable text but as a "living" statement forged in an historical context. On the two hundredth anniversary of the founding of the Republic and on the eve of the forty-ninth presidential election, we wanted to raise our voices against misinterpretation and simplification.

This book of essays constitutes a broad-ranging reflection on the Constitution and gives some of our leading scholars—historians, specialists in literature and philosophy, educators, and experts in the law—a chance to express their thoughts on culture and politics. Many of the authors here take up the larger question of what it means to the culture as a whole to be able to point to a time in the past and say, Here is the founding moment, the root basis for our identity. Here, in the writing of the Declaration of Independence and the Constitution, is the seed to which all legitimate branches of the American social and political tree must trace themselves.

Not all the writers in this volume are in harmony with one another; some disagree fundamentally over the meaning of the American past, some over the individuals who helped shape American institutions and ideas. In three of the essays Thomas Jefferson is alternately viewed as a farsighted scientist, as a thinker hostile to genuine individualism, and as a great figure of liberation. These divergent perspectives on Jefferson are offered in the best spirit of intellectual inquiry; they show that no view of a complex person, idea, event, or document is totally definitive, no conviction or theory foolproof. All can command our attention in reconstructing the complex nature of original intent.

As a whole this book challenges the mythopoeic tendencies of ideologues. Far from interpreting the Constitution and the American past as linear and "one-dimensional," the writers here are sensitive to the *tensions* that shaped the past and constitutional interpretations, tensions between original intent and context, between the realistic and the utopian, between the principles of the past and the imperative needs of the present. From the very moment the Constitution was written, another "Constitution" was emerging.

This "Constitution" grows out of the demands of each new generation, out of the changing character of American society and economy, out of the shift from an isolationist to an internationalist foreign policy, and out of courageous appeals for social justice and equality on the part of women, blacks, and minorities of all kinds. It is this "second" Constitution, which is implicit in the first, that ideologues seek to dismantle and destroy, and it is this Constitution that the contributors to *America in Theory* seek to examine, defend, and preserve.

Theory

We have divided the essays in this volume into five parts: "Theory," "Rights," "Domestic Policies," "Foreign Policy," and "Epilogue." The essays on theory set the tone of the volume by refuting the idea of a unified "Theory of America" and by pointing out that the Founding Fathers were both pragmatic and suggestive. They criticize "strict constructionists" for failing to be sufficiently historical or contextual. These essays suggest that we would be mistaken to be bound by a fixed view of the past and by some exaggerated belief in the utopian idealism of the framers.

In the essay that opens the volume, "Theory and the American Founding," John Diggins asks whether there was anything approaching an abstract utopian theory held by the men who wrote the Constitution. These framers were not dreamers, says Diggins, but realists interested in confronting power and in creating a document and a government that accurately reflected the character of human experience.

David Richards's essay, "Founders' Intent and Constitutional Interpretation," bolsters Diggins's argument and shows how the Constitution evolved from a subtle interplay between theory and an interpretative sense of history. He emphasizes how devoted the framers were to practical critical thinking. Richards also believes that today's conservative ideologues have seriously misunderstood the intentions of the Founders.

In the concluding essay of this section, "New York in Theory," Thomas Bender takes us away from the realism of the Constitution to the world of founding myths. What kind of myths or theories, Bender asks, do Americans turn to to explain their origins? Do these myths accurately reflect reality and do they do justice to the urban complexity of much of American life? According to Bender, traditional American myths are inadequate to our cultural needs and must be replaced by a new myth, by an urban "theory of New York" that captures and celebrates cosmopolitanism and diversity.

Rights

Over the years there have been many disputes about what kind of rights are protected in the Constitution and what kinds are not. Was the Constitution meant to be a flexible document designed to incorporate the rights of many groups? Or was the Constitution written only with a core set of rights—such as freedom of religion—and an exclusive group in mind?

In the essay on "Equality," J. R. Pole confronts these issues head on by claiming that the idea of "equality of rights" lay at the heart of the Constitution and, therefore, at the heart of the American political system. Equality for all people, he says, is an ideal inherent in the Constitution; the only problem Americans have had is in translating the ideal into action. At the same time, in a controversial argument, Pole denies that affirmative action is consistent with the traditional idea of equality in American life.

John Sexton demonstrates how central the constitutional right to religious freedom is and how easily it can be violated, in spite of the fact that the Constitution explicitly guarantees it. He argues that the equilibrium that has long existed between American religions and the State has been jeopardized recently by the failure of American courts to resolve the controversy over how to interpret the religion clauses of the First Amendment.

The essays that follow deal with inherent rights or those rights that are implicit in American political thinking but cannot be linked to the 1787 Constitution (although addressed in later amendments). Deborah Rhode discusses the difficulties women have had, from the early nineteenth century into our own times, in claiming the legacy of constitutional rights. The battle has been even grimmer for blacks, as Nell Painter writes in her essay, describing how Southern blacks have struggled to maintain a hold, in face of opposition from the Reagan administration, on the civil rights achievements of the 1960s.

Can a woman's right to an abortion be justified on constitutional grounds? Can affirmative action? Is the right to privacy constitutionally assured, even though the Constitution never mentions it? Norman Dorsen affirmatively answers these questions in his essay "Rights in Theory, Rights in Practice." Dorsen blasts Meese and Reagan for arguing to the contrary and for clinging to interpretations based solely on "original intentions." Like David Richards, he is certain that the Constitution was meant to be understood in a way congruent with the changing needs of men and women.

Domestic Policies

"Domestic Policies" provides a multifaceted picture of how Americans have succeeded or failed in fulfilling some of the political and social promises inherent in the Constitution and the Bill of Rights. The Founding Fathers were silent on such matters as universal public education and about such concrete rights as the right to health and welfare. Nonetheless, these entitlements have become part of the American political agenda. Each of the essays in this part suggests that American policies on such issues as health, education, social welfare, and science have been disappointing, especially in the Reagan years.

In his essay "Jefferson, Science, and National Destiny," Gerald Holton shows how the ideas of Thomas Jefferson on science and scientific inquiry represented a remarkable blend of the pursuit of knowledge for its own sake with the need to protect and strengthen the national interest. Holton believes that modern national policies on science are narrow and insufficient to our needs and that policy-makers would benefit from a look at Jefferson's ideas.

The next four essays underscore the problems besetting American policies on education, health, and social welfare. Daniel Fox describes the weakening of the public health sector, which historically has been a privileged domain but was undermined by the conservative commitment to market individualism and by the abandonment of federal responsibility to maintain the general welfare. The state of education, John Brademas and Michael Katz contend, is also no cause for rejoicing. Brademas, who spent twenty-two years in Congress leading the fight for support of educational programs, reveals the consequences of Ronald Reagan's slashes in federal funds to education. He urges a return to common sense, to quality education, and to responsible intervention on the part of the federal government.

Michael Katz finds modern educational policies bankrupt. He deplores what he calls the "meritocratic bias" of American education and its profound failure, at all levels, to deal with the needs of people without property and power. Katz underscores the contradiction between the American failure to give all peoples access to the educational system and the promise of equality and human dignity articulated in the Constitution and the Bill of Rights.

"Philanthropy as Moral Discourse," the essay by Robert Payton, examines the origins of modern American social welfare practice. According to Payton, it is philanthropy, not the federal government or the marketplace, that has spawned the moral ideas leading to social welfare policy. Payton maintains that it is the philanthropic tradition of this nation that has located the moral problems in society and illuminated the "gap between the ideal and the actual."

Foreign Policy

In the practice of foreign diplomacy Americans have often reached beyond the domain of constitutional principles to astonish the world with unrealistic and even irrational behavior. As the American role of international watchdog has expanded, so too has the power of the executive branch, thus contributing to the destabilization of the constitutional balance of powers. This development and the consequences of America's commitment to "manifest destiny" are the underlying themes of the section "Foreign Policy."

In his essay "The True Sentiments of America," Denis Donoghue criticizes the Founding Fathers more vigorously than any of the previous essayists. Indeed, he traces to such leaders as John Adams two basically dangerous beliefs—a millennial conviction that Americans are destined to save the world from corruption and tyranny, and a belief that Americans are "exceptional" individuals outside history and culture and obedient to no one. Such convictions, Donoghue contends, have produced a huge imperialistic apparatus and fueled a foreign policy that has threatened the stability and peace of the world.

James Chace describes the evolution of the United States from an isolationist nation to an expansionist giant and focuses on the moral criteria used to justify this transformation. In his "Dreams of Perfectibility: American Exceptionalism and the Search for a Moral Foreign Policy," Chace claims that the American "dream of perfectibility" and the desire to play a role of crusader and exemplar in the world has haunted and often wrecked American foreign policy over the course of many administrations.

In the essay "Presidents and Nuclear Weapons and Truth: Some Examples, from Roosevelt to Nixon," McGeorge Bundy concludes the section with a lucid assessment of the way American presidents have handled nuclear weapons. He makes clear that atomic arms are irrelevant ultimately to the resolution or solution of international disputes. Bundy observes the enormity of modern presidential powers and responsibilities in an age of dangerous technologies. Like the other writers in this volume, he encourages us to find new solutions that reflect the demands of our times and are in the spirit of the "second Constitution."

⁂

ALTHOUGH E. L. DOCTOROW'S THOUGHTS COME at the end of the volume in the epilogue, they deal eloquently with the beginning. Doctorow takes the reader through the history of the creation of the Constitution. He writes of the men who dared to write the Constitution and of the men who fostered the revolutionary climate, men like Jefferson, who, in Doctorow's estimate, possessed "the radical voice of national liberation." Doctorow reminds us how astonishing it was that the nation's greatest national document, as well as the very phrase "we the people," emerged out of the near chaos and conflict of the colonial period.

The essays in this volume are a tribute to the dynamic quality of American life and thought. They call upon us to avoid the simplifications of ideology and extremism. They urge succeeding generations to return to the founding documents and to find within them a frame of broad intent and confidence in the power of reason to govern and effect change. They challenge us to read and to interpret the Constitution through a thoughtful and informed historical perspective, if we are to capture the "theory of America."

New York
March 1988

L.C.B.

I

THEORY

Theory and the
American Founding

JOHN PATRICK DIGGINS

Ever since the eighteenth century American political thinkers have sought to resolve two questions: Does the American Republic have an essential meaning? And what is America's relationship to the rest of the world in the light of its meaning and purpose? As if these questions were not ambitious enough, there is also a third, which has received less attention, though it is implicated in any attempt to answer the first two. Was America consciously founded on a specific theoretical basis, or did it evolve organically from tradition and practical experience? The question of theory versus experience yields still a further one that bears upon the first two. Whether America was founded upon abstract doctrine and ideology or developed from custom and seamless processes, can we explain it by returning to and grasping the deliberate intentions of its Founders?

Any effort to discuss the place of theory in American history must begin with a definition of that elusive term. In the original Greek, *theoria* implied the act of seeing, with the suggestion that beholding and contemplation preceded action. With the rise of scientific thought, however, theory could not so readily be separated from practice, since empirical knowledge required verification. In modern scientific philosophy, especially the pragmatism developed by John Dewey, it was even conceded that the object of knowledge is transformed by the experimental methods employed in the process of knowing it. The framers of the Constitution, influenced by Locke and Hume as well as Montesquieu, were fully aware of such epistemological issues, which rendered problematic the relationship of the knower to the known. They were also aware of the modern problem of trying to interpret political conduct through political ideas and the "cloudy" medium of language, which distorts communication. Unlike Thomas Jefferson, those who either drafted or defended the Constitution—Alexander Hamilton, James Madison, John Adams, and others—rarely invoked the notion of "self-evident" truths. In what sense, then, were they theorists?

The framers were convinced, first of all, that the Constitution should be adopted after the arguments for its ratification had been made, arguments that purported to present a reasoned, systematic view of the problems facing the country. Thus Hamilton begins *Federalist* number 1 by challenging Americans to consider the body of principles to be set forth and to ask themselves "whether societies of men are really capable or not of establishing good government from reflection or choice, or whether they are forever destined to depend for their political constitutions on accident and force." Aside from asking readers to exercise the faculties of mind, the framers were theorists of power as opposed to morality. For they did not set out to judge history by some external standard, the domain of the speculatist and idealist; rather, they were realists who translated the data of history into the problem of power and its control. Such an effort required what contemporary philosophers call "action theory," an understanding of the causes, motives, and "springs" of human action without which the political thinker is helpless to preserve liberty by balancing power. In this enterprise they rejected "reason" in favor of "experience" as their guide. But they also recognized that historical experience provided insufficient evidence of the success of republican forms of government, and the decline and fall of Rome haunted them no less than it did Edward Gibbon. Thus the American "experiment" would be based upon "the new science of politics," which predicted not how men ought to act but how they would act. In this bold endeavor, the framers believed they could draw upon the "maxims of geometry" and other scientific theories to establish explanations of behavior and power that would make possible their political control.

The precise nature of this daring "experiment" has become the subject of intense controversy in recent historiography. Were its origins in ancient classical republicanism, the Scottish Enlightenment, New England Calvinism, or modern liberalism and economic individualism? The question of the origins and meaning of America is presently being debated by exponents of these discrete schools of thought.[1] But another question has gone relatively unexplored. What would be the role of "theory" in the new Republic after its founding? More specifically, would the theorist as intellectual have any role?

In the *Federalist* Madison addresses this question directly. The anti-Federalists, in addition to denying the need for a new centralized government, had been arguing that many structural mechanisms of the Constitution were also not needed to control power and adjudicate clashing interests. Such problems as "factions," they contended, could be handled in the future by men of superior learning. "It is vain," Madison replies to this argument, "to say that enlightened statesmen will be able to adjust these clashing interests, and render them all subservient to the public good. Enlightened statesmen will not always be at the helm."[2] Here clearly is a curious combination of pride and prescience. Although the framers' generation saw itself as one of reason and virtue, its leaders felt that they must use their talents to construct a Constitution that would not have need of men of such caliber, for America could never again count upon their appearance. Henceforth it would be not the moral qualities of man but the "machinery of government" that would perpetuate the Republic. The American framers did not see the intellectual as the one member of society capable of rising above mundane concerns to offer an enlightened and disinterested perspective. Even though Hamilton hoped that the "rich, well-born, and able" might serve the Republic as administrators, Adams gave ample reason, in his *Defence of the Constitutions*, why an "aristocracy" was not to be trusted as leaders under any circumstances. Thus it took intellectual men of letters to conceive of a new system of government that would not require the activity of intellect to run it.

The skeptical conclusions of the framers yield two implications that deserve comment; one relates to the matter of theory, the other to America's relationship with the world. It could be said that with the American framers the authority of theory and political philosophy comes to an end, or at least enters a modern phase in which the older promise of politics and civic virtue can no longer be counted upon to command the citizens' obedience. Although the Federalist authors were steeped in the classics, they departed from Aristotle's dictum that political man can overcome the imperfections of natural man. In Adams and Madison there is no suggestion that politics provides the means by which a rational society could be ordered, and Hamilton felt the same doubts about commerce and enterprise functioning independently of government surveillance. The turbulent "passions and interests" are "sown in the nature of man"; hence the causes of factions can never be eliminated but can only be controlled. Those who think otherwise, who want to bring about uniformity and deny that diversity is the essence of liberty are, Madison warned, "theoretic politicians."[3]

The second implication involves the issue of American exceptionalism. The Federalist authors, and Adams in particular, scarcely glimpsed the peculiar conditions of American society that would make the New World unique. Curiously, many of the rebels had done so in 1776. Such figures as Gouverneur Morris, John Adams, and Samuel Adams had insisted that the American Revolution was sui generis and incapable of being emulated by France and the Old World. When it came to writing the Constitution, however, the Federalists saw many problems of the Old World being replicated in the New, and thus they went to the Philadelphia convention in 1787 to draft a constitution for a country seething with class conflict. Their assumptions about the antagonisms between the few and the many and the necessity of a "mixed" government to balance conflict may have proved ill-founded, as Alexis de Tocqueville would later point out. But the framers were consistent in rejecting politics and political theory, whether in America or in Europe, as redemptive. Thus America had little to teach the Old World other than avoiding its mistakes and regarding history as the study of power and corruption—teaching by bad examples. To be sure, there remained in America a residue of messianism that could lead to a righteous arrogance about the nation's superior virtue and a "mission" to spread its way of life to the four corners of the earth. But the framers themselves doubted that America would be morally exemplary. There was "no special providence for Americans," observed Adams after the élan of revolutionary years had subsided, "and their nature is the same as that of others." To Hamilton the universality of the "fallen" human condition was obvious to everyone except those who had succumbed to the deceits of doctrines and theories.

> Have we not already seen enough of the fallacy and extravagance of those idle theories which have amused us with promises of an exemption from the imperfections, weaknesses, and evils incident to society in every shape? Is it not time to awake from the deceitful dream of a golden age, and to adopt as a practical maxim for the direction of our political conduct that we, as well as other inhabitants of the globe, are yet removed from the happy empire of perfect wisdom and perfect virtue?[4]

The twofold thesis of the framers—that political theory would not be needed after the founding and that America would not be exceptional but would instead be subject to the same corruptions as the Old World—was contested almost as soon as it was articulated. Many French writers, though critical of the new Constitution, had hailed the American Revolution and its political accomplishments as the fruit of the Enlightenment's theories, the triumph of "liberty, virtue, and reason" over "prejudice, dogma, and superstition."[5] Edmund Burke, in contrast, defended both the American Revolution and the Constitution as the natural outgrowth of customs and habits rooted in British legal traditions. To Burke, the stability of political institutions was due not to the innovations of abstract theory but to the unseen force of convention and repetition. So great was Burke's desire to defend a traditionalist interpretation of political liberty against a rationalist counterinterpretation that he not only equated validity with antiquity but also insisted that the origins of government must remain veiled in secrecy.[6]

In American history, however, generations of intellectuals have probed the origins of their government, and their findings seemed only to have reinforced their suspicion that they had been excluded from the constitutional system bequeathed to them by the Founders. Ralph Waldo Emerson and Henry David Thoreau complained that the "machinery of government" condemned human nature to forever distrusting the self and stunting the "oversoul." James Russell Lowell may not have gone so far as to protest that the framers had their priorities wrong when they made property, instead of morality, the object of government, but he, too, concluded that the Constitution was "a machine that would go of itself" and thus had no place for men of theory and vision. Abraham Lincoln called upon Americans to reconceive the origins of the Republic and to look to the Declaration of Independence, not the Constitution, as foundational, since it is in the former document that the principles of equality and natural right are grounded. Woodrow Wilson, displeased with what he took to be the fixed, mechanistic structural assumptions of the framers, wanted a government based on the principles of growth and adaptation, a government "accountable to Darwin, not to Newton." Walter Lippmann wanted to see government as something more than a system of rules and routines that left untouched man's moral and aesthetic nature.[7]

All such thinkers were theorists in that they wanted to see government accountable to ideas. To them, theory was the liberating faculty that enabled the mind to conceive of government and history as something more elevating than the inexorability of interests and power. If America's political institutions had indeed been influenced by conscious theoretical premises, as opposed to a Burkean grounding in prerational tradition, then America might be able to engage the world in some form of intellectual discourse. Hence the question: Did theory have an important role in American history? The remainder of this essay will deal with Daniel J. Boorstin, who denies the importance of theory; Hannah Arendt, who affirms it; Henry Adams, who wants to believe in theory but in the end cannot; and Alexis de Tocqueville, who asks Americans to rethink the theoretical foundations of their Republic.

HEGEL'S NOTION OF the "cunning" of history seems to plague Daniel J. Boorstin's illustrious career. Having written in the fifties several articles and books that downplayed the importance of book-learned ideas in early American history, he found himself in the eighties, as Librarian of Congress, going before legislative committees to ask for further budget allocations on the grounds that books are vital to America's culture.[8] Boorstin's earlier assault on abstract "ideas" and "theories" was, of course, part of a general assault on the bugaboo of "ideology" that haunted the Cold War generation, whose members, many of them former radicals, had witnessed the horrors of totalitarianism. Daniel Bell's well-known "end of ideology" declaration was accompanied by a pervasive critique of the communist mentality as "a mania of absolutism" (Reinhold Niebuhr), the curse of the "monist and dogmatist" (Arthur Schlesinger, Jr.), the "tyranny of logicality" (Hannah Arendt), and the translation of "universal principles" into their "utter depravity in action" (Hans Morgenthau).[9] Fair enough; one can understand the bitter disillusionment with radical political ideas that afflicted that "twice-born" generation, which, as Bell poignantly put it, grew old before its time.

But the equation of ideology with "fanaticism" pure and simple—the argument of Eric Hoffer's widely read *The True Believer*—played havoc with intellectual history. In the eighteenth century Jefferson and others had no difficulty accepting Destutt de Tracy's concept of ideology as simply the scientific study of ideas and the social phenomena they represent. The concept, to be sure, did not impress John Adams, who dismissed it as "idiocy." But then what could?

> I have been a Lover and a Reader of Romances all my life. From Don Quixote and Gill Blas to the Scottish Chiefs and a hundred others.
>
> For the last year or two I have devoted myself to this kind of Study: and have read 15 Volumes of Grim, Seven Volumes of Tuckers Neddy Search and 12 Volumes of Dupuis besides a 13th of plates and Traceys Analysis, and 4 Volumes of Jesuitical History! Romances all! I have learned nothing of importance to me, for they have made no Change in my moral or religious Creed, which has for 50 or 60 Years been contained in four short words *"Be just and good."* In this result they all agree with me.
>
> My conclusion from all of them is Universal Tolleration.[10]

Adams boasts to Jefferson of the number of books he has read to indicate which did or did not influence his thinking. Boorstin, in contrast, advises the intellectual historian that he is mistaken to assume that "in a period like the eighteenth century the content of a man's library was roughly the same as the content of his mind." American thinkers like Adams and Jefferson, Boorstin insists, learned primarily "from common experience in their particular place, rather than from books or the ideas of distant philosophers."[11]

Boorstin's minimizing of the philosophical curiosity of early American thinkers and his dismissal of the Enlightenment as a "myth" on this side of the Atlantic were part of an effort to deny any role for the theoretical mind in America's founding. His *The Genius of American Politics* (1953) rhapsodically described an American mind that ever accommodated itself to a changing environment. The chapter on the Puritans ("From Providence to Pride") would have readers believe that the first settlers happily accepted their transformation from Calvinists to Yankees with scarcely any sense of loss or betrayal of their earlier spiritual ideals, as indicated in the jeremiads that so fascinated Perry Miller. The chapter on the Revolution ("Revolution Without Dogma") depicts the episode as a pedestrian affair of legal technicalities and practical politics. As to the Constitution, it too required no exercise in political philosophy but merely "an unspoken assumption, an axiom, so basic to our thinking that we have hardly been aware of it at all. This is the axiom that institutions are not and should not be the grand creations of men toward large ends and outspoken values; rather they are organisms which grow out of the soil in which they are rooted and out of the tradition from which they have sprung." Because the American people respond primarily to the "whisperings" of the environment rather than to the temptations of the intellect, because their history is "doctrinally naked," the Constitution was born before it was conceived and thus "the American future was never to be contained in a theory."[12]

Boorstin made no attempt to conceal that his notion of the "genius" of the American people aimed to render them immune to the "garret-spawned" ideologies that presumably were responsible for fascism and communism. Yet embedded in his argument lies an embarrassing paradox. While it purports to disavow every semblance of theory and ideology, the argument itself rests on a mode of reasoning that is nothing if not theoretical.

Americans had no need of theory, Boorstin contended, because the raw experiences of the natural environment shaped the mind. Thus early Americans, having abandoned unworkable doctrines like Calvinism, came to accept the "growing sense of 'givenness,' the growing tendency to make the 'is' the guide to the 'ought,' to make America as it was (or as they now made it) a criterion of what America might be." The concept of "givenness" builds upon another theoretical concept, that of "the preformational ideal"—the notion that values existed in a "perfectly preformed theory" that rendered unnecessary the reflective activity of mind. It is "the idea that all parts of an organism pre-exist in perfect miniature in the seed. . . . It assumes that the values and theory of the nation were given once and for all at the very beginning." On top of the "preformational" concept is still another, one that could lead Americans into believing that they were growing not out of but into a theory: "Our theory of society is thus conceived as a kind of exoskeleton, like the shell of a lobster. We think of ourselves as growing *into* our skeleton, filling it out with the experience and resources of recent ages. But we always supposed that the outlines were rigidly drawn in the beginning."[13]

It is at once consoling and disturbing to see the American mind celebrated for its mindlessness. For Boorstin is not the first philosopher of history to reconcile the "is" and the "ought" in order to give ontological priority to doing over being and to action over thinking. The entire edifice of his argument is strikingly similar to Hegel's concept of the "Preformation Hypothesis," upon which Marxism builds its theory of history. Hegel's description of the organic unity of the "bud" and the "blossom" as a means of dramatizing the continuity within all change has its echo in Boorstin's worship of the "unity of our history" and his conviction that American institutions were not conceived, but somehow sprouted as "organisms which grow out of the soil in which they are rooted and out of the tradition from which they have sprung." Hegel advised the historian that "thought must be subordinated to what is given, to what is real."[14] But Hegel no less than Boorstin derided theory and philosophy, because the Enlightenment mind, like the owl of Minerva, gets too late a start to do any good. And Boorstin was not the first to dismiss ideology as a snare and a delusion. Did not Marx denounce it as the "illusion of an epoch"?

Those who categorized Boorstin as a "consensus" historian were obviously dissociating him from Charles Beard, Marx, and the theory of class conflict. Yet the consensus was broad enough to allow Boorstin to agree with Marx that the scholar cannot grasp the meaning of historical events by reading political doctrine. One author who would disagree emphatically with that position is Hannah Arendt. Although Arendt, like Boorstin, was responding to the "tyranny" of European ideology and totalitarianism, although she too made comparative analyses between the New World and the Old, and although she also favored the life of action to contemplation, Arendt sought to emphasize the extent to which the framers were influenced by European political thought in order to give the American Republic theoretical credentials.

IN *On Revolution* (1963), ARENDT AGREES with Boorstin that America's colonial experience with English legal traditions was important, but she rejects his argument that the American mind is inherently antitheoretical. Even though thinkers like Adams and Jefferson distrusted metaphysical philosophy, they and others were willing to "consult books for guidance to action." More important, the Declaration of Independence and the constitution-making that took place in the thirteen colonies are evidence that "the inhabitants of this world spoke and thought in terms of the Old World and referred to the same sources for inspiration and confirmation of their theories."[15] But why, if the colonists drew upon Old World ideas, did the eighteenth-century revolutions succeed only in the New World? For Arendt, what explains the success of American politics is not the absence of theory but the absence of "the social question," the problem of misery and poverty, the solution of which led the French revolutionaries to push far beyond their original political goals and in the process to betray their original ideals. Arendt's argument is questionable when one considers the threatening presence of class conflict in *The Federalist*—not necessarily Marx's specter but the authors' fear that unless majority factions were controlled there would arise "a rage for paper money, for the abolition of debts, for an equal division of property, or for any other improper or wicked project."[16] Why the framers were possessed of such fears remains a problem for which only Tocqueville seems to have had an explanation, and he suggests, as we shall see, that both the fears and the theories on which they were based were misplaced.

But it was Arendt who first saw that the Constitution is primarily about not only liberty (Tocqueville) or even property (Beard) but power. The colonists, wanting to limit the authority of the Crown and Parliament, faced a power vacuum after the Revolution, when America became what Hamilton called "an awful spectacle"—a nation without a national government. Arendt admires Adams and the Federalists for unlocking the secret of power by showing how it can be simultaneously augmented and arrested. In relocating power in the new central government, the Federalists made it possible both for Congress and the executive to exercise power and for it to be controlled through the system of checks and balances among the departments of government, bicameral representation in the legislature, and judicial surveillance on the part of the Supreme Court. Yet, having overcome the impotence of the Articles of Confederation, the Constitution resolved the problem of power but not that of freedom. To grasp the nature of freedom, Arendt shifts her admiration from Adams to Jefferson, and here her study drifts off into never-never land.

Implicit in Arendt's interpretation of the American Republic are two theories involving the nature of politics and the nature of revolution. The first was elaborated in *The Human Condition* (1958), where she drew a distinction between work and labor on the one hand and politics and governance on the other. The distinction was addressed in part to Marxism, which had invested the working class with the "mission" of history. But it also had implications for the liberal tradition, which had drawn upon the Lockean idea of labor as the means by which man creates value. The trouble with *animal laborans*, according to Arendt, is that all productive work merely answers to the needs of the body and thus can never rise above the level of biological necessity that confines man to the private realm of existence. Politics, in contrast, brings man into the public realm, where he relates to fellow human beings without the mediation of things but simply through speech and action. Having identified classical, participatory politics as the highest of human activities, Arendt then proceeded in *On Revolution* to identify freedom with the ability to begin and inaugurate, with "the act of founding." Arendt believed she could see such a phenomenon flowering in the town meetings during the Revolution and, afterward, in the small, decentralized state governments that characterized the Articles of Confederation. But the spirit of the Revolution, which created the organs of "public space" that made possible local politics, became America's "lost treasure." The vital participatory ethos on which freedom was founded failed to become incorporated into the Constitution, which, as Charles Beard and the Progressive historians had earlier pointed out, had more to do with controlling democracy than with expressing it.[17]

Thus Arendt's heroes are Jefferson, Paine, and the anti-Federalists, those who resisted the consolidation of power in the new Constitution. It never seems to have occurred to her that Jefferson and Paine placed little value on politics and wanted to see the scope of political authority reduced to a minimum, at times going so far as to identify the best form of government as that which "governs least." Even anti-Federalists who wrapped themselves in classical garb, like the pseudonymous "Cato," had reasons for opposing the new Constitution that would warm the cockles of Ronald Reagan's heart. "I know there are politicians who believe you should be loaded with taxes, in order to make you more industrious . . . but it is an erroneous principle. For what can inspire you with industry if the greatest measure of your labor are to be swallowed up in taxes?"[18] Not only did the anti-Federalists value labor and its rewards more than politics and its demands, they were also distrustful of democracy and believed the Constitution needed more, not fewer, checks to control the branches of government. No doubt their lasting contribution to the Constitution was their demand that a bill of rights be included, but such a demand had more to do with preserving what Isaiah Berlin has called "negative" liberty than with "positive" liberty. The anti-Federalists were less interested in securing the ability to participate in government than in resisting it. No wonder Cecelia Kenyon described them as "men of little faith."[19] Even the Virginian anti-Federalists who demanded the Bill of Rights, George Mason and Patrick Henry, feared the new Constitution would allow the North to predominate and would threaten not only state sovereignty but black slavery.

If Jefferson had his own private agonies about slavery, he never lost faith in democracy and human nature. Yet Arendt's attempt to develop a theory of political freedom on the basis of Jeffersonian ideology must be judged as desperate as Boorstin's attempt to save the Founders from the disease of all theory. In view of Jefferson's warm response to the Shays uprising, which chilled the spines of the Federalists, and in view of his conviction that the tree of liberty needed to be "bathed" in the blood of rebellion each generation, Arendt had good reason to hold up Jefferson as the exemplar of revolutionary revitalization. She was delighted to discover among his personal writings a reference to Cato's injunction "to divide the country into wards." In *On Revolution* she uses Jefferson's reference to the "ward system" to establish him as the supreme philosopher of freedom, and the Arendtian definition of freedom is the continuous reenactment of the founding at the most local level of spontaneous political activity:

Jefferson himself knew well enough that what he proposed as the "salvation of the republic" actually was the salvation of the revolutionary spirit through the republic. His expositions of the ward system always began with a reminder of how "the vigor given to our revolution in its commencement" was due to the "little republics," how they had "thrown the whole nation into energetic action," and how, at a later occasion, he had felt "the foundations of government shaken under his feet by the New England townships," "the energy of this organization" being so great that "there was not an individual in the States whose body was not thrown with all its momentum into action." Hence, he expected wards to permit citizens to continue to do what they had been able to do during the years of revolution, namely, to act on their own and thus to participate in public business as it was being transacted from day to day. By virtue of the Constitution, the public business of the nation as a whole had been transferred to Washington and was being transacted by the federal government, of which Jefferson still thought as "the foreign branch" of the republic, whose domestic affairs were taken care of by the state governments.[20]

Arendt's conviction that freedom has its birth in the spontaneity of small-group activity had wide appeal for the New Left of the sixties, whose members assumed that students could begin the revolution by taking over the campus and then the neighborhood. Jefferson, it is true, did advocate the need for generational rebellion, but not necessarily for the reasons Arendt claims. "The basic assumption of the ward system, whether Jefferson knew it or not, was that no one could be called happy without his share in public happiness, that no one could be called free without his experience in public freedom, and that no one could be called either happy or free without participating, and having a share, in public power." Actually there is no mention of "public" at all in Jefferson's discussion of wards:

It is not by the consolidation, or concentration of powers, but by their distribution, that good government is effected. Were not this great country already divided into States, that division must be made, that each might do for itself what concerns itself directly, and what it can do so much better than a distant authority. Every State is again divided into counties, each to take care of what lies within local bounds: each county again into townships or wards, to manage minute details; and every ward into farms, to be governed by its individual proprietor. Were we directed from Washington when to sow, and when to reap, we should soon want bread. It is by this partition of cares, descending in gradation from general to particular, that the mass of human affairs may be best managed, for the good and prosperity of all.[21]

Instead of defining freedom as the ability to participate in the noble life of political action, Jefferson identified it as the autonomous individual growing his crops and managing his own affairs. Arendt's classical prejudice against work and labor in favor of politics and government is totally alien to America's essentially liberal political culture. In the eighteenth century that culture had been inspired by the Lockean conviction that productive man was moral man and the Jeffersonian conviction that men were freer, happier, and more just when farming than when working at any other occupation, including government, which he found "oppressive."[22] Freedom required property, not politics.

However questionable was Arendt's neoclassical interpretation of America's founding, she did hint that America had something to teach the world. She found it odd that in modern political thought the American Revolution is dismissed as provincial, whereas the French Revolution is esteemed for its worldwide repercussions even though it ended in disaster. Apparently she did not believe that American exceptionalism rendered American political theory completely irrelevant to the rest of the world. Just before her death she had been steeped in the writings of John Adams, who had predicted the course of the French Revolution several years before Burke's better-known reflections. But her real affinity was with Jefferson and localism, and that legacy had been lost forever.

IT IS CURIOUS that Arendt, who never left the contemplative solitude of her American academic life to participate in public affairs, remained so convinced that the only noble vocation is politics. Other intellectuals who have experienced directly the real world of politics, writers like Conor Cruise O'Brien and Daniel Patrick Moynihan, have said that they hardly know which is worse, its monotony or its mendacity.[23] But one American intellectual who knew more about politics than he could stomach, and who also knew that politics itself kills theory, was Henry Adams, the historian who also knew what Arendt never wanted to consider—that Jeffersonianism died at the hands of Jefferson himself.

Today Henry Adams is attacked from both ends of the political spectrum. The Left suspects him of being an elitist trying to prop up the "hegemony" of the capitalist order, and the neoconservatives flay him for his alleged "hatred" of America.[24] It is good to see the Left and Right agreeing on something, but the Adams who spent the last years of his life plotting a scheme of "chaos" and "entropy" did more to undermine the idea of order than Marx himself, and a scholar who spent his earlier years writing more than a dozen volumes on American history perhaps loved his country too much not to be disappointed by its unfulfilled promises.

At the most philosophical level, Adams's disappointment with America arose from his discovery that history, defined as "the movement of power," had eluded and defied the theoretical constructions that promised to control it. In his monumental nine-volume *History of the United States of America during the Administrations of Thomas Jefferson and James Madison* (1889–91) and his lesser-known *The Life of Albert Gallatin* (1879), Adams follows the course of the Jeffersonian Republican party to show how sixteen years of history leaves it unrecognizable, without a theory, identity, or purpose. Assuming that they formed the party of idealism, the Republicans declared, in Adams's words, that "government must be ruled by principles; to which the Federalists answered that government must be ruled by circumstances." The theoretical principles of the Republicans had their roots in agricultural Virginia, where Jefferson had instructed Americans that "those who labor in the earth are the chosen people of God" and the depository of "genuine virtue." Jefferson suffered, Adams observed, from "the temptation of omniscience," the tendency to see all reality from a single value system and to regard Virginia as "the typical society of a future Arcadian America. To escape the tyranny of Caesar by perpetuating the simple and isolated lives of their fathers was the sum of their philosophy."[25]

Nothing appalled Adams more than the spectacle of statesmen enunciating one set of principles when out of office and, once in the White House, embarking upon an entirely different course of action. Thus Jefferson the philosopher and Jefferson the president become for Adams almost separate entities. The philosopher wanted to preserve the values of rural life in the name of Republican simplicity, to restrict the power of the national government in the interest of human liberty, and to uphold the principle of state sovereignty as the best guardian of the will of the majority. The philosopher also distrusted the power of the executive and the Supreme Court, and he called for a reduction in taxes and of the national debt and for the elimination of the tariff and the Bank of the United States. Jefferson the president, however, violated his own principles in allowing the old Federalist banking system to remain and the debt to increase, in failing to revise the Judiciary Act, and, most of all, in negotiating the Louisiana Purchase without the advice and consent of Congress or the states—a move that boldly expanded executive power, negated the philosopher's own strict construction of the Constitution, and ensured that America would be a continental empire in which the precious "ward system" and "Little Republics" would be more irrelevant than ever.

Today, libertarian conservatives have become impatient with President Reagan for allowing many programs to stand that he had promised to eliminate. It was not for nothing that former Budget Director David Stockman titled his memoir *The Triumph of Politics*. "There is a startling disconnection between Reagan the campaigner, the scourge of big government, and Reagan the chief executive officer of the American government," Stockman has recently complained in an interview. "There is no consistent, credible or serious intellectual content to Reaganism, only a very popular kind of rhetoric—and by content I mean ideas." Asked what he now thinks of Reagan's "new beginning," Stockman replied: "The gap between Reagan's policy position and his public rhetoric is wider by orders of magnitude than in any administration we've ever experienced."[26] Those who know little history can be granted a little hyperbole.

Adams, it should be noted, was not complaining that Jefferson failed to carry out his promise to dismantle the government. He was not opposed to federal programs that would enhance public authority over the private realm—indeed, his ancestors Presidents John Adams and John Quincy Adams advocated such programs. What he wanted were statesmen with a consistent theory of government, so that principle would guide conduct and theory control power. Instead, he observed in Jefferson's America politicians in both parties who "care nothing for fine-spun theories of what government might or might not do, providing government did what they wanted."[27]

Any hope that theory and political ideas could influence interests and power collapses in Adams's America. In the *History* he shows how the fateful course of events in Napoleon's Europe forced Jefferson and his followers to adopt domestic policies more autocratic and sweeping than Hamiltonianism at its boldest: an embargo that violated state sovereignty, revenue and financial measures that drained the economy, and manufacturing that spelled ruin to arcadian America. As the needless War of 1812 approached, Jefferson and successor James Madison had to compromise their old classical aversion to war and standing armies, which once had been seen as the beginning of imperialism and the end of republicanism. Again and again the forces of history compelled Americans to abandon old doctrines, but between 1800 and 1816 not one important thinker came forth with a new theory of politics. Henceforth the American mind would adapt to change and yield to reality, and history would be determined not by theory but by the inexorable movement of interests and power.

In recent times Henry Adams has been all but ignored by American historians and appreciated mainly by philosophers and literary critics. More humanistic scholars treat *The Education of Henry Adams* and *Mont-St. Michel and Chartres* as works of art confronting the chilling meaninglessness of the twentieth century. Literary critics in particular admire Adams's strategy of impersonal narration, his view of the relentless movement of power and the causeless indeterminacy behind it, and his brilliant and witty sense of irony, which may be the mind's ability to deal with the wounds of the heart. But before Adams became disillusioned with the limitations of the mind he had become even more disillusioned with the activity that Arendt claimed would nurture character, nobility, and public spirit—politics.

During the Civil War Adams assisted his father, Charles Francis Adams, who served as Lincoln's minister to England. After the war Henry worked in Washington as a journalist, where he did what today would be called "investigative reporting" on corruption and civil-service reform. It was not only the "machines," "bosses," and "rings" that sullied American politics; Adams saw that American politics could never be elevating, because the party system itself presupposed the division and factionalism that classical republicanism had regarded destructive to the public good.

Since parties meant opposing forces struggling for domination, politics had more to do with opportunity than with duty, and politicians themselves behaved as though they were characters in an Edward Albee play. Of Senators William Seward and Charles Sumner, Adams observed: "The two men would have disliked each other by instinct had they lived in different planets. Each was created only for exasperating the other; the virtues of one were the faults of his rival, until no good quality seemed to remain of either. That the public service must suffer was certain." If the ruling passion of a democracy is "envy," according to Tocqueville, then Adams had every reason to conclude that politics could never be anything more than "the systematic organization of hatreds."[28]

IN THE *Education* ADAMS CONCLUDED that "the moral law had expired—like the Constitution," so convinced was he that "the system of 1789 had broken down, and with it the eighteenth-century fabric of a priori, or moral principle."[29] The conclusion must be qualified, for, as we have seen, Adams's great-grandfather did not believe that the Constitution depended upon the efficacy of any theory of morality or moral law. The Federalist authors sought to counterpoise faction against faction, and John Adams even went so far as to assume that he and the framers had successfully structured the government to deal with the familiar categories of monarchy, aristocracy, and democracy—the one, the few, and the many as in the English Constitution. The assumption rested on the theory of "mixed" government, a classical republican conviction that government can control power to the extent that its departments and branches accurately reflect society's class divisions. It remains one of the embarrassments of history that it took a Frenchman to point out that the framers were wrong:

> I have always considered what is called a mixed government to be a chimera. There is in truth no such thing as a mixed government . . . since in any society one finds in the end some principle of action that dominates all others.
> Eighteenth-century England, which has been generally cited as an example of this type of government, was an essentially aristocratic state, although it contained within itself great elements of democracy, for laws and mores were so designed

that the aristocracy could always prevail in the long run and manage public affairs as it wished.

The mistake is due to those who constantly see the interests of the great in conflict with those of the people, have thought only about the struggle and have paid no attention to the result thereof, which was more important. When a society really does have a mixed government, that is to say, one equally shared between contrary principles, either a revolution breaks out or that society breaks up.[30]

Many of the framers' theoretical assumptions collapse in Tocqueville's *Democracy in America*. The *Federalist* authors were determined to control popular majorities as "overbearing factions" that threatened the property interests of the few; Tocqueville demonstrates that the democratic will prevails in America as "the tyranny of the majority." But revolution does not break out and society does not break up. The class tensions upon which the framers structured government did not materialize, because America was not Europe. Having skipped the feudal stage of history, Americans were "born free." With no real aristocracy to denigrate labor and resist the "virtuous materialism" of an emergent capitalism, Americans enjoyed "equality of condition," and they identified wealth not with privilege but with work and natural right. Once property is seen as compatible with democracy, all expectations of class warfare become the fallacy of pure theory, and hence neither the framers' fears nor Marx's hopes will come to pass in America. To understand America, Tocqueville advised, one must shift attention from its political institutions to its beliefs, sentiments, mores, and "habits of the heart." With Tocqueville, political theory yields to sociological theory and to society itself, and the Constitution, instead of being the bulwark of republican liberty, is now seen as a secondary institution, a "recipe" and "precious piece of paper."[31]

What, then, of the meaning of the American Republic, and how can it be made relevant to the modern world? Boorstin insists that we cannot return to 1787–89, for America's constitutional system was not the product of rational design. Arendt believes that the spirit of the Revolution became the "treasure" that had been lost among the labyrinth of checks and balance devised at Philadelphia. Adams concludes that the whole fabric of eighteenth-century constitutional principles had expired. And Tocqueville suggests that the ideas of the framers do not explain America anyway, since their thoughts had been shaped by the categories of European political institutions and social structures. Assuming that America would replicate Europe's class system, the framers created a Constitution to control conflict, when in reality the new political system worked only because of the extent of consensus. American theory, in short, cannot account for American reality.

Tocqueville's perspective seems worth pondering since it is the most disturbing—so much so that it drove one brilliant scholar to a nervous breakdown.[32] Tocqueville is not only the first theorist of "consensus" but also the first to formulate what the Old Left used to call "exceptionalism," the idea that America is unique and must be explained by new categories that are almost sui generis. Some Americans may regard consensus and uniqueness as blessings, yet there is another, more sobering side. To the extent that America's historical experience was unique, America cannot readily offer a model to the world or expect to understand the predicament of people elsewhere who were not "born free" and who must struggle to become so against backwardness and the remnants of feudalism. Henry James once observed that America lacks the "imagination of disaster." A country that skipped feudalism, achieved freedom without having to overcome poverty, won power and succeeded in controlling it, and made a revolution that was truly exceptional in not devouring its own children—such a country may also lack the imagination of oppression. Yet America still feels it has something to teach the world. And today we are in the awkward position of judging others by our own standards and even calling for human rights that are universal in countries that have their own uniqueness.

One problem that might be pondered is the pronouncements of our own political leaders. If the ultimate meaning of the American Republic eludes scholars, it is perfectibly accessible to presidents. F. Scott Fitzgerald once observed that to be able to hold in the mind two contradictory ideas and still function rationally is the mark of a first-rate intelligence. Ronald Reagan deserves the compliment when he invokes the Puritan John Winthrop and the atheist Tom Paine. In calling for a "city upon a hill," Winthrop was asking seventeenth-century Americans to submit to authority; in describing government as "the badge of lost innocence," Paine was urging eighteenth-century Americans to overthrow it. The irony is that our leaders hail not the Constitution's framers but its opponent, Paine. In his first inaugural address, Reagan quoted Paine's exhortation that America has it in its power "to begin the world over again." The demand to "get government off our back," a theme that actually started with Jimmy Carter, reached a red-blooded crescendo in Reagan's inaugural. "Government is not the solution to our problem. Government is the problem."[33] The framers, one feels bound to point out, would never have assumed that government was all bad and the people all good. "What is government itself," exclaimed Madison, "but the greatest of all reflections on human nature." "Why has government been instituted at all?" asked Hamilton. "Because the passions of men will not conform to the dictates of reason and justice without constraint."[34] He who promises to get a wicked government off the backs of a virtuous people would probably be dismissed by the framers as a "theoretic politician."

Notes

1. The leading exponent of the classical republican school is J. G. A. Pocock and his magisterial *The Machiavellian Moment: Florentine Political Thought and the Atlantic Republican Tradition* (Princeton: Princeton University Press, 1975); the influence of the Scottish Enlightenment is emphasized in Gary Wills's *Inventing America: Jefferson's Declaration of Independence* (New York: Doubleday, 1978), and *Explaining America: "The Federalist"* (New York: Doubleday, 1981); the Calvinist-Lockean themes are explored in John P. Diggins, *The Lost Soul of American Politics: Virtue, Self-Interest, and the Foundations of Liberalism* (New York: Basic Books, 1984); and the emergence of economic individualism in Joyce Appleby, *Capitalism and a New Social Order: The Republican Visions of the 1790s* (New York: Columbia University Press, 1984).

2. *Federalist*, no. 10.

3. Ibid.

4. Ibid., no. 6; Adams is quoted in Gordon S. Wood, *The Creation of the American Republic, 1776–1787* (Chapel Hill: University of North Carolina Press, 1969), p. 571.

5. René Remond, *Les Etats-Unis devant l'opinion française, 1815–1852* (Paris: A. Colin, 1962), pp. 552–58.

6. *Burke's Speeches*, ed. F. G. Selby (London: Macmillan, 1956), pp. 64–84.

7. Ralph Waldo Emerson, "Self-Reliance," in *Ralph Waldo Emerson: Selected Prose and Poetry*, ed. Reginald Cook (New York: Holt Rhinehart and Winston, 1966), p. 179; Michael Kammen, *A Machine That Would Go of Itself: The Constitution in American Culture* (New York: Knopf, 1986); Woodrow Wilson, "What Is Progress?" in *The New*

Freedom, ed. William E. Leuchtenburg (Englewood Cliffs, N.J.: Prentice-Hall, 1962), pp. 41–42; and John P. Diggins, "Republicanism and Progressivism," *American Quarterly*, 37 (1985): 572–98.

8. For his earlier dismissal of books and theoretical ideas, see Daniel J. Boorstin, "The Place of Thought in American Life" and "The Myth of the American Enlightenment," in *America and the Image of Europe: Reflections on American Thought* (Cleveland: Meridian Books, 1960), pp. 43–78.

9. Reinhold Niebuhr, *The Irony of American History* (New York: Scribner's, 1952), p. 85; Arthur Schlesinger, Jr., "The Varieties of Communist Experience," in *The Politics of Hope* (Boston: Houghton Mifflin, 1962), p. 292; Hannah Arendt, *The Origins of Totalitarianism* (New York: Meridian Books, 1958), pp. 472–73; Hans Morgenthau, *Politics among Nations* (New York: Alfred A. Knopf, 1960), p. 259.

10. John Adams to Thomas Jefferson, Dec. 12, 1816, in *The Adams-Jefferson Letters*, ed. Lester J. Cappen (New York: Simon & Schuster, 1971), p. 499.

11. Boorstin, "Myth," pp. 73–78.

12. Daniel J. Boorstin, *The Genius of American Politics* (Chicago: University of Chicago Press, 1953), pp. 1–98.

13. Ibid., 8–16.

14. John P. Diggins, "Consciousness and Ideology in American History: The Burden of Daniel J. Boorstin," *American Historical Review*, 76 (Feb. 1971): 99–118.

15. Hannah Arendt, *On Revolution* (New York: Viking, 1963), pp. 221–22, 318.

16. *Federalist*, no. 10.

17. Arendt, *On Revolution*, pp. 252–85.

18. "Cato" is excerpted in *The Essential Antifederalist*, ed. W. B. Allen and Gordon Lloyd (New York: University Press of America, Inc., 1985), pp. 159–69.

19. Cecelia M. Kenyon, "Men of Little Faith: The Anti-Federalists and the Constitution," *William and Mary Quarterly*, 3d ser., 12 (1955): 3–43.

20. Arendt, *On Revolution*, p. 254.

21. *The Writings of Thomas Jefferson*, ed. Andrew A. Lipscomb (Washington, D.C.: 1853), 1:82.

22. So did many other Founders find politics insufferable. See this author's *The Lost Soul of American Politics*, pp. 62–63.

23. See O'Brien's comments in the symposium "The Responsibility of Intellectuals," *Salmagundi*, 70–71 (Spring–Summer 1986): 190–95.

24. Norman Podhoretz, *The Bloody Crossroads: Where Literature and Politics Meet* (New York: Simon & Schuster, 1986).

25. Henry Adams, *History of the United States of America during the Administrations of Thomas Jefferson and James Madison* (New York: Library of America, 1986), p. 95.

26. Stockman's interview appeared in *Omni* and was reported in the *Japanese Times* (Tokyo), Aug. 24, 1986, p. 4.

27. Adams, *History*, p. 440.

28. Henry Adams, *The Education of Henry Adams* (New York: Modern Library, 1930), pp. 7, 102–03, 147.

29. Ibid., pp. 36, 180, 280–81.

30. Alexis de Tocqueville, *Democracy in America* (New York: Anchor-Doubleday, 1966), p. 251.

31. Alexis de Tocqueville to Claude-François de Corcelle, Sept. 17, 1853, in

Alexis de Tocqueville: Selected Letters on Politics and Society, ed. Roger Boesche (Berkeley: University of California Press, 1985), pp. 292–95.

32. The late Louis Hartz, author of the brilliant and despairing analysis *The Liberal Tradition in America* (New York: Harcourt Brace Jovanovich, 1955), a book to which I have been indebted.

33. Reagan is quoted in Arthur Schlesinger, Jr., *The Cycles of American History* (Boston: Houghton Mifflin, 1986), p. 219.

34. *Federalist*, nos. 15, 51.

Founders' Intent and Constitutional Interpretation

DAVID A. J. RICHARDS

The American Constitution is the longest-lasting written constitution in the world. Americans are famously self-conscious of this
fact, which gives to our legal and wider political discourse its
special sense of history. Today Americans very actively debate, for
example, how we should understand the intent of the Founders
who wrote and ratified the Constitution in 1787–88, the Bill of
Rights in 1791, and the Fourteenth Amendment and its due-
process and equal-protection clauses in 1868. Two remarkable
features of the American constitutional tradition are that the
Founders aspired to this kind of long-term durability and that
generations of Americans have regarded it as common sense. It is,
of course, nothing of the kind.

No less a figure than Thomas Jefferson (who did not attend the
Constitutional Convention) had suggested an alternative approach,
namely, that each generation should revolt against the old political
order and establish a new one by its own best lights.[1] Jefferson did
not object in principle to a written constitution. On the contrary, as
a prominent figure of the revolutionary era, he was far too alive to
the potential for oppression in British parliamentary supremacy to
trust legislative supremacy in the way the British did. For this
reason he defended the importance of a written constitution in

defining appropriate limits on executive, legislative, and judicial power.[2] But he did object to the idea that any generation's conception of the best form of written constitution should be authoritative for later generations. Madison, one of the greatest of the Founders, disagreed with his good friend and associate Jefferson on precisely this point in *The Federalist* number 49.[3] Madison's view of the intergenerational authority of the written constitution was the view of the Founders; it is a tribute to their success that this view is now the common sense of almost all sides in the continuing American controversies over constitutional interpretation.

There is, of course, a yawning logical gap between what the Founders may have intended (namely, that the Constitution should endure over many generations of their posterity) and what role, if any, their intentions should play in subsequent interpretive debates. The great architects of the British common-law tradition (for example, Lords Coke and Mansfield) may have intended their work to last forever, but the interpretation of that tradition today cannot reasonably be understood as a search for their intentions. Indeed, whatever weight the idea of authorial intent may properly have in the interpretation of what a speaker says or a writer writes does not naturally transfer to the interpretation of culture in general or of a legal tradition in particular. A complex legal culture—whether the British unwritten or the American written constitution—embodies highly abstract and densely structured collective understandings about the legitimate use of the modern state's monopoly of coercive power. Those collective understandings are the work of many generations of shared historical experience, and their interpretation cannot be based on the model of a speaker's or writer's meaning.[4]

But American constitutional interpretation *does* give central play to Founders' intent in a way that suggests at least to some Americans a closer analogy to a speaker's meaning; there is something indigenously American in conceiving American-style constitutional interpretation in this way. We can (Raoul Berger, for example,[5] argues) only make sense of the specifically American commitment to an enduring written constitution if we limit the current application of pertinent constitutional language to the things the Founders would have thought properly identified by that language; and we must not apply that language to anything the Founders would have excluded from its scope of application. We can thus properly apply the prohibition on cruel and unusual punishment in the Eighth Amendment to torture, but not to the death penalty;[6] we can apply the requirement of equal protection in the Fourteenth Amendment to racial discrimination by states in access to the criminal and civil law, but not to racial segregation or antimiscegenation laws or blatant gender discrimination.[7]

The converse of this view of constitutional interpretation is the liberals' ill-considered response: constitutional interpretation can only mean what Berger tells us it means, but it is constitutionally legitimate for the judiciary to engage in open-ended moral prophecy nonetheless.[8] The consequence of such an uncritical theory of interpretation is, of course, a parody of liberal constitutionalism as a theory of constitutional law, acting out, as it were, a kind of conservatives' nightmare of constitutional lawlessness.

This essay is an investigation both into why Founders' intent plays the role it does in American constitutional interpretation and how we should interpret this idea. There is no good reason, I argue, why arguments of Founders' intent should be monopolized, as they currently are, by conservative critics of much "liberal" contemporary constitutional jurisprudence, including Attorney General Meese.[9] A deeper understanding of the premises of the American commitment to an enduring written constitution powerfully explains both the weight of Founders' intent and how and why conservative ideologues misinterpret that intent.[10]

I. Historiography and Constitutional Interpretation

American constitutional interpretation incorporates a sense of history in a way peculiarly guided by its self-interpretation as an ongoing historical project of a distinctive sort of political theory. That sense of history naturally organizes itself around three interlocking points: first, the historical sense of the framers themselves about the traditions on which they built; second, our current sense of what the Founders aspired to achieve; and third, our historical sense of the interpretive elaboration of constitutional law and doctrine over time.

1. THE FOUNDERS' SENSE OF HISTORY

The constitutional "experiment" (as the Founders referred to it)[11] was designed, discussed, and ratified with a remarkably developed and articulate critical self-consciousness about its place in a complex fabric of thought about and practice of legitimate government in Western culture. The Constitution, followed shortly by the Bill of Rights, is thus the product of self-conscious reflection on past republican experiments (Greece, Rome, the Florentine and Venetian republics, the Cromwellian commonwealth) and the republican political theory and science of their emergence, stability, and decline (Polybius, Machiavelli, Guicciardini, Giannotti, Sarpi, Harrington, Locke, Sidney); on various ancient and modern federal systems and their comparative success and failure; on both explanatory and normative theories of federalism, separation of powers, a mixed or balanced constitution, and the British Constitution (Aristotle, Hume, Montesquieu); on historical traditions of respect for basic rights of the person, including the rights of conscience and free speech (Locke, Milton); on the practical political experience of colonial self-government: the struggles with Britain centering on concepts of political representation, the republican experiments in the states after the American Revolution, and the abortive federalism of the Articles of Confederation; and much else besides.[12]

James Wilson, one of the greatest of the Founders, aptly expressed in the Pennsylvania ratification convention the manner in which this sense of history framed the work of the Founders:

> Government, indeed, taken as a science may yet be considered in its infancy; and with all its various modifications, it has hitherto been the result of force, fraud, or accident. For, after the lapse of six thousand years since the Creation of the world, America now presents the first instance of a people assembled to weigh deliberately and calmly, and to decide leisurely and peaceably, upon the form of government by which they will bind themselves and their posterity.[13]

The point was not just that no government had been reflectively designed by and for an enlightened "legislator," for the history of Western political theory from Plato onward was littered with such designs. The idea, rather, is that no such design had ever been so much the product of the collective deliberations of a free people, a people absorbed by a sense of unique historic opportunity to use the best political theory and political science of an enlightened age to achieve enduring republican government in a large territory.

There were undoubtedly some among the Founders (for example, Edmund Randolph of Virginia[14] and Alexander Hamilton of New York)[15] who frankly shared Montesquieu's enthusiasm for the British Constitution. From their perspective, republican government was, as Montesquieu appeared to conclude,[16] essentially the government of small, often economically backward, militaristic city-states. But the American government contemplated an enormous territory, a potentially huge population, and a thriving commercial life, and the British Constitution—with its mixture of hereditary and republican elements—was the historically validated model for such governance. These Founders thought of the Constitution as a solution *faute de mieux*, the best that could be consensually achieved consistent with an unfortunate American republicanism that rejected, in principle, the legitimacy of any form of the hereditary principle.

But there were other Founders (James Wilson of Pennsylvania and James Madison of Virginia notably among them) who argued both at the Constitutional Convention[17] and in the ratification debates[18] that, properly understood, the design of the American Constitution afforded a unique opportunity to defend republican principles against their contemporary and classic conservative critics. In order, however, properly to exploit this opportunity, we must, they argued, assess the critical errors of both the theory and practice of past republican and federalist experiments so that our own experiment will not stupidly repeat their mistakes.

Accordingly, all discussion of the Constitution gravitates around examination and reexamination of an extraordinarily broad range of both ancient and modern "experiments" in republican and federal government, including, of course, both the republican experiments in the states since the American Revolution and the defects in America's first federal experiment, the Articles of Confederation.[19] Founders used and discussed such examples very much in the spirit of the political science of Montesquieu[20] and Hume[21]—that is, the application to human institutions of the experimental philosophy of Bacon, Newton, and Locke.[22] But the appeal to experience was not, however, understood in a narrow inductive way as if any American republican experiment must not go beyond what history shows can work. If that had been the dominant empirical philosophy of the Founders, the Constitution would *not* have been the result, for none of the relevant historical "experiments" contained anything like the Constitution. That, indeed, was the empiricist objection made to it at the Constitutional Convention: "Where we have no experience there can be no reliance on Reason,"[23] or "Experience must be our only guide. Reason may mislead us" (appealing to British political experience).[24] But the proponents of the Constitution appealed to history as a way of identifying and analyzing blunders in the theory and practice of republican and federal systems of government, not as an exhaustive catalogue of constructive republican and federalist alternatives, and they were quite prepared, if necessary, to experiment with self-consciously utopian federalist proposals, works of imaginative political reason, not of experience (for example, Hume's utopian commonwealth).[25] Indeed, their constructive political imagination was in the service of a new departure in political thought and value, which they in part pioneered.

When Madison, for example, drew his classical distinction between republics and democracies,[26] he both analyzed a vice in Athenian-style participatory democracy and innovated a republican design keyed to new virtues. The vice of direct participatory democracy was, for Madison, its naive indulgence of a larger moral vice of human nature in groups, namely, the pathology of group psychology (the practice of oppressing outsiders), which, after Hume,[27] he calls "faction." He defined the idea precisely:

> By a faction I understand a number of citizens, whether amounting to a majority or minority of the whole, who are united and actuated by some common impulse of passion, or of interest, adverse to the rights of other citizens, or to the permanent and aggregate interests of the community.[28]

But Madison, like Wilson, understood faction as a vice from the perspective of the political virtue of respect for republican equal rights, which both (unlike Hume)[29] considered, following Lockean political theory,[30] fundamental to political legitimacy as such. That political theory was, of course, a new departure in the history of political thought, and, for Madison and Wilson, the American Constitution was a practical experiment in the institutionalization of its consequences. One such consequence is institutional respect for inalienable equal rights, like the right of conscience that Madison passionately defended in his great Remonstrance[31] and later

in his design of the First Amendment,[32] and that Wilson invoked
as the central purpose of government: "The cultivation & improvement of the human mind was the most noble object."[33]
Another consequence of this republican political theory, correlative with its protection of the right to conscience, was the limitation of state power to the pursuit of general (nonsectarian) political and economic goods—the common denominators of life,
liberty, and security, which persons require to pursue their more
ultimate aims, whatever they are.[34] For this reason, Madison
regarded the vaunted virtues of participatory republicanism
(namely, people "perfectly equalized and assimilated in their pos-
sessions, their opinions, and their passions")[35] as another name
for the illegitimate pursuit of sectarian aims by the state, that is,
as an unfettered dominance by religious, political, or economic
faction that Madison considered a vicious parody of the pluralism
of republican equal liberties of moral independence.

Since Madison thus identified the rationale of participatory
republicanism as a corruption of republican principles, he saw no
merit in the view of Montesquieu and others that the virtue of
republics requires a small, ideologically homogeneous, often economically backward and militaristic city-state (e.g., Sparta).[36] To
the contrary, what opponents of the Constitution[37] identified as
its antirepublican vice (the nation's large territory, heterogeneous
populace, and commercial interests) could be the key to its enduring republican virtue. With brilliant political irony, Madison, like
Wilson,[38] thus reversed the reigning republican assumptions of
the age: the small size and homogeneity of participatory republics
was their vice; the largeness and religious and commercial heterogeneity of the American representative republic would be its
virtue. In particular, the use of the representative principle in the
constitutional design operates over so large a territory and so
diverse a people that national representatives could only achieve a
common ground for democratic governance if they learned not
only to think about the factionalized interests of the Congregationalists of Massachusetts, or the Quakers of Pennsylvania, or
the Catholics of Maryland, or the Anglicans of Virginia, but to
identify and pursue the common interests of life, liberty, and
security that all such groups share, forming coalitions on the basis
of such common interests.[39] And collective deliberation of such
representative bodies (with "total exclusion of the people in their
collective capacity")[40] would advance republican values of reason-

able democratic discourse among free and equal persons. Properly designed representative bodies would thus structure the exercise of republican political rights in ways more consistent with deeper republican principles of equality, namely, principles both of respect for equal rights and of pursuit of the common good. The demonic exercise of faction, which the politics of participatory republics had unleashed, could at last be cured and the basic principles of republican government could be vindicated against Plato's indictment of the Athenian democracy's judicial murder of Socrates. The fault, Madison suggested, lay not in republican principles but Athenian mass political democracy: "Had every Athenian citizen been a Socrates, every Athenian assembly would still have been a mob."[41]

Even the American absorption in commercial interests was not, from this perspective, a republican vice. Montesquieu and Hume had, of course, sharply contrasted the malign insularity and thirst for glory of the participatory republic of civic virtue[42] with the way commercial life and exchange under constitutional monarchies like Britain created incentives to peace and broader ties of reciprocal mutual cooperation among diverse peoples.[43] Madison interpreted these views as arguments that an appropriately designed national framework of commercial exchange is essential to a civilized polity and conjoined them to the distinctively American (and Lockean) theme that a core right reserved from state power is the right to conscience. Madison's two examples of faction are thus religious sectarianism and "unequal distribution of property,"[44] and he sees the representative structure of the federal system as an appropriate way to limit the factionalized exercise of these forces and therefore to heighten the liberating force of respect for rights of both conscience and property.[45] For Madison, the enumerated power of the federal government to regulate interstate and international commerce is thus one with its lack of power over religion. State regulation of secular interests like commerce and the absence of regulation of religion are complementary ways of fostering the civilizing bonds of a community that treats persons as both free and equal.

As I have noted, Madison and Wilson did not find these arguments in history, for their institutional innovations had been experimentally tested nowhere. But past political experience was, as Wilson saw, "the result of force, fraud, or accident,"[46] and the American opportunity was precisely its freedom, its theoretical clarity and fidelity to fact, and its exercise of collective deliberative choice. Their sense of history thus both uses the best critical historiography of the age and yet interprets that history in a way that advances brilliantly imaginative institutional innovations, sometimes freely adapted from the utopian speculations of an anti-Lockean political philosopher of Hume's stature,[47] that both clarify and elaborate the meaning of Lockean constitutionalism— or, at least, that variant of Lockean constitutionalism which is the United States Constitution.[48]

2. OUR HISTORICAL SENSE OF THE FOUNDERS

The interpretive sense of history that Founders brought to their task laid the foundation for the sense of history that informs all serious discussion of how to interpret their work. The point is not just that our understanding of their work is often advanced by taking seriously the ways in which they both use and revise past political traditions. But constitutional interpretation today is so absorbed by the Founders because our interpretive project, suitably updated, *is* their project.

That interpretive project centers on the authority of a certain kind of written constitution, achieving in America what had never been achieved elsewhere: enduring republican government in a large territory. "The ends" of such institutional constraints, as Madison put it at the Constitutional Convention, "were first to protect the people agst. their rulers: secondly to protect [the people] agst. the transient impressions into which they themselves might be led."[49] The authority of such constraints is, for the Founders, a product of a certain kind of constitutional politics, namely, that the "ends" are those of a "people deliberating in a temperate moment, and with the experience of other nations before them, on the plan of Govt. most likely to secure their happiness."[50] That authority is, I believe, crucial in *Federalist* number 49, when Madison defends the conception of a long-enduring written constitution against Jefferson's idea of a written constitution remade by each generation.[51]

Madison's argument is an appeal to the extraordinary sort of liberty, opportunity, and reflective capacity collectively and democratically brought to bear on the framing and ratification of the United States Constitution. The authority of the framers' conception of a written constitution is precisely that such a document is not the product of garden-variety democratic politics, in which competitors for political power bring to all disputes their factionalized perceptions of issues of principle and policy. Madison thought of the legislative debates of such normal politics as "so many judicial determinations, not indeed concerning the rights of single persons, but concerning the rights of large bodies of citizens,"[52] that is, as a substantive debate about justice in which all parties interpret such claims of justice through their factionalized commitments as either creditors or debtors, farmers or manufacturers, Quakers or Anglicans. The authority of the Constitution, in contrast, is the sort of impartiality brought to bear on the construction of constraints that are themselves immune from such politics and that supply reasonable substantive and procedural constraints on the exercise of such politics consistent with a larger republican conception of principles of justice and equal rights and the effective use of collective power to advance the common good. Madison's objection to Jefferson's view of a written constitution is that the sense of a written constitution easily changed erodes the distinctive authority of the framers' conception, undermining its distinctive virtue of constitutional impartiality by the factionalized perceptions of constitutional constraints that necessarily arise in normal politics. And that would mean unleashing yet again the demons of democratic faction, which it was the very point of the Constitution to tame and civilize, in contrast to previously existing republics whose example the Founders self-consciously repudiated. For this reason, the very authority of the written constitution must place it beyond any change resembling normal democratic politics.

This conception of impartiality pervades both the theory and practice of the constitutional design. Not only had the Founders experienced such impartiality in their collective deliberations, they institutionally designed the three great institutions of the federal system (the legislative, judicial, and executive branches) to give proper scope to a more impartial exercise of each of these functions. The vice of which impartiality is the correlative virtue is the partiality of faction, or being judge in one's own case.[53] Accordingly, the three branches are designed to secure institutional independence in the exercise of their respective functions. In striking contrast to both the legislative and executive branches, the judiciary is thus constitutionally accorded lifetime tenure, because only independence of that sort would tend to ensure the kind of impartiality that the Founders knew was needed to maintain fidelity to the deeper impartiality of an enduring written constitution immune from ordinary politics.[54] That deeper impartiality expresses a conception of the collective republican reasonableness of the Constitution itself,[55] and amendment thereof, Madison argues,[56] must be structured to approximate the same sort of collective exercise of deliberative republican reflection on enduring constitutional design.

Madison's argument is, of course, implicitly contractarian in Locke's sense; that is, political legitimacy is tested against a moral ideal of acceptability to free, rational, and equal persons.[57] When Founders like Wilson thus characterize the democratic legitimacy of the Constitution, their model is clear: "The great and penetrating mind of Locke seems to be the only one that pointed towards even the theory of this great truth."[58] This Lockean theory of political legitimacy bases the authority of the Constitution on its deliberative justifiability to the free, rational, and equal persons subject to its requirements. Thus, for Madison, the authority of the Constitution was the way in which it imposed constraints on the power of the state and of the people that could be and often were publicly justified to all persons subject to them as reasonable—for example, by arguments like those in *The Federalist*.[59] Reasonable justification, in this normative sense of justifiability, is the basis of constitutional impartiality, and thus of the authority of the written constitution itself.

When I say, then, that the Founders' interpretive project is our project, I mean that both the making of the Constitution and its interpretation are a continuous project of a certain kind of reasonable justification of substantive and procedural constraints on the power both of the state and of the people. It was therefore essential, as republican Founders like Wilson and Madison insisted,[60] that the Constitution be ratified by one of the most inclusive deliberative processes of democratic ratification that any working democracy had ever seen; such ratification precisely made the authoritative point of reasonable justification. It is equally essential, I believe, that interpretation of the Constitution be similarly justifiable.

The authority of an enduring written constitution is, Madison argues, the impartial reasonableness of its written constraints. But Madison also thinks of these constraints as an enduring heritage to posterity, namely, standards of an impartially conceived republican morality enforceable against both the state and the people. That heritage will, Madison clearly understands, be accorded by later generations "that veneration which time bestows on everything, and without which perhaps the wisest and freest governments would not possess the requisite stability";[61] he defends the idea because an enduring written constitution will use the deeply human sense of historical tradition in the service of such a morality.

Madison here remarkably anticipates the normative role that the historical commitment to a written constitution (and its founders) must have if that constitution is to perform its essential role in binding the people into an enduring republican community of free and equal persons. The United States Constitution conceives of itself in the same way, as a structure of governance that would endure over long generations: in the express words of the Preamble, to "secure the blessings of liberty to ourselves and our posterity."[62] That commitment to an enduring written constitution shows itself also in the equally self-conscious way the Founders linked both their style of drafting the Constitution and the style of interpretation they anticipated. For example, an important document used in their drafting of the final Constitution states:

> In the draught of a fundamental constitution, two things deserve attention:
> 1. To insert essential principles only; lest the operations of government should be clogged by rendering those provisions permanent and unalterable, which ought to be accomodated [sic] to times and events; and 2. To use simple and precise language, and general propositions, according to the example of the (several) constitutions of the several states. (For the construction of a constitution necessarily differs from that of law).[63]

The interpretation of such a constitution best uses the sense of history that Founders like Madison anticipated when that sense of history is itself interpreted in the same way Madison defended the legitimacy of the Constitution itself: as a historically continuous interpretive enterprise of principle constitutive of an enduring community of free, rational, and equal persons (i.e., as a historically self-conscious community of principle over time).

For this reason, constitutional interpretation not only reflects the sense of history that the Founders themselves used as well as anticipated but itself construes that history on the model of a historically continuous community of principle:[64] the claims of the community over time must be justifiable to all on terms of its constitutive principles of equal rights and pursuit of the public good. Since that enterprise enjoys the historical continuity sponsored by an enduring written constitution, the interpretation of the Constitution exhibits arguments of principle as the condition of the legitimacy of constitutional interpretation.[65] American controversies over constitutional interpretation thus standardly debate whether a decision is unprincipled, or what its principle might be—for example, the prolonged academic debate over the "neutral principle"[66] of *Brown v. Board of Education*.[67]

All sides to the academic debate conceded that the decision was substantively just, but they differed over whether its substantive justice corresponded to a coherently reasonable justification of the relevant constitutional provision, its history, and other actual or likely cases interpreting the provision.[68] The consequence of that debate over an issue of interpretive principle was what one expects and should expect from debates over principle: reasonable discussion among a community of equals leading, eventually, to agreement that a range of principles justify *Brown*— namely, either that all racial classifications are invalid, or that all invidious racial classifications are invalid.[69] Through the kind of reasoning sponsored by debates over principle, we now understand that *Brown* is based on a constitutional principle of substantive equal justice, though we still debate the relative merits of the alternative principles in other cases where they dictate different results (for example, in cases involving the policy of affirmative action).[70]

3. THE HISTORICAL SENSE OF DOCTRINAL AND INTERPRETIVE CHANGE

The idea of a historically continuous community of principle sponsors as well the ways in which constitutional interpretation incorporates an internal sense of the history of both doctrinal and interpretive change over time.

As we have seen, American interpretation of the written constitution naturally gives weight to arguments of Founders' intent centering on an enduring community of principle, but any reasonable attention to these arguments shows ways in which the Constitution and the Bill of Rights—remarkable achievements that they are—contain compromises, and even sacrifices, of republican principles, of which the Founders were themselves all too painfully aware. Madison, for example, regarded equal representation of states in the senate as a clear violation of basic republican principles of justice in voting,[71] would have preferred a guarantee of religious liberty and free speech that extended to both the states and the federal government,[72] and knew—as did many of the Founders—that the institution of slavery in Southern states was obscenely violative of the republican equal liberty of all persons.[73] Some constitutional compromises were perhaps not as disastrous in fact as some of the Founders feared, but the evil of blatant sacrifices of principle, like the legitimation of slavery and the absence of an inhibition on the powers of states to deprive persons of basic rights, worsened with cumulative historical experience. The Founders' sense of basic flaws in the community of principle was confirmed, and—in the wake of the Civil War— many of them were expressly addressed by the Reconstruction Amendments.

The "Founders" of the Reconstruction Amendments brought to bear on their work the same kind of interpretive sense of history that we earlier saw in the Founders of the 1787 Constitution, namely, an attempt to learn from past republican and federal mistakes in institutional design, including here the 1787 Constitution itself.[74] They were not institutional innovators in the sense of the 1787 Founders, however, for their interpretive sense of history accepted, indeed elaborated, many of the substantive and procedural constraints of the 1787 Constitution and 1791 Bill of Rights. Of course, they addressed central defects in the earlier constitutional design: the Thirteenth Amendment (1865) abolishes slavery, the Fourteenth Amendment (1868) extends guarantees of basic rights against the states, and the Fifteenth Amendment (1870) prohibits racial discrimination in voting. But, these changes do not innovate principles as much as they elaborate the scope of application of standing constitutional principles in ways often defended by the 1787 Founders themselves. For example, when the Fourteenth Amendment extends guarantees of basic rights against the states, it does not make new rights, but rather takes standing guarantees of the 1791 Bill of Rights and expands them from the federal government to the states; one of the great lacunae of the Constitution is thus filled. Even the adoption of new terminology of constitutional protection (notably, the equal-protection clause of the Fourteenth Amendment) builds on standing constitutional guarantees.[75] Undoubtedly, the equal-protection clause introduces new themes into the fabric of American constitutional principle, namely, a prohibition of the expression through public law of degrading prejudices like racism. But even this theme of the suspectness of certain classifications (for example, race) is anticipated by the Constitution's rejection of all religious qualifications and its pervasive concern with factions (the propensity of groups to hate outsiders). In short, the most novel normative innovation of the Reconstruction Amendments (the equal-protection clause) builds on standing constitutional principles and on concerns of the Constitution and Bill of Rights. The community of principle has, if anything, been expanded by the Reconstruction Amendments to encompass a more coherently principled and certainly less flawed conception of the persons and rights protected by republican equality.

We naturally bring to the interpretation of the Reconstruction Amendments the same interpretive sense of history that its "Founders" brought to it, in the same way we earlier saw that Madison's interpretive project was also ours. A historically continuous community of principle sponsors this pervasive sense of constitutional interpretation as a historically self-conscious elaboration of republican political theory. It sponsors as well a continuing concern of all constitutional interpretation not only for its Founders, whether in 1787, 1791, or 1865–70, but for patterns of constitutional interpretation over time. The American conception of an enduring written constitution expresses, I have argued, the normative conception of public justification of coercive power to free, rational, and equal people. Since that conception expresses a historically continuous community of principle, its interpretation must be sensitive to relevant contextual factors that bear upon the forms that public justification must take in different circumstances and periods. Only such contextual sensitivity enables us to read the Constitution as a continuing community bound to a common thread of principles; failures of such sensitivity may constitute powerful paradigms of interpretive mistake, a failure to understand or articulate enduring strands of principle.

II. The Contextuality of Constitutional Interpretation

The style of constitutional interpretation in the United States has taken a form historically sensitive to the Founders' sense of history, to our sense of the Founders, and to interpretive practice over time. But it has remained capable of being both faithful to text and history and contextually sensitive to changing circumstances. As I have observed, the Founders of the Constitution (in contrast to Jefferson) self-consciously conceived the written constitution as a structure of governance that would endure over generations, and they drafted the Constitution in anticipation of an interpretive practice that would be historically sensitive to their aspiration to establish an enduring community of principle.[76]

Consistent with that design, the success of the enterprise has been made possible by a distinctively American style of constitutional interpretation that has insisted on framing its interpretive task in terms of what John Marshall called "a constitution intended to endure for centuries to come, and, consequently to be adapted to the various *crises* of human affairs."[77] Marshall's argument is, I believe, that the framers' aspiration to an enduring constitutional government binding on future generations can only be given effect if we read the often general language of the constitutional text in ways contextually sensitive to changing circumstances. Marshall makes the argument in his classical examination in *McCulloch v. Maryland*[78] of the appropriate interpretation of article 1, section 8, the grant of enumerated powers to Congress. *McCulloch* is concerned with whether implied grants of power to Congress (specifically, the power to create a national bank) can be imputed to article 1, section 8. Among the expressly granted powers is the grant to Congress of the power to regulate interstate and international commerce.[79] What are the implications of Marshall's argument for interpretation of the commerce clause?[80]

We may usefully understand that argument in terms of the commonplace semantic distinction between the denotative and connotative meaning of sentences.[81] Very roughly, the denotative meaning of a sentence identifies the things in the world to which the speaker refers; its connotative meaning is, in contrast, the propositional content of the sentence. When the framers of the Constitution gave Congress the power to regulate commerce, they did so by language with both a denotative and a connotative meaning. Denotatively, the framers used the language to refer both to things that could and things that could not be regulated in a way consistent with the language used; for example, such a 1787 denotative meaning would clearly give Congress power to regulate trade among the states, but it could not fairly give Congress power to regulate purely intrastate farm production, reserved, say, for home consumption. Connotatively, we would identify the meaning of the commerce clause as the propositional content of "Commerce . . . among the several States," that is, business that affects more states than one.[82] The denotative and connotative meaning are related in the following way: because the connotative meaning of "Commerce . . . among the several States" is "business that affects more states than one," the denotative meaning of the text includes trade among the states (since it is business that affects more states than one) but would exclude farm production for home use (which does not affect other states).

Marshall's argument is in part that we best construe the Founders' aspiration to an enduring constitution when we read the text connotatively in the light of contemporary circumstances, not denotatively as of 1787. If we read the text denotatively as of 1787, we could reasonably apply the textual grant only to the things to which the Founders in their circumstances would have applied the language. But such an interpretive approach would freeze constitutional interpretation to the circumstances of 1787; it would not be contextually sensitive to relevantly changed circumstances (for example, the change from the agrarian economy of 1787 to the industrial and postindustrial technological civilization of the twentieth century). The denotative meaning would thus forever forbid the application of the commerce clause to farm production of home-consumed products, because the 1787 denotation could not encompass such economic events. But this denotative meaning of the clause would conflict with a fair reading of its connotative meaning: "business affecting more states than one" would in the twentieth century plausibly include even such farm production if appreciable parts of the aggregate of such production now withheld from the market might under changed economic circumstances (rising demand for farm goods) be sold in the market and thus appreciably affect market transactions in a now integrated national economy. On this reading, congressional power could regulate home farm production.[83]

Marshall's argument is that we should here interpretively prefer the connotative meaning because it is equally consistent with the text and, in contrast to the 1787 denotative meaning, advances and does not frustrate the Founders' unambiguous aspiration to a long-term durability of the grants of power to Congress.[84] James Wilson, for example, distinguished two kinds of liberty that were the subject of the constitutional contract: civil liberty and federal liberty.[85] Civil liberties included many of the rights guaranteed by state bills of rights and, as such, subject to arguments of principle, but federal liberty identified the public policy purposes granted to the federal government because state regulation thereof—though affecting other states—had neither effectively realized their benefits, nor fairly distributed their benefits and burdens. The scope and distribution of such federal liberty were, Wilson argued, a highly discretionary judgment of policy remitted under the Constitution to a fairly representative Congress. Consistent with Wilson's views, Marshall argues that the interpretation of congressional powers is so much a contextually sensitive and highly discretionary issue of policy that we must interpret these grants, including the commerce clause, in a way that will enable Congress to make these judgments responsive to its interpretation of public purposes under changed circumstances. The connotative interpretation of the commerce clause allows Congress to make these contextually sensitive policy judgments in a way that the denotative interpretation would not, and it should be preferred for that reason. Accordingly, we regard the decisions of the Supreme Court that for a period limited the interpretive power of Congress over these issues as examples of grave interpretive mistake,[86] for they impute to the commerce clause and related clauses precisely such an unwarranted denotative interpretation.[87]

I have so far discussed the American preference for connotative as against denotative interpretations of the written text regarding congressional powers. But the same point applies to constitutional language protecting the rights of the person. For example, the Fourth Amendment to the Constitution protects the "right of the people to be secure in their persons, houses, papers, and effects, against unreasonable searches and seizures."[88] When the Founders wrote and ratified that language in 1791, they clearly meant denotatively to forbid certain invasions of the home by arbitrary police power, as a way of protecting the connotative proposition of the principle of the right to a private life immunized from arbitrary state intrusions.[89] If we only read the Fourth Amendment denotatively, as Justice Black once suggested we should,[90] we could not appeal to it to protect invasions of privacy not historically imaginable in 1791—for example, electronic bugging. This would, of course, introduce the same structural kind of conflict between denotative and connotative meaning we have just examined in the area of the commerce clause: the 1791 denotative meaning would clearly frustrate the connotative meaning read to protect privacy against the new technological threats that have arisen in contemporary circumstances. But the denotative interpretation compromises the integrity of the community of principle fundamental to the American commitment to an enduring written constitution: it reads a constitutional text—imposing constraints on state power reasonably justifiable to persons understood as free, rational, and equal—in a way that cannot be so justified, indeed that is crudely insensitive to relevantly changed technological circumstances bearing on the understanding and protection of its underlying principle. Such an unprincipled reading is compelled neither by text nor by history, and indeed it frustrates the contextually sensitive community of principle that motivates the very legitimacy of an enduring written constitution. For this reason, our interpretive tradition has preferred here as elsewhere the connotative over the denotative meaning as the better reading of such guarantees, and has rejected contrary judicial constructions as examples of grave interpretive mistake.[91]

Americans now largely agree (Raoul Berger perhaps excepted) that connotative meanings are to be preferred in interpreting the scope of congressional powers and guaranteed rights like those of the Fourth Amendment. But there is another level of interpretation about which there is more controversy, namely, the interpretation of abstract constitutional guarantees like due process or equal protection or the prohibition on cruel and unusual punishments. These guarantees, in contrast to the others so far examined, appeal to the most abstract kinds of ethical and political values. Due process is nothing less than the most abstract requirement of justice: giving people their due; equal protection states the core requirement of justice: treating like cases alike.

Controversy over the interpretation of these guarantees is not over denotative versus connotative meaning but over different levels of interpretation of connotative meaning. The equal-protection clause, for example, may be taken to protect a wide range of different connotative meanings—some more concrete, others much more abstract. One concrete interpretation forbids state-endorsed racial discrimination in a certain narrow list of civil rights, but not in education or in marriage.[92] More abstract interpretations would forbid all state-endorsed racial discrimination in distributing all rights and benefits,[93] or, more generally, all state-endorsed prejudice through law (including sexism as well as racism).[94] A still more abstract interpretation would forbid state use of all constitutionally unreasonable classifications, including both those that express constitutionally unreasonable prejudices and those that unjustly abridge fundamental rights.[95] There is a wide range of such alternative connotative meanings, each subject to even further interpretive discussion and refinement into subinterpretations.

Which interpretation should be preferred? There are a few American advocates of the concrete interpretation view, who reject all constitutional law inconsistent with such interpretations (for example, Raoul Berger[96] rejects *Brown v. Board of Education* on this ground). These views, however, represent neither dominant conservative nor dominant liberal opinion in the United States. American conservatives like current Attorney General Meese defend, for example, the judiciary's prohibition of state-sponsored racial segregation,[97] though this application of the equal-protection clause is outside the consensus of Berger's "Founders."[98] Rather, dominant interpretive controversy is over different views of the preferred abstract interpretation (for example, over whether the abstract prohibition on racial discrimination legitimates or forbids racial preferences,[99] or should be extended beyond racial to gender discrimination).[100] In order to understand why this is so, we must interpret, not parrot, history.

This task requires not only that we read constitutional principles in ways responsive to changing economic circumstances (the commerce clause) or technological innovations (the Fourth Amendment) but that we bring to bear on the elaboration of arguments of constitutional principle those factual and normative arguments that can offer the most reasonable justifications for the exercise of the state's coercive power. The factual and normative premises underlying the consensus of the 1868 "Founders" about the constitutionality of state-imposed racial segregation (i.e., the theory of race differences)[101] are today no longer reasonable, and the attempt to limit the interpretive scope of equal protection by such an appeal insults the intelligence and morality of a community of principle that finds it no longer reasonable.

The most powerful objection to Berger's approach is that it flouts the very principles fundamental to equal protection. In fact, the factual and normative assumptions that interpretively explain the 1868 consensus almost certainly reflect the false and vicious theory of race differences at the root of the racism that the equal-protection clause clearly condemns as a ground for state action. But the reason why racism is an interpretive paradigm of suspectness is that facts and values are themselves factitiously manufactured by a history of unjust racial degradation and then used in the justification of further degradation.[102] We now know that the corruptive evil digs deeper than the 1868 "Founders" understood, that, indeed, their very acceptance of their generation's "common sense" of race differences rests on this evil. The enforcement of the 1868 consensus about race (like gender) today would therefore introduce a fundamental incoherence into the law of equal protection: it would enforce a now constitutionally unreasonable and anachronistic concrete interpretation that in fact perpetuates the very evil that its more abstract principle condemns. Neither conservative nor liberal constitutionalists today are inclined to accept that argument, not because it is immoral or bad policy (though it is both), but because it is interpretively unprincipled.

III. Conclusions

My argument has tried to explain the role of Founders' intent in American constitutional interpretation and to show that conservative strict constructionists have no exclusive purchase on the idea. To the contrary, the strict constructionism of Founders' denotations is, I have argued, a travesty of the constitutional text, its history, its interpretive practice, and its political theory of a community of principle. Founders' intent simply cannot be reasonably understood on this model of speaker's meaning.

American constitutional interpretation is absorbed in Founders' intent, but that absorption, I have suggested, is one with its commitment to an enduring written constitution and the community of principle that this commitment expresses. The important and responsible debates over constitutional interpretation are not over rejecting the notion of criteria of Founders' intent, but over how we should interpret Founders' intent—in particular, how we should understand the abstract connotations that the constitutional text often expresses. Interpretive controversies over *this* issue are often debates in the abstract political theory of justice: for example, over whether the better principle of the suspectness of race is the prohibition on use of immutable characteristics like race or the more limited prohibition on use of classifications tainted by invidious prejudice and contempt.[103] We often display the result of such debates by imputing our preferred interpretation to Founders' intent, but that is, in this context, a kind of figure of speech: all the important work is going on elsewhere. Why, then, must we dress all constitutional controversy in originalist garb?

Certainly, some of the appeal of the originalism is ideological. Conservative discourse about constitutional interpretation often criticizes "liberal" constitutional jurisprudence (for example, the unconstitutionality of school prayer) on this ground. But these arguments are no stronger than their interpretive cogency, and they are often very flimsy indeed. For example, the appeal to Founders' intent in the controversy over school prayer is constitutionally and historically illiterate, failing, for example, to understand or give weight to the uniquely American commitment to strong constitutional principles both of antiestablishmentarianism and free exercise.[104] In other cases, it cannot reasonably explain why *Brown v. Board of Education* is interpretively right, but the incorporation of the Bill of Rights is wrong. Often, its conception of the just scope of majority rule fails to take seriously distinctive features of the American conception of constitutional republicanism and its procedural and substantive constraints on both the state and the people[105]—that constitutional democracy is in the service of the democratic equality of equal liberties and reasonable deliberation about and pursuit of the common good, and must be justifiable to all people in such terms. Indeed, such justifiability is, I have suggested, the normative basis of arguments of principle as a requirement of interpretive constitutional legitimacy. The Founders well understood the evils of majority rule and designed a form of government intended to cabin its populist demons by a theory and practice of democratic equality enforced by contextually sensitive arguments of principle. It would be the bitterest of betrayals to abandon that great work of democratic political intelligence in the name of Founders' intent.

But originalism also has a broader appeal for Americans, an appeal no less deep than the structure of the American political imagination. That structure is what I have called a historically continuous community of principle, a framework of contractarian political legitimacy. That framework expresses a powerful sense of the good fortune and opportunity remarkably seized by its Founders in a great work of collective democratic deliberation and achievement. But that framework—an enduring written constitution—carries with it as well the critical need for each generation of Americans both to interpret and to elaborate its community of principle as a continuing work of historical criticism and contextually sensitive aspiration. That tradition is, I believe, misinterpreted if either pole of its demands—its history or each generation's rearticulation of its principles in the light of constitutional reasonableness—is ignored.

America's constitutional originalism amounts to ideological deception and betrayal when it is unharnessed from any responsible engagement with the complex strands of history and political theory fundamental to constitutional legitimacy. Properly understood and used, however, the work of America's Founders is as moving a legacy in collective democratic deliberation and experiment as any nation has ever had. It is a mark of the imaginative power of their achievement that we regard our most constitutionally decent impulses and aspirations as a carrying forward of that legacy and that project.

Notes

1. See, e.g., Adrienne Koch, *Jefferson and Madison: The Great Collaboration* (New York: Knopf, 1950), pp. 62–96.

2. See, e.g., Thomas Jefferson, *Notes on the State of Virginia*, ed. William Peden (Chapel Hill: University of North Carolina Press, 1955).

3. *Federalist*, no. 49. Page references are to *Federalist Papers*, ed. Clinton Rossiter (New York: Mentor, 1961).

4. See, in general, Ronald Dworkin, *Law's Empire* (Cambridge, Mass.: Harvard University Press, 1986); David Richards, *Toleration and the Constitution* (New York: Oxford University Press, 1986), pp. 20–45.

5. See Raoul Berger, *Government by Judiciary* (Cambridge, Mass.: Harvard University Press, 1977) and *Death Penalties* (Cambridge, Mass.: Harvard University Press, 1982).

6. Berger, *Death Penalties*.

7. Berger, *Government by Judiciary*.

8. See Michael J. Perry, *The Constitution, the Courts, and Human Rights* (New Haven: Yale University Press, 1982).

9. For the views of Attorney General Meese and the opposing views of Justice Brennan and Justice Stevens, see "Addresses—Construing the Constitution," *University of California at Davis Law Review* 19 (1985): 2.

10. Cf. Richards, pp. 20–64.

11. For example, at the Virginia ratification convention, Madison observes: "I can see no danger in submitting to practice an experiment which seems to be founded on the best theoretic principles." Jonathan Elliot, ed., *Debates in the Several State Conventions on the Adoption of the Federal Constitution* (Philadelphia, 1836), 3:394. At the South Carolina convention, Charles Pinckney admits that "our Constitution was in some measure an experiment" and "that he considered it the fairest experiment ever made in favor of human nature." Ibid., 4:262.

12. For citations to pertinent secondary literature regarding all these influences on the making of the American Constitution, see Richards, p. 56.

13. Merrill Jensen, ed., *Documentary History of the Ratification of the Constitution* (Madison: State Historical Society of Wisconsin, 1976), 2:342.

14. At the Constitutional Convention, Randolph observes of the British Constitution: "He did not mean however to throw censure on that Excellent fabric. If we were in a situation to copy it he did not know that he should be opposed to it; but the fixt genius of the people of America required a different form of Government." Max Farrand, ed., *The Records of the Federal Convention of 1787* (New Haven: Yale University Press, 1911), 1:66.

15. At the Constitutional Convention, Hamilton admits: "This view of the subject almost led him to despair that a Republican Govt. could be established over so great an extent. He was sensible at the same time that it would be unwise to propose one of any other form. In his private opinion he had no scruple in declaring, supported as he was by the opinions of so many of the wise & good, that the British Govt. was the best in the world: and that he doubted much whether any thing short of it would do in America." Farrand, 1:288.

16. See Thomas L. Pangle, *Montesquieu's Philosophy of Liberalism* (Chicago: University of Chicago Press, 1973), pp. 48–106.

17. See, e.g., Farrand, 1:134–36 (Madison), 218–19 (Madison), 260–61 (Wilson).

18. See, e.g., Jensen, 2:167–72 (Wilson), 339–63 (Wilson); Elliot, 3:128–32 (Madison), 399–400 (Madison). See also *Federalist*, nos. 10, 37, 47–51 (Madison).

19. See, in general, Gordon S. Wood, *The Confederation and the Constitution* (Washington, D.C.: University Press of America, 1979).

20. See, e.g., Montesquieu, *The Spirit of the Laws*, trans. Thomas Nugent (New York: Hafner, 1949), pp. 1–20, 40–70, 149–206.

21. See, e.g., David Hume, "That Politics May Be Reduced to a Science," in *Essays: Moral, Political and Literary* (Oxford: Oxford University Press, 1963), pp. 13–28.

22. For example, at the Virginia ratification convention, Wythe opines: "He thought that experience was the best guide, and could alone develop its consequences. Most of the improvements that had been made in the science of government, and other sciences, were the result of experience." Elliot, 3:587.

23. Farrand, 1:264.

24. Farrand, 2:278.

25. See David Hume, "Idea of a Perfect Commonwealth," in *Essays*, pp. 499–516. For commentary on Hume and Madison, see Douglass Adair, *Fame and the Founding Fathers* (New York: Norton, 1974), pp. 75–106.

26. See *Federalist*, esp. pp. 81–84.

27. See, e.g., David Hume, "Of Parties in General," in *Essays*, pp. 54–62.

28. *Federalist*, p. 78.

29. See, e.g., David Hume, "Of the Original Contract," in *Essays*, pp. 452–73.

30. See, for pertinent discussion, Richards, pp. 89–102.

31. James Madison, "Memorial and Remonstrance," in *The Mind of the Founder*, ed. Marvin Meyers, rev. ed. (Hanover and London: University Press of New England, 1981), pp. 5–13.

32. See, e.g., Leonard Levy, *Judgments* (Chicago: Quadrangle, 1972), pp. 169–224; Thomas J. Curry, *The First Freedoms* (New York: Oxford University Press, 1986), pp. 193–222.

33. Farrand, 1:606.

34. In his first *Letter Concerning Toleration*, John Locke characterized the just limits of state power in terms of "[c]ivil interest . . . life, liberty, health, and indolency of body; and the possession of outward things, such as money, lands, houses, furniture, and the like." *The Works of John Locke* (London, 1823), 6:10.

35. *Federalist*, p. 81.

36. See, e.g., Pangle, pp. 48–106.

37. See, e.g., Herbert J. Storing, ed., *The Anti-Federalist* (Chicago: University of Chicago Press, 1985), pp. 113–14.

38. See, e.g., Jensen, 2:340–44.

39. See, e.g., *Federalist*, pp. 81–84.

40. *Federalist*, p. 387.

41. *Federalist*, p. 342.

42. See, e.g., Pangle, pp. 48–106; James Moore, "Hume's Political Science and the Classical Republican Tradition," *Canadian Journal of Political Science* 10 (1977): 809; David Miller, *Philosophy and Ideology in Hume's Political Thought* (Oxford: Clarendon Press, 1981), pp. 121, 150–51.

43. For Montesquieu, such commerce is nothing short of world revolutionary; see Pangle, pp. 200–48. For Hume, such commerce has been an essential cause of the growth of public liberty in civilized societies; see Duncan Forbes, *Hume's Philosophical Politics* (Cambridge: Cambridge University Press, 1975), pp. 296–98.

44. *Federalist*, p. 79.

45. On the liberating force of capitalist commercial life in early America, see Joyce Appleby, *Capitalism and a New Social Order* (New York: New York University Press, 1984).

46. Jensen, 2:342.

47. For Hume's skepticism about contractarian political theory, see, e.g., Hume, "Of the Original Contract," pp. 452–73.

48. For defense of this position, see Richards.

49. Farrand, 1:421.

50. Ibid.

51. See, in general, Koch, pp. 62–96.

52. *Federalist*, p. 79.

53. See, e.g., *Federalist*, p. 79.

54. See *Federalist*, no. 78 (Hamilton). The lifetime tenure of the federal judi-

ciary, unique among federal officials, may be understood as the functional equivalent to the use of the hereditary principle, by Montesquieu and Hume, as a key
feature of the balanced constitution and its protection of civil and political liberty.
See, in general, Pangle and Forbes. Of course, the Founders of the United States
Constitution could not, consistent with their republicanism, accept a class-bal-
anced constitution (including hereditary classes), which Montesquieu and Hume
contemplated as one way of resisting oppressive super-factions.

55. See *Federalist*, no. 78 (Hamilton), which makes this point.

56. See *Federalist*, pp. 316–17.

57. See, in general, Richards. Cf. John Rawls, *A Theory of Justice* (Cambridge,
Mass.: Harvard University Press, 1971), and "Kantian Constructivism in Moral
Theory," *Journal of Philosophy* 77 (1980): 515.

58. Jensen, 2:472.

59. Cf. Albert Furtwangler, *The Authority of Publius* (Ithaca: Cornell University
Press, 1984).

60. See, e.g., Farrand, 1:122–23 (Madison), 123 (Wilson), 127 (Wilson); 2:92
(Madison), 468–69 (Wilson), 469 (Madison), 475–76 (Madison), 477 (Wilson), 561–
62 (Wilson).

61. *Federalist*, p. 314.

62. See U.S. Constitution, Preamble.

63. Farrand, 4:37–38.

64. See, e.g., Richards, pp. 20–64.

65. See, in general, Dworkin.

66. See Herbert Wechsler, "Toward Neutral Principles of Constitutional
Law," *Harvard Law Review* 73 (1959): 1.

67. 347 U.S. 483 (1954).

68. For a sampling of this commentary, see Wechsler; Louis Pollak, "Racial
Discrimination and Judicial Integrity: A Reply to Professor Wechsler," *University of
Pennsylvania Law Review* 108 (1959): 1; C. L. Black, Jr., "The Lawfulness of the Segrega-
tion Decisions," *Yale Law Journal* 69 (1960): 421. See also Alexander Bickel, "The
Original Understanding and the Segregation Decision," *Yale Law Journal* 69 (1955): 1.

69. See, e.g., Dworkin, pp. 355–99.

70. See, e.g., *Regents of Univ. of California v. Bakke*, 438 U.S. 265 (1978).

71. See, e.g., Farrand, 1:151–52.

72. Madison originally proposed to the House of Representatives the following amendment to the 1787 Constitution: "No state shall violate the equal rights of
conscience, or the freedom of the press, or the trial by jury in criminal cases." Levy,
p. 179. The proposed amendment was not adopted.

73. At the Constitutional Convention, Madison observed that the mention of
the slave trade "will be more dishonorable to the National character than to say
nothing about it in the Constitution." Farrand, 2:415.

74. My understanding of these issues is indebted to the forthcoming book of
my colleague William E. Nelson, *The Adoption and Early Interpretation of the Fourteenth
Amendment* (in press).

75. Cf. Richards, pp. 296–303.

76. Cf. H. Jefferson Powell, "The Original Understanding of Original Intent,"
Harvard Law Review 98 (1985): 885.

77. See *McCulloch v. Maryland*, 4 Wheat. 316 (1819).

78. 4 Wheat. 316 (1819).

79. See U.S. Constitution, art. 1, sec. 8, cl. 3.

80. Marshall himself examined this issue in *Gibbons v. Ogden*, 9 Wheat. 1 (1824), and *Willson v. Black Bird Creek Marsh Co.*, 2 Pet. 245 (1829).

81. Frege formulated the distinction as between reference (the things referred to by "the evening star" and "the morning star") and sense (the proposition that would be used to characterize, for example, "the evening star"—that is, "a star that arises and is seen at evening time"). In fact, modern science tells us that both linguistic expressions have the same referent (namely, the planet Venus), but they have, of course, different senses. On Frege, see Gareth Evans, *The Varieties of Reference* (Oxford: Clarendon Press, 1982), pp. 7–41.

82. See Robert Stern, "That Commerce Which Concerns More States than One," *Harvard Law Review* 47 (1943): 1335.

83. See, e.g., *Wickard v. Filburn*, 317 U.S. 111 (1942).

84. Cf. *Gibbons v. Ogden*, 9 Wheat. 1 (1824).

85. See, e.g., Jensen, 2:346–47; Farrand, 1:166.

86. See, e.g., *United States v. Darby*, 312 U.S. 100 (1941); *West Coast Hotel Co. v. Parrish*, 300 U.S. 379 (1937); *United States v. Butler*, 297 U.S. 1 (1936).

87. Felix Frankfurter's classic criticism of these decisions is precisely along these lines. See Felix Frankfurter, *The Commerce Clause under Marshall, Taney, and Waite* (Chicago: Quadrangle, 1964).

88. See U.S. Constitution, Amend. 4.

89. See, e.g., Polyvios G. Polyviou, *Search and Seizure* (London: Duckworth, 1982), pp. 1–19.

90. See Justice Black's dissent in *Katz v. United States*, 389 U.S. 347 (1967).

91. See *Katz v. United States*, 389 U.S. 347 (1967), overruling *Olmstead v. United States*, 277 U.S. 438 (1928).

92. Raoul Berger takes this view in *Government by Judiciary*.

93. See, e.g., Justice Rehnquist's dissent applicable to both *In re Griffiths*, 413 U.S. 717 (1973) and *Sugarman v. Dougall*, 413 U.S. 634 (1973).

94. See, e.g., John Hart Ely, *Democracy and Distrust* (Cambridge, Mass.: Harvard University Press, 1980).

95. See, e.g., Richards, pp. 296–303.

96. See Berger, *Government by Judiciary*.

97. For the views of Attorney General Meese and the opposing views of Justice Brennan and Justice Stevens, see "Addresses—Construing the Constitution," *University of California at Davis Law Review* 19 (1985): 2.

98. See Berger, *Government by Judiciary*, pp. 117–33.

99. See, e.g., *Regents of Univ. of California v. Bakke*, 438 U.S. 265 (1978).

100. See, e.g., *Craig v. Boren*, 429 U.S. 190 (1976).

101. See, e.g., Stanley M. Elkins, *Slavery* (New York: Grosset & Dunlap, 1963), pp. 164–93; Richard Hofstadter, *Social Darwinism in American Thought*, rev. ed. (Boston: Beacon Press, 1955); Thomas F. Gossett, *Race: The History of an Idea in America* (New York: Schocken, 1965); Stephen Jay Gould, *The Mismeasure of Man* (New York: Norton, 1981).

102. See, e.g., Gunnar Myrdal, *An American Dilemma* (New York: Pantheon, 1972), 1:75–78, 101, 144–49, 207–09.

103. See, e.g., Dworkin, pp. 355–99.

104. See Richards, pp. 146–55.

105. Cf. Richards, pp. 34–45.

New York in Theory

THOMAS BENDER

When New Yorkers and others speak of New York as being different, as being something other than America, which they often do, they seem to have in mind some special quality in the city's culture and politics, perhaps associated with its ethnic makeup. Such perceptions, however imprecise, have a ring of truth. Culture and politics in New York are based on fundamentally different premises, premises not shared by the dominant American culture.

The dominant myths of America, those that have been incorporated into the culture of our national life as founding myths, are, curiously enough, easily identified in their origins with quite specific regions: Puritan New England and Jeffersonian Virginia. Neither place is as representative of America as the harder-to-characterize middle colonies are. Yet in spite of the narrowness and purity of their originating context, the dreams of a city upon a hill and of Jeffersonianism have been able to associate themselves with a presumptively real America, with the agricultural frontier and with the small town.

An earlier version of this essay, with a different title, appeared in a special New York City issue of *Dissent*, September 1987.

It is puzzling but true that the less provincial ideology born of New York's more cosmopolitan experience has been unable similarly to establish itself as an American standard. The other two myths—or, to use a more contemporary terminology, these other two representations of the American ideal—have managed to deflect, if not completely obliterate, the alternative standard that has been an abiding theme of cultural and political discourse in New York City since the eighteenth century.

Scholars a generation ago devoted themselves, perhaps too much, to the study of the communitarian myth of the American town and the agrarian myth of the American landscape. It is worth returning to the theme and the point of that scholarship. Our acceptance of these myths of America, whether passively or, as in the case of recent national political leaders, aggressively and instrumentally, has limited our ability to grasp the value as well as the distinctiveness of the culture and politics of New York City.

When we examine these myths we can better see what makes New York City uncomfortable with America and America uncomfortable with, even fearful of, New York City. While the New York experience and the ideology associated with that experience posit a political and cultural life based upon difference, the myth of rural and small-town America denies difference and excludes it from politics and culture. Such exclusion impoverishes civic life; it thins and trivializes the notion of public culture.

CAN ONE REALLY bracket Puritanism and Jeffersonianism? Everything about them, it seems, is different: one religious, the other secular; one hierarchical, the other egalitarian; one urban, the other rural; one reminiscent of the medieval worldview, the other participating in the modernity of the Enlightenment. More differences could be enumerated, but I want to point out a crucial similarity: both reject difference. Neither can give positive cultural or political value to heterogeneity or conflict. Each in its own way is xenophobic, and that distances both of them from the conditions of modern life, especially as represented by the historic cosmopolitanism of New York and, increasingly, daily experience in other cities in the United States and abroad. Let us look more closely, then, at these two "theories" of the promise of American life.

Few phrases reverberate more deeply through American history than John Winthrop's celebration of the Massachusetts Bay Colony as "a Citty upon a Hill." "We must," Winthrop urged his party as they sighted Massachusetts Bay, "be knitt together in this worke as one man." Never has the ideal of community been more forcefully stated in America. The Puritans envisioned a single moral community, one that acknowledged no distinction between private and public values. "Liberty," Winthrop explained in his famous "Little Speech" in 1645, permitted "that only which is good, just, honest"—something to be determined by the consensus of the community.[1]

Contrary to much American myth-making, neither individualism nor democracy was nourished in the New England town of fond memory. Its significance, Michael Zuckerman has argued, is rather for nourishing "a broadly diffused desire for consensual communalism as the operative premise of group life in America." One had a place in a Puritan village or town only if one's values coincided with those of one's neighbors. Instead of incorporating difference, Puritan town leaders were quick to offer strangers, in their own language, the "liberty to keep away from us."[2]

The myth of consensus and sameness was sustained in the towns by a peculiar pattern of "democratic" practice. Votes were taken in the town meeting, of course, but the minutes of those meetings did not record split votes, thus making a single opinion the only recorded history. The ideal of concord and sameness underlay religion as well as democracy. When Jonathan Edwards described heaven for his congregation, it was the New England town ideal made eternal. Heaven, he explained, is a place "where you shall be united in the same interest, and shall be of one mind and one heart and one soul forever."[3]

Although the social basis for such an experience of consensus was undermined by the beginning of the nineteenth century, enough remained to sustain the ideology. The ideal of the covenanted community persisted into the nineteenth century, particularly rooting itself, as Page Smith has demonstrated, in the Midwest.[4]

Even in the seventeenth century, this theory of America accommodated inevitable difference, but in a quite limited way. You cannot be in our town, but you are free to establish your own with your own type of people and beliefs. This sort of pluralism, argued before the Supreme Court as recently as 1982 (in defense of school library censorship in the suburban Long Island district known as Island Trees), is the pluralism of many supposedly consensual communities.[5] The dream of living surrounded by sameness thus persists. It is at the heart of much suburban development, but it is also evident, as Frances FitzGerald has recently shown, in a rather diverse group of contemporary self-segregating communities, ranging from the "Castro" to Jerry Falwell's church.[6]

The dark side of the New England communal ideal is intolerance, as many a seventeenth-century New England Quaker accused of witchcraft learned. Otherness is a problem for such communities; difference becomes indistinguishable from subversion.[7]

⚬❧⚬

THOMAS JEFFERSON, OF COURSE, was less worried about subversion. He even recommended frequent revolutions, always trusting the democratic practice of the living. It is this spirit that prompted Alexis de Tocqueville to refer to Jefferson as "the most powerful advocate democracy ever had."[8] However much we are moved by Jefferson's magnificent democratic professions, we must attend as well to the theory of society that underlay them. Jefferson could trust democracy because he assumed a consensus of values. He opposed places like New York, calling them cancers on the body politic, in part because they would produce citizens whose values and interests would be marked by difference and even serious conflict.

It is only lately, since Garry Wills publicized the Scottish influences on Jefferson's thought, that the communitarian basis of his social theory has become evident. Jefferson believed men were naturally endowed with a "sense of right and wrong" because they were "destined for society."[9] Yet this "moral sense" was honed in actual social relations, making common sense, as Wills puts it, actually "communal sense." The approbation of the community, in other words, provided the basis for assessing virtue.[10] For example, Jefferson granted blacks a moral sense, going on to explain that "their situation" accounted for their evident "disposition to theft."[11]

Jefferson's admiration for Native American tribal cultures has been much remarked. But we must grasp more fully the centrality of such communalism to his general theory of society. It was the basis for his confidence that Leviathan was not needed in the agrarian society he envisioned.[12] Sociability and affection, not the artifice of government, would make the good society. All of this depended, however, upon shared values. Such a consensus would derive, in Jefferson's view, from a common social experience. If cities multiplied social differentiation, a geographically expansive nation of yeoman farmers would by a process of replication encourage a welcome sameness. Not only were cities sacrificed in this vision, but so were immigrants. His commitment to uniformity made Jefferson very hesitant about any policy that would encourage immigration. He explained that "it is for the happiness of those united in society to harmonize as much as possible in matters which they must of necessity transact together." For Jefferson, homogeneity and the duration of the Republic were interlinked.[13]

Jefferson's fear of the heterogeneity associated with immigration provides a clue to his inability to contemplate a republic comprised of former masters and former slaves. Historians have long tried to determine the sources of Jefferson's peculiar position on slavery and freedom: he strongly criticized slavery, but he declined to become publicly identified with any antislavery movement. Even in his private dreams he always assumed that freed blacks would have to be deported. Some Jefferson scholars have focused on his racist language and assumptions, others upon economic interest, still others on his inability to transcend the culture, the worldview, of his time, place, and class. Some have even suggested that slavery was fundamental to his republicanism: freedom was defined by slavery. All of these explanations, and others, contain part of the answer. But no one, at least to my knowledge, has noted the way in which his theory of society as necessarily conflict-free made an interracial republic of former masters and former slaves impossible.

This was the explanation given by Jefferson himself. In his *Notes on the State of Virginia* (1784), he explained why freed slaves, if ever there were such a population, must be removed from society, why it was not possible to "incorporate blacks into the state":

> Deep-rooted prejudices entertained by the whites; ten thousand recollections by the blacks, of the injustices they have sustained; new provocations; the real distinctions which nature

> has made; and many other circumstances, will divide us into
> parties and produce convulsions, which will probably never end
> but in the extermination of the one or the other race.[14]

Jefferson was thus paralyzed. Writing in 1820, he observed that
"we have a wolf by the ears, and we can neither hold him, nor
safely let him go. Justice is in one scale, and self-preservation in
the other."[15] When real conflict of interest and values were present, the happy revolutionary retreated to the conservative standard of self-preservation. He feared even the divisiveness of public antislavery agitation, hoping, quite unrealistically, for a natural
and conflict-free moral progress that would somehow remove the
blot of slavery.[16] There was nowhere else for Jefferson to go.

Certain elements of the Jeffersonian tradition thus appear in
a new light. It is clearer why Jefferson wanted a happy and undif-
ferentiated yeomanry, why he opposed the development of cities
with their complex social structures, their diverse values and
interests. The great defender of democracy based upon sameness,
Jefferson could not in theory accommodate difference. He found
himself compelled to discourage immigration, to maintain slavery,
and to oppose urbanization. Hardly a democratic theory for our
time.

The theory of society embedded in the Jeffersonian myth
impoverishes the public realm. It denies the difference that makes
both politics and the public realm significant. Such a notion of
society and of civic life prepares the way for the acceptance of an
illusory market as the natural law of society. Jefferson's theory of
social harmony was noncapitalistic at its core, yet it led to the
immunization of the marketplace from politics, safe from acknowledged social contest. An assumed social harmony justifies
the market and renders the public realm inert. Hence the peculiar
quality of Americans, who, as William Pfaff has observed, are
inclined to submit themselves "to the proposition that the market
must arbitrate, and that it is scientifically impartial, choosing
necessity."[17]

Both the Puritan and the Jeffersonian myths nourish a distrust of democracy—at least any democracy that proceeds from
difference, whether of culture or of interest. Both undermine a
theory of democracy that proposes to use politics to determine the
allocation of social resources. More than any other American city,
New York historically has proposed this sort of redistributional

politics. One cannot claim as much success for this approach as one might hope for, but there has been some.

When New York has been stopped or even turned back in such ambitions, it has been in the name of dominant American values, not in the name of New York's values. As early as the 1830s, Tocqueville proposed that the blacks and immigrants in cities (what he called the "rabble" of New York) be governed by an "armed force" under the "control of the majority of the nation" but "independent of the town population and able to repress its excesses." In 1840, the conservative Philip Hone, a former mayor, recorded in his diary that universal suffrage might work in the American countryside, but not in New York, with its "heterogeneous mass of vile humanity." After the Civil War, E. L. Godkin, the founding editor of the *Nation*, insisted that economic and social relations were beyond the legitimate reach of politics. If the mass of urban workers could not be dissuaded from pursuing interest politics, he was ready to disenfranchise them, thus removing them from municipal politics.[18]

Most recently, Felix Rohatyn has taken aim at New York's best traditions. In place of the tumult of a politics of difference, he proposes to rescue the city and even the nation from excessive democracy with an elite council of conciliation, much like the leaders of a Puritan church, charged with persuading the wicked of the one true way. For Rohatyn the only strategy for making New York City acceptable to America is to depoliticize the city, substituting—in the Municipal Assistance Corporation and the Emergency Financial Control Board—a suprapolitical authority, "publicly accountable but . . . run outside of politics."[19]

∂₯

IS THERE INDEED a tradition of cultural and social theory in New York City that suggests an alternative to the dominant American myths? a more vital politics? a richer notion of public culture? Does New York offer even a rudimentary alternative myth that deserves recovery? I think it does.

The special character of New York was evident from the beginning. If religion inspired the Puritans and the dream of wealth drove the Virginians, the practicality of trade engaged the first settlers of New Amsterdam. If churches and regular church service came quickly to both Massachusetts and Virginia, it was the countinghouse, not the church, that represented early New

Amsterdam. There was little impulse to exclusion; trading partners were sought whatever their background and values. By the 1640s eighteen languages were spoken in the area that is now New York City.

This very different history became the material for an alternative vision of society in New York, one that embraced difference, diversity, and conflict. By the middle of the eighteenth century William Livingston, who would later be a signer of the Constitution, was beginning to articulate in New York City a remarkable—for its time—theory of society and culture.

Born in 1723, Livingston graduated from Yale College before beginning the study of law in New York City in 1742, the year before Jefferson's birth. A decade later the trustees of the proposed King's College (today's Columbia) requested a charter of incorporation that privileged one religion at the expense of others (it prescribed an Anglican president in perpetuity), and Livingston responded with an innovative vision of city culture that was cosmopolitan and pluralistic.

At a time when all colonial intellectual life was organized in denominational terms, Livingston proposed a radically different premise for culture, one that implied a politics based upon difference. Writing in his own magazine, the *Independent Reflector*, Livingston described a "free" college, one not tied to any private group. It was rather to be governed by the people in their public character—that is, through public authorities.

> While the Government of the College is in the Hands of the People . . . its Design cannot be perverted. . . . Our College, therefore, if it be incorporated by Act of Assembly, instead of opening a Door to universal Bigotry and Establishment in Church, and Tyranny and Oppression in the State, will secure us in the Enjoyment of our respective Privileges, both Civil and religious. For as we are split into a great Variety of Opinions and Professions; had each Individual his Share in the Government of the Academy, the Jealousy of all Parties combating each other, would inevitably produce a perfect Freedom for each particular Party.[20]

This sense of city culture, born of the social history of New York, not only tolerated difference but depended upon it.

Almost exactly one hundred years later, Walt Whitman transformed these same social materials into a work of art, *Leaves of Grass*, first published in 1855. Whitman's greatest poems at once reveled in and reconciled difference. But Whitman's achievement was aesthetic; emotion and imagination, not theory, was the glue that enabled him to encompass difference. *Leaves of Grass* was not an ideological expression of New York. Such expression found its best voice another half-century later, in the person of Randolph Bourne.

The symbolic leader of the first generation of American writers to call themselves intellectuals, Bourne was in fact the prototype of the later New York intellectual, working at the intersection of politics and culture. Bourne gave ideological expression to the cosmopolitan ideal that decisively distinguished New York from the provincial values of America and supplied the context for the emergence, as David A. Hollinger has pointed out, of a left intelligentsia in New York between the wars.[21]

Bourne embraced the immigrants who were transforming New York City. They were his chosen allies against the constraints of the Anglo-Saxon provincialism of his family experience in suburban New Jersey and much of his education. For Bourne, the conjuncture of difference in the metropolis meant neither chaos nor conflict. Instead, it offered freedom from narrow orthodoxies. The diversity of the metropolis was a solvent that worked against the impulse to make one's own, usually limited, interpretation of reality universal.

Bourne's essay, "Trans-National America," published in the *Atlantic* in 1916, amidst the intolerance of war, proposed a cosmopolitan ideal that combined an acceptance of persistent particularism with a commitment to the making of a common or public culture. This cultural theory, deriving from the social experience of New York, was offered by Bourne as a vision for America. Cosmopolitanism, as Bourne defined it, must be distinguished from both cultural pluralism (a form of separatism) and the "melting pot" (a form of assimilation). One could characterize Bourne's notion as a sort of *via media*, but that tells us too little. In fact, his idea was driven by the desire to use ethnic difference to deprovincialize politics and culture in America.

Bourne associated his cosmopolitan image of society with a pragmatic test of truth that rejected absolutes. Having learned from John Dewey, his teacher, that truth or knowledge was the product of inquiry, an actual social experience that explicitly accommodated different social perspectives, Bourne understood culture not as something fixed but as the product of a historical process. American culture, Bourne insisted, "lies in the future." Rejecting the claims of the Anglo-Saxon tradition, Bourne declared that American culture shall be "what the immigrant will have a hand in making it."[22]

It was an audacious claim when made, and it could have been made only in New York. The editor who published the piece, Boston's Ellery Sedgwick, stood for more traditional and homogeneous American ideals. He had agreed to publish the essay only because of his long-standing relationship with Bourne as a contributor and because the piece was so well written. But he informed Bourne in his letter accepting the article, "I profoundly disagree with your paper." In the incredulous voice of genteel Boston confronted by cosmopolitan New York, he continued: "You speak as if the last immigrant should have as great effect upon the determination of our history as the first band of Englishmen." Insisting that the United States had neither political nor literary lessons to learn from Eastern Europe, he bridled at Bourne's equation of an old New Englander and a recent Czech as "equally characteristic of America."[23]

꩜

IF WE MAY now leap to the present—and toward a conclusion—it is precisely Bourne's vision of New York and America that is endangered by both national and local cultural and political developments. No current cultural and political issue better illustrates these stakes, better shows what gives New York its distinctive quality and what New York would be like if it were America, than does the controversy over the future of Times Square. Is it to remain and be renewed as a New Yorkish public space? Or is it to be transformed, with vastly overscaled corporate towers designed by Philip Johnson, into a corporate campus? Is it to remain the product of the multiple and contending forces that have historically made the bowtie formed by Broadway and Seventh Avenue one of the world's great public spaces, or is it to be reduced to a mere episode in crass government-sponsored but private real-estate development that could exist anywhere in America?

A government that seemingly recognizes only one constitu-

ency is trying to give to that constituency a space that has historically represented all classes. What Johnson proposes, and what the
political and financial elite sponsoring the scheme desire, is the
transformation of a public space historically marked by a multi-
voiced public culture into a monotonal space without public significance.

To thus destroy Times Square is to destroy our most potent
symbol of New York's peculiarly cosmopolitan politics and culture. Times Square, like Union Square before it, has historically
represented the complexity of the city's culture. Here for all to
see, for all to experience, the city has represented itself in all its
fullness to itself and to the world. No other American city has an
equivalent to Times Square.

The question, however, is whether it is necessary to destroy
the diversity and public quality of this space in order to save it. Is
inclusion, is difference, necessarily incompatible with safety?
What is the source of the loss of confidence that is eroding our
historic cosmopolitanism? From whence the idea that in New
York it is necessary—or even possible—to remove completely all
sources of tension, or even struggles for visibility, in a public
space? Of course, a sense of physical safety is necessary for a
space to function as a public space, but one must have the confidence to weigh, with some delicacy, the legitimate claims of security against the dynamic, even messy elements that make a space
public and that impel the process of making public culture. To say
that the space is in some sense contested terrain is not to deny its
public character; rather, it is to confirm it. Times Square has been
a celebration of and a very complicated reconciliation of difference, remaining so even today, when it has lost much of its
centrality and vitality.

Current proposals—such as those of the Municipal Art Society, the Landmarks Preservation Commission, the City Planning
Commission, and other ad hoc committees and boards—to save
the theaters and the lights at Times Square totally miss the point.
They do not grasp the real historical and political stakes at Forty-
Second Street and Broadway. This complex intersection is a representation of an important tradition, and it is a contemporary
symbol for an alternative to the dominant American presumption
of sameness. Perhaps New York's own myth, to say nothing of its
practice, has never been fully elaborated and achieved, but New
York and America would both lose if it were casually abandoned.

Times Square symbolizes the difference between New York and those Puritan and Jeffersonian founding myths that continue to find resonance across the Hudson. If New York gives in, if New York abandons engagement with difference, who will be left in America to stand against the rising intolerance for difference, against the virulent new provincialism?

A theory of society and culture such as I have described does not, of course, constitute a politics. But without it, without a symbolic representation of diversity and difference, the much-discussed but perpetually unrealized progressive politics of a "rainbow" coalition is an impossibility.

New York has never been completely alone in standing for a cosmopolitanism in culture and politics. In fact, much of twentieth-century reform in American national politics has been driven by an urban coalition led by New York. The founding of the United States Conference of Mayors in 1933, for example, was the work of New York's Fiorello LaGuardia and Detroit's Frank Murphy. Surely one finds rich patterns of cultural difference in Chicago, Boston, and Los Angeles, to name only a few large American cities. But even more must be said on this point. Modern society, wherever one looks, is more like heterogeneous New York than like the homogeneous yeoman empire or Puritan utopia of American myth. General American experience, even in the suburbs, may be, however reluctantly, going the way of New York.

Certainly this is not the time for New York to lose confidence in its historic cosmopolitanism. America's metropolis, so long beleaguered in a land drawn to Jeffersonian and Puritan mythology, may, after all, prove prophetic. Perhaps New York may yet in theory become one with America.

Notes

1. Edmund Morgan, ed., *Puritan Political Ideas* (New York: Bobbs-Merrill, 1965), pp. 92–93, 139.

2. Michael Zuckerman, *Peaceable Kingdoms* (New York: Knopf, 1970), pp. 4, 5.

3. Zuckerman, p. 51.

4. Page Smith, *As a City upon a Hill* (New York: Knopf, 1966), esp. ch. 3.

5. For a historically grounded critique, see Thomas Bender, "One for the Books," *New York Times*, Feb. 19, 1982, p. A31.

6. Frances FitzGerald, *Cities on a Hill* (New York: Simon & Schuster, 1986).

Note the modification of Winthrop in her title. The change makes my point in the fewest possible words.

7. See the very powerful argument in Christine Leigh Heyrman, *Commerce and Culture* (New York: Norton, 1984).

8. Alexis de Tocqueville, *Democracy in America* (New York: Knopf, 1945), 1:280.

9. Adrienne Koch and William Peden, eds., *The Life and Selected Writings of Thomas Jefferson* (New York: Random House, 1944), p. 430.

10. Garry Wills, *Inventing America* (Garden City, N.Y.: Doubleday, 1978), p. 197.

11. Koch and Peden, p. 261.

12. Richard Matthews, *The Radical Politics of Thomas Jefferson* (Lawrence: University of Kansas Press, 1984), pp. 17–18.

13. Koch and Peden, pp. 216–17.

14. Koch and Peden, p. 256.

15. Quoted in David B. Davis, *The Problem of Slavery in the Age of Revolution, 1770–1823* (Ithaca: Cornell University Press, 1975), p. 183.

16. Koch and Peden, pp. 641–42.

17. William Pfaff, "Reflections: Elitists and Egalitarians," *New Yorker*, Sept. 28, 1981, p. 123.

18. Tocqueville, 1:299n–300n; Allan Nevins, ed. *The Diary of Philip Hone* (New York: Macmillan, 1927), p. 508; E. L. Godkin, "The Real Objection to the Candidacy of Henry George," *Nation*, Sept. 30, 1886, pp. 264–65; Godkin, "Classes in Politics," *Nation*, June 27, 1867, pp. 519–20; Godkin, "The Real Nature of the Coming Struggle," *Nation*, April 9, 1874, pp. 230–31.

19. Felix Rohatyn, "Reconstructing America," *New York Review of Books*, March 5, 1981, pp. 16–20.

20. Milton Klein, ed. *The Independent Reflector* (Cambridge, Mass.: Harvard University Press, 1963), pp. 194–95.

21. David A. Hollinger, *In the American Province* (Bloomington: University of Indiana Press, 1985), ch. 4.

22. Randolph S. Bourne, *War and the Intellectuals*, ed. Carl Resek (New York: Harper & Row, 1964), pp. 114, 108.

23. Ellery Sedgwick to Randolph Bourne, March 10, 1916, Randolph S. Bourne Papers, Special Collections, Columbia University.

II

RIGHTS

Equality:
An American Dilemma

J. R. POLE

The admissions committee of a professional graduate school is deliberating on the claims of three candidates for the one remaining place in the incoming class. The three candidates, whose names are A, B and C, have scored similar grades, and the nonacademic considerations may be taken into account. A, the son of an unemployed steelworker, has worked hard and saved from his own earnings; he is of Polish descent with no history of professional aspiration in his family. B is Hispanic, the daughter of a single-parent mother who works as an office cleaner; father unknown, possibly Indian. C is the son of a black law professor; his mother, a white, is a civil servant. C has perhaps had to work less hard than A or B to get this far. Is the committee considering three ethnic or gender representatives, or three individuals? Readers are invited to form their own committees.

The dilemma—in this case a trilemma—has become familiar from the lawsuits and policy debates of recent years. Most of them have been settled with the aid of common sense assisted by informal private judgments. But there are hard cases, and marginal decisions arising under the Civil Rights Act of 1964 as well as the Fourteenth Amendment have become the subject of anguished debates on constitutional law. And because constitutional law is invoked, these discussions are constantly referred back to issues of general principle; general principles are thus involved in each decision, necessarily setting precedents for future cases.

But general principles have to be defined in individual cases. In all these cases the issue is equality. That, however, is to state the problem, not to resolve it, because definitions of equality differ; they have differed at different historical periods and among conflicting interests in the same period—never more so than now. The problem involves a search for the complex but often fascinating interplay between the history of the idea of equality and the logical analysis of its meaning.

First as a social ideal, then as a constitutional principle, the idea of equality has a primacy in America that it generally lacks in other Western democracies. When, as in the American case, a country commits itself to a philosophical principle as a specific reason for its existence, it inevitably invites a certain philosophical scrutiny—not least, in America's case, because equality has not been the only important ideal. It is indeed not the only ideal enumerated in the Declaration of Independence. Liberty, in a practical sense, has often mattered more, and to more people. So we should begin by asking exactly why equality deserves the primary status so often claimed for it.

To begin with the logic. The Declaration of Independence *begins* with equality. It then proceeds to name certain natural rights, among which are mentioned the rights to "life, liberty and the pursuit of happiness." If, however, all men are created equal, they cannot logically have unequal shares in the rights that follow from this equal creation: their claims to the enumerated rights must in the nature of the case be equal claims.

Liberty, I have suggested, has been a more active force in American history than equality—it might be said that equality has been called into play from time to time as a corrective to the economic and social effects of liberty. And the two have often been held to be in conflict, so that America seemed to be dedicated to two inconsistent ideals. Their rival claims are often presented as posing one of the irreconcilable dilemmas for American political science. No American political scientist ever made this dilemma more ruthlessly clear than William Graham Sumner in his essay *What Social Classes Owe to Each Other*, published in 1883, where equality is a pernicious doctrine because it puts a stop to evolutionary progress.

But once we have granted the premise of the individual condition of equality of rights, it must follow logically that no American can be entitled to *more* liberty than any other: Americans enjoy a right to liberty, but the shares they hold in that right must be equal shares.

There is some question as to whether we can know that rights exist. Like certain chemicals, they are colorless, odorless, and tasteless; we can conceive of them, but only in connection with the objects to which they are attached. At the founding of the Republic, one of the rights principally in view was the right to property. So, when these abstractions are translated into more concrete terms, the Founders would have perceived no contradiction, no inconsistency of principle, between the equal right to acquire property on the one hand and on the other hand the quite unequal amounts of property held by different people as a result of the free exercise of these rights.

In the language of Douglas Rae and his associates,[1] the kind of equality the Founders believed in was "person-regarding" equality, not "lot-regarding" equality. This group's rigorous analysis has shown that a strict attachment to "lot-regarding" equality, which requires constant equal distribution of goods, can be maintained only in a static society. In principle this aim could be maintained in a steady state. But to do so would require suppressing the functioning of natural inequalities among people, because the exercise of natural inequalities leads *inevitably* to the growth of acquired inequalities in goods and opportunities.

If the Constitution has any continuous meaning from the time of its foundation, there must be a connection between what it originally meant and what it means now; but it is a tortuous connection, fraught with epistemological problems. It is certainly not a direct connection, but a connection certainly exists. To infer the meaning of the Constitution we must read the text of the Constitution. We could hardly have equal confidence of its meaning from the Decalogue or the plays of Shakespeare. Among contemporary commentaries, *The Federalist* is the best-known testimony to the Founders' belief in the existence of wide natural inequalities among men. The most significant were those differences in ability and character that led to differences in social position and property. According to James Madison, differences of faculty gave rise to differences of property: to protect the free exercise of these differences of faculty was one of the positive aims of the state—the object which, above all others, justified the state's claim to exercise authority over its citizens.

It has been remarked—most recently by John P. Diggins[2]—that the concept of rights, which inspired the Revolution, got lost in this constitutional argument. But I think this comment is misplaced. We must assume that men have rights to the exercise of their own faculties, if they have any rights at all; that part of the theory is implicit in the whole position; and it was not the purpose of *The Federalist* to restate familiar assumptions. We are entitled to retain the idea of a dedication to rights as *basic* to American constitutional thought.

The object of these remarks is to emphasize that the Constitution was founded at a time when the rights and interests of the individual had acquired primary status in America—as was the case to a rather more limited and uncertain extent in the thought of the Enlightenment. When I refer to "the individual" I have in mind the existing, historically derived conventions that permitted only individuals in certain understood categories to enjoy the favor of this form of public regard—in effect, to *be* the public: for the most part, adult white men paying taxes or owning some small portion of personal property. These limitations could be lifted, and civic recognition extended to other classes, without having to rewrite the individualist principle at the core of the new system.

The Founders of the American Republic had many intellectual debts, not least to the civic principles of the Italian Renaissance.[3] Renaissance political thought, however, had little general interest in rights; Machiavelli neither advised the prince to respect human rights nor advised him to ignore them: they did not exist. Republican thought emphasized the civic value of equality for reasons of civic stability, not for justice or fairness. Everyone was supposed to have a common or equal interest in stability.

The great example of egalitarian legislation from the ancient world, well known to Americans not only from classical education but because of its prominent place in the *Oceana* of James Harrington (1656), was the famous Agrarian Law of the Gracchi. J. G. A. Pocock has suggested that, in the United States, the West took the place of the Agrarian Law. But for Harrington, the Agrarian—as he called it—did not prevent considerable and lasting disparities of wealth; its aim was to ensure that no group of great landowners could grow by acquisition into the "over-mighty subjects" who had threatened the stability of the English kingdom in the Wars of the Roses.

Whatever we may think of the role the West actually played in American development, its presence was not thought of as an equivalent to the Gracchian law in 1787, and although it certainly played an important role in the anticipations of the nation's future, that role was not to be mediated through egalitarian land laws.

What I am suggesting is that, at the founding of the United States—Pocock's "Machiavellian moment"—the radical transformation which had taken place in the idea of the state took concrete form in the Constitution. The concept of individual rights had assumed pride of place in the configuration of the objects of public concern which were supposed to have called the state into existence. And in the United States of America, as nowhere else, "the State" was being called into existence in a sense that many contemporaries regarded as analogous with the original social contract they had learned about from John Locke.

The Constitution as adopted at Philadelphia does not begin with a statement of general principles, as the Declaration of Independence had done; in fact, it does not declare any rights at all, it assumes them. But it also makes certain prohibitions and confers certain powers that unmistakably imply general views of society. It forbids titles of nobility and precludes any idea that inherited social status could confer political privilege. (It has hardly been entirely successful in this aim.) Although political representation was left to the states, where it was generally restricted to adult white males with a modicum of property, there was a strong presumption that one man's vote counted equally with another's. This meant that electoral districts were expected to be of approximately equal population—fixed at 30,000 in the House of Representatives.

The Constitution reinforced this view by acting directly on individual citizens—an indisputable principle in a form of government that was to be national rather than a league of sovereign states. Wherever the federal government was concerned, it knew of no distinctions between persons. It could not treat one person, or members of one group, as having rights or privileges or protections that placed them in a different constitutional category from the others. The Constitution could not claim to be "color-blind," since it obliquely protected black slavery, and it was not sex-blind either,[4] but among male citizens it was class-blind, and that form of blindness could be extended without impairing the principles on which it was based—principles of individuality.

When the Bill of Rights was adopted in 1791 the principle of individual equality under the Constitution was formally codified. The concept of equal protection—though not that of "substantive due process"—was already implicit in these clauses.

The social nature of man was well understood. Eighteenth-century thought assumed the fundamentally social objectives of society when it did not make them explicit. For this reason, it seems to me important to dwell on the corollary at this crucial moment in the formation of statehood—the countervailing strand of positive political thought that insisted on the rights of individuals as legitimating the very existence of the state.

The Constitution was a very loose-fitting garment. It would be impossible to draw a map of American society with nothing but the Constitution as a guide; and it was very tolerant of any number of different, voluntary arrangements of people in various forms and groups. But the rights of individuals under the Constitution were always to be equal rights. This means, in my view, that the Constitution would be obliged by its own *internal* principles to withhold its protection from any form of group arrangement that restricted the rights of members of any one or another group, *as individuals.* In this sense the Constitution was committed to an equality of individual rights, at least as far as it reached its own citizens.

The reason I am insisting on this theme, which to many may appear obvious, is that often and over long periods the Constitution has been committed to interpretations that specifically recognized unequal political and social consequences resulting from defining individuals by group membership. Exactly what kind and degree of such organization ought to be tolerated by the Constitution will always remain a matter of debate because it will always tend to arise in circumstances where the intended benefits are debatable. A familiar example of the problem of interpretation is that of the laws which were enacted to protect women from exploitation and are now regarded as oppressive to women. Such laws treated women as a class, with the best intentions, but failed to allow for individual differences among women, as the laws normally did among men.

The evidence for this insistence on the individualistic basis of formal American political principles is not confined to the Constitution: it can be found in the political philosophy underlying the state governments formed in the revolutionary period, where it makes its appearance in bills of rights preceding the first state constitutions. It was highly articulate in the mind of Thomas Jefferson, and the philosophical background is clearer in his Rough Draft of the Declaration of Independence than in the final form of the document. "We hold these truths to be sacred and undeniable," Jefferson had originally written, "that all men are created equal and independent; that from that equal creation they derive rights equal and inalienable."[5]

The dynamics of American development in the next century placed the idea of equality under severe stress. A historical analysis has shown that it was susceptible of different emphases, of different meanings to different classes, and even of internal conflicts.[6] Equality before the law was an original Enlightenment category; political equality in effect came in with the Constitution, and equality of religious conscience with the First Amendment (though only as far as the federal government was concerned). But the most popular slogan of nineteenth-century individualistic capitalism was "equality of opportunity," which was similar in principle to the French notion of *la carrière ouverte aux talents*. A different category, transfusing the others and constituting the driving force of social protest, was that of equality of esteem. (Michael Walzer speaks of "equality of respect," Ronald Dworkin of "concern and respect" meaning the same thing;[7] but I prefer my term.) Sexual equality has also emerged as a distinct historical category. But it is not desirable to extend these categories until they represent a mere table of special interests. The reason why I do not make room for a category of racial equality is that races (whatever they may be; the concept itself is suspect) consist of individuals, and individuals are the very subjects of the egalitarian principles we have been discussing.

Both the individualist principles at the root of American political philosophy and many of the open conditions of American society made room for the emergence in the nineteenth century of an idea that I have called "the interchangeability principle."[8] It can be illustrated freely from Mark Twain, who was particularly fond of it. In his fable "The Prince and the Pauper," the two central characters, both of them children and therefore innocent of the adult world and its values, change their garments—and with the change of garments they literally change places: the prince becomes a pauper, the pauper child, a prince. The idea is developed at greater length in *A Connecticut Yankee at King Arthur's Court.*

The idea is disarmingly simple, and it could make no claim to be completely new: the English peasants, at the time of Wat Tyler's rebellion in 1381, had sung "When Adam delv'd and Eve span / Who was then the gentleman?" But despite its moral appeal, it begs the question of whether people *really are* what they have become—from circumstances not only of parentage but of region and culture, religion and education, if we exclude genetics. It seems in a sense to preempt the meaning of cultural history. But the interchangeability principle had tremendous appeal, and seems to have entered into American folklore quite early in the nineteenth century. Part of its attraction is that it converts so easily into the recognized ideal of equality of opportunity. The trouble, for the idealist of equality, was that in a highly competitive economy, it was going to run into conflict with equality of esteem. Americans wanted a society run on equal principles without wanting a society of equals.

"Interchangeability" took its force from defiance of distinctions of rank, economic class, inherited status. In this sense I think its passage may have been made easier by an underlying assumption of homogeneity—essentially of white, mainly north European Protestants. It may be thought of as a moral counterpart of the "equality of conditions" that formed such an important part of Tocqueville's exposition of the social character of the Republic as he found it in the early 1830s.

In the later nineteenth century, Lester Frank Ward, an anthropologist of strong egalitarian convictions, gave powerful support to this idea and ideology of interchangeability. Ward broadened the concept in the developing context of a society of racial, ethnic, and religious groups, with all the familiar accompanying complex of prejudices and exclusions. He insisted that existing inequalities, between groups of men and between men and women, were the product of circumstance—not of class, or race, or "blood." "There is no better or nobler blood; there are no inferior peoples, only undeveloped or stunted ones. The same is true of individuals."[9] (The reference to "undeveloped or stunted" peoples of course reflects the contemporary preoccupation with evolution as a social force.) Ward brought the American ideology of equality to the affirmation that equalization of opportunity would bring equalization of intelligence.

By that time, however, this was a minority voice. By the end of the nineteenth century, the law of the Constitution was being brought to bear not to redress individual inequalities but to validate bloc inequalities. The most notorious case, though not the first, was *Plessy v. Ferguson* (1896), which effectively permitted Jim Crow legislation under the plausible but specious doctrine of "equal but separate."

The Supreme Court was articulating views generally held in white America. But I have always found it difficult to acquit Justice Brown, who rendered the judgment, of deliberate cynicism when he denied "the assumption that the enforced separation of the two races stamps the colored race with a badge of inferiority" and asserted instead that such an opinion of the act in question could exist "solely because the colored race chooses to put that construction on it."[10]

The decision was clearly accepted for many years as a satisfactory resolution of a vexatious if rather minor problem; constitutional histories written in the 1920s and 1930s pay little attention to it. People were able to satisfy themselves that equality and separateness were compatible because all the members of both racial groups were treated alike with respect to each other. All blacks and all whites were affected by the law, and if it restricted personal liberty, it did so in the same way for all of them.

Race relations were not the only area in which bloc-defined assumptions of individual identity were taking over American public thought. They were the most influential, however, in the sense of being fraught with the most pervasive consequences from the point of view of the dilemma that begins this essay; there was a strong sense now in which ethnic or religious identity was becoming the acid test of *American* identity. It was certainly becoming the acid test of personal opportunity in the American economic system.

Common sense rather than constitutional law suggested toleration of a good deal of informal or semiofficial pluralism in all sorts of ways in a society that had become pluralistic beyond the dreams—or fears—of the Founders. But neither common sense nor constitutional law required the kind of reasoning employed in *Plessy*. The same principle would have equally well constituted grounds for requiring comparable forms of separation between

Protestants and Catholics, Jews and non-Jews, Hispanics and other minorities. I believe this kind of reasoning to be incompatible with the constitutional requirements of a society based on individual rights and sustained by constitutional law; it is incompatible with equal protection under the Fourteenth Amendment. But in spite of the immense wealth of discussion, the basic reasons have not been made clear. They are essentially individualistic reasons, neither derived from nor compatible with the view that people can best be considered as representative members of socially or ethnically defined groups.

The point can be demonstrated from the crucial test of intermarriage. Let us suppose that the law lays down that Greens and Blues must not marry each other, and further that this law has the consent of the majority of both communities. So Person A, a Green, may marry any other Green, and Person B, a Blue, may marry any other Blue. All Greens and all Blues being subject to the same law, the majority are satisfied that the law of equality has been preserved. And so are the judges.

The trouble is that A and B do want to marry each other. And they, as individuals, are not being treated equally with other Greens or Blues in the matter that is of the highest importance to the individual, because *their* liberty is restricted by a law that defines them not as free individuals but as members of two groups—to which, incidentally, they never chose to belong. If the argument, presented in this way, carries conviction, it must be said that it has not done so for very long. It was as recently as 1967 that the Supreme Court overturned southern laws forbidding interracial marriage.[11]

The political and ethical convictions that gradually overturned racial and religious discrimination in the years after the Second World War were the result of a historically extraordinary concentration of forces. But the results were not harmonious. It began to appear that the categories of equality, as listed earlier in this essay, did not form an indivisible conceptual ideal, but on the contrary that some categories might be in conflict with others. This discovery, which has made former allies into enemies, was, I think, not widely contemplated until *after* the passage of the Civil Rights Act of 1964.

In 1965 President Lyndon Johnson made a famous speech at Howard University. It was then that he said, "We seek not just freedom but opportunity—not just legal equity but human ability—not just equality as a right and a theory, but equality as a fact and a result."[12] He meant that minority Americans now had a right to expect results in terms of employment, income, education, housing, and hopes for the future of their families, rather than pious incantations.

His phraseology quickly adapted itself to a new concept, which had not been apparent in the drive for the Civil Rights Act; and leaders claiming to speak for blacks, and soon for other groups, claimed that "equality of result" must be reflected in the actual numbers of these groups in the allocation of jobs, promotions, and other placements throughout their communities. It soon became conventional to distinguish between "equality of result" and the older concept of "equality of opportunity."

In the sense in which it has come into general use, "equality of result" is an evasive expression. It conceals a transition of intent from a rights-based individualism to a new typology of group determination in which the outcome of any particular case can no longer be determined by an appeal to individual rights. Nathan Glazer has called it "statistical parity,"[13] but that is misleading because parity is not the aim. I think a better term, which I propose as a substitute, is *proportional pluralism.* This formula implicitly recognizes the pluralistic view of American society on which the policy is based and the policy's intention to work that pluralism into the foundations of American law.

Defenders of proportional pluralism maintain, with some reason, that while opportunities in America remain badly skewed against blacks, action is continually needed to keep on redressing the imbalance until the distribution is right. And, they go on to argue, we can *know* that the distribution is right only when we can *ascertain* that it is proportional.

The political consequences were only to be expected; they were what in Britain is known as the "knock-on effect." Other minorities put in their claims, and politicians accede to them in the spirit of bargain and compromise, not at all unlike the way in which nineteenth-century tariff acts reflected all the economic interests who wanted protection and could make themselves heard in Washington.

Opponents of the proportional pluralist case should recognize that it can make an important contribution to the debate about American civil-rights policy. Not least among its strengths is a passionate desire to set right the wrongs resulting from injustice in the past. (I myself would go as far as to say that anyone who does not share that desire is on weak ground to take part in the debate.)[14] It is argued that the Civil Rights Act was intended and expected to produce this kind of proportional result; it follows, notwithstanding the express language of the act, that it cannot be misrepresented if results obtained under it are forced into a pattern conforming to this fundamental aim. In *U.S. Steel Workers v. Weber* (1978), a case decided under the act of 1964, not under the Fourteenth Amendment, the Supreme Court opined that "interpretation of the sections forbidding all race conscious affirmative action programs would bring about an end completely at variance with the purposes of the statute." In other words the statute was in certain ways at variance with itself, so that it fell to the judiciary to decide which portions were more fundamental than others. But the Supreme Court also recognized that the race-conscious training scheme that gave rise to the *Weber* case was a temporary measure: no sanction was given to any idea of using affirmative action to maintain racial proportions on a permanent basis.

The proportional pluralist case is at its strongest when a black or other member of a minority can claim that he or she is discriminated against, that is, evaluated not as a neutral individual, on the basis of appropriate qualifications for the job, but as someone who is black—or, *pari passu*, Hispanic, female, and so on. There are obvious difficulties, as has often been remarked in the course of these controversies, in mounting a racially neutral defense against a racially conscious attack. That is the dilemma central to the civil-rights theory.

Apart from these concessions, however, the proportional pluralist case represents a profoundly significant departure from both the aims and the underlying principles of the earlier civil-rights movement. In the *Brown* case, the NAACP team of lawyers, led by Thurgood Marshall, argued for the abolition of *all* color-conscious allocations; it is interesting—and sobering—that Marshall seriously considered the advisability of accepting a modified reaffirmation of *Plessy*, qualified by the insistence that this time conditions must really be made equal, because he feared that this might be the best they could get from the Court.[15]

I want now to suggest, however, that such an outcome—that is, a modified and modernized version of *Plessy*, accepting "separate but equal" on the basis that the separate conditions really were equal—would actually have laid a more appropriate foundation for the policies that are now widely advocated—equality of result, or, as I prefer to call it, proportional pluralism—than do the foundations laid by the Warren Court in *Brown* and its successors. The principles underlying proportional pluralism, or the misnamed "equality of result," are at least compatible with the doctrines of equal but separate employed by the Court in 1896 to uphold the worst forms of racial segregation.

I should stress here that I am talking at the level of principle and that the issues are not identical; the comparison should not be pressed too far. Proportional pluralism does not prevent intermarriage; it does not prevent people from sitting next to each other in railroad cars, living side by side, or entering business partnerships. It does not represent one race's forcing physical or social separation on another. Most important, its motives are benign, and it is impelled by a basic desire for fairness among groups, where *Plessy* and the legislation behind it were the expression of one group's repugnance toward another.

These qualifications are important. In practice, they modify the effects of policy. They make possible a reasonable amount of fair-minded give-and-take in difficult cases, and they have the beneficial tendency of raising local common sense above the level of refined constitutional law. But in the end, they do not alter the fact that different principles are at work and that if these principles *become* constitutional law the situation for future generations will be changed. (It will be argued that under a Rehnquist Court this turn of events is unlikely, but that does not diminish the importance of understanding the principles at issue; indeed, it may give a breathing space for taking stock of them.)

Proportional pluralism, as I have chosen to call it, does predicate extremely important individual choices on a basis of social or ethnic identification of the individual, and the principle sustaining this identification is a source of immense cultural value in all modern mixed societies; nothing is being said here to detract from these values. But strictly as a basis for qualified appointments, promotions, and responsibilities it tends to be arbitrary and irrational; from the individual's point of view, generally speaking (there are some exceptions, even legally authorized ones) it is also involuntary rather than personally chosen. Ultimately, moreover, it is irrational because it is also indeterminate. In a free society, ethnicity is itself a fluid and unfixable condition, and a law that attempts to fix it will enforce injustices on individuals as well as perpetually losing touch with reality. The system of reasoning that upholds both *Plessy* and proportional pluralism recognizes group or ethnic affinities as having the power to determine the application of rights associated with the individual status of the person. It imposes that determination on the individual and goes on to give that kind of imposed identity a status in constitutional law.

Whatever social policies people in this or the next generation may wish to enact, it is vital to be analytically clear about the distinctions between them: there is a fundamental distinction between using interventionist policies to redress historic injustices and maintaining, as a *general* social policy, an economic or educational balance among permanently identified social groups—however the identification may have been arrived at.

Americans are free to alter the Constitution by reinterpretation, and when this is done, as after *Plessy v. Ferguson*, later generations have to live and contend with the consequences. But the conclusion of this argument links with its beginning, because it is the bloc-conscious orientation of proportional pluralism that represents the real departure from the individualist and rights-based principles laid down by the Founders. To put the matter in the least contentious way, it is the proportionalists, not the individualists, who have to make their case at the bar of the Constitution.

I am concerned not to be misunderstood. These remarks are not intended as an attack on affirmative-action programs or principles. Such programs have done a great deal of good and will continue to have work to do until the point is reached when no presumption of disadvantage attaches to persons of any sort of ethnic or gender status on specific account of that status. But that is an individualist aim, not a pluralist aim. At the deeper level of general principle with which I began, these are different aims, sustained by incompatible philosophies. If the United States, under some future dispensation, were to move deliberately in the direction of proportional pluralism, it would assuredly have a good foundation in the discriminatory laws and customs of its discarded history. It does not seem to me impossible, however, to imagine policies that seek to identify social and educational deprivations and needs, and to devise effective remedies for them, without defining those deprivations and needs in terms of the discredited terminology of race or the unpredictable and insecure status of ethnicity.

Notes

1. Douglas Rae et al., *Equalities* (Cambridge, Mass.: Harvard University Press, 1981).

2. John P. Diggins, *The Lost Soul of American Politics* (New York: Basic Books, 1984), p. 61.

3. J. G. A. Pocock, *The Machiavellian Moment* (New York: Oxford University Press, 1975).

4. Technically, of course, it says nothing to confine political participation to the male sex, but only because this condition was taken for granted. It took a constitutional amendment to extend the suffrage to women throughout the nation.

5. Julian P. Boyd et al., eds., *The Papers of Thomas Jefferson* (Princeton: Princeton University Press, 1951), 1:423–28.

6. J. R. Pole, *The Pursuit of Equality in American History* (Berkeley: University of California Press, 1978).

7. Michael Walzer, *Spheres of Justice* (New York: Basic Books, 1983), pp. 267, 277–78; Ronald Dworkin, *Taking Rights Seriously* (Cambridge, Mass.: Harvard University Press, 1977), pp. 180–83.

8. Pole, pp. 293–94, 295.

9. Pole, pp. 240–41.

10. 163 U.S. 551.

11. Loring *v.* Virginia 388 U.S. 1 (1967).

12. Quoted by Sidney Verba and Gary Orren, *Equality in America: The View from the Top* (Cambridge, Mass., and London: Harvard University Press, 1985), p. 47.

13. Nathan Glazer, *Affirmative Discrimination* (New York: Basic Books, 1975), ch. 2.

14. And compare Glazer, p. 73.

15. Richard Kluger, *Simple Justice* (New York: Vintage, 1977), pp. 290–91.

Of Walls, Gardens, Wildernesses, and Original Intent: Religion and the First Amendment

JOHN SEXTON

I.

Congress shall make no law respecting an establishment of religion, or prohibiting the free exercise thereof . . .[1]

The constitutional law of church and state is at an impasse. For four decades, the Supreme Court has struggled to articulate a coherent interpretation of the religion clauses of the First Amendment. Yet today the enterprise is stalled, with the justices sharply divided over the meaning of the clauses—and with some justices apparently even willing to discard previous doctrine in favor of new approaches. At the same time, significant groups who never were happy with the Court's church-state decisions have mobilized a vigorous assault—often with the assistance of the Reagan administration—on the intellectual roots of those decisions and the doctrines they produced.

The present impasse has many causes, but one undoubtedly is the selective and self-contradictory use of historical evidence by advocates on both sides. In no area of American constitutional law have judges and scholars more consistently resorted to historical materials as the foundation of their analytical structures than in the church-state area. Yet, to date, they generally have used these materials in a way that has obscured the meaning of the First Amendment's provisions on religion.

In this essay, I describe the traditional focus of judicial and scholarly commentary on the meaning of the religion clauses. After identifying the two major competing interpretative positions and the standoff now existing between them, I highlight some of their more obvious shortcomings. In particular, I demonstrate how each major interpretative camp is, in its own way, guilty of doing what others have called "lawyers' legal history"—a phrase describing the advocate's tendency to view historical evidence solely by reference to how it affects his or her position, a tendency that encourages the use of nonhistorical or even antihistorical criteria to select and analyze historical data.[2]

My principal aim, however, is to expose a fundamental flaw in the major premise of both major interpretative camps: limiting the historical inquiry to what I call the "Period of Formulation" (the fifteen years between the adoption of the Virginia Declaration of Rights in 1776 and the ratification of the federal Bill of Rights in 1791). By so limiting their inquiry, both camps are guilty of doing what I call "freeze-frame history"—the tendency, in examining the history of a constitutional provision (here, the religion clauses), to neglect the developing understanding of the provision throughout the constitutional era, during what I call the "Period of Elaboration."

My thesis is that any valid interpretation of the religion clauses must address not only the history that preceded and surrounded their adoption but also the history that followed it, that unfolded as the life of the nation and its law was shaped or (just as important) left untouched by the constitutional provisions. Thus, as we enlist history in the enterprise of constitutional interpretation, we must *both* cultivate a sense of the complexity and ambiguity of the historical record in the Period of Formulation *and* honor the essential character of history as a chronicle of change and development during the Period of Elaboration.[3]

II. The Contending Interpretations

> No provision of the Constitution is more closely tied to or given content by its generating history than the religious clause of the First Amendment. It is at once the refined product and the terse summation of that history.[4]

Though Justice Wiley Rutledge voiced this blunt assertion while dissenting from the Supreme Court's 1947 decision in *Everson v. Board of Education* (the "New Jersey school bus" case),[5] he and Justice Hugo Black (who wrote for the Court) shared the view that the "generating history" of the religion clauses was the key to understanding their meaning. Moreover, though they came to opposite conclusions about the case before them, the two Justices based their opinions upon virtually identical historical accounts.

Over the three decades after *Everson*, in dozens of cases, the Supreme Court reiterated the view that understanding the Period of Formulation was the key to understanding the religion clauses, and various justices repeated the history of that period provided by Justices Black and Rutledge. Whether it was right or wrong, the *Everson* Court's "history" of the religion clauses became the orthodox view.

Over the same three decades, critics of the Supreme Court's church-state decisions generally conceded the *Everson* Court's major premise—to wit, that the "generating history" of the religion clauses was the key to understanding their meaning. They made a more modest attack: the account of the Period of Formulation offered by Justices Black and Rutledge was wrong; therefore, the doctrines based on that version must be discarded. Thus, the historical battle was joined on narrow ground.

THE ORTHODOX HISTORY OF THE RELIGION CLAUSES

Everson was a challenge to a New Jersey statute authorizing local school districts to provide bus transportation to all school children, even those attending sectarian schools. When the school board in Ewing Township offered to reimburse parents for the cost of sending their children to school on public buses, a taxpayer challenged the constitutionality of the payments to parents of students attending Catholic schools. He argued that the aid constituted an "establishment of religion" prohibited by the First Amendment.[6]

Justice Black's opinion for the Court began by noting that European history to the time of the American Revolution was marked by rampant religious persecution and that the nasty habits "of the old world were transplanted and began to thrive in the soil of the new America."[7] This brought him to a pivotal point in his argument:

> *No one locality and no one group throughout the Colonies can rightly be given entire credit for having aroused the sentiment that culminated in adoption of the Bill of Rights' provisions embracing religious liberty. But Virginia, where the established church had achieved a dominant influence in political affairs and where many excesses attracted wide public attention, provided a great stimulus and able leadership for the movement.* The people there, *as elsewhere,* reached the conviction that individual religious liberty could be achieved best under a government which was stripped of all power to tax, to support, or otherwise to assist any or all religions, or to interfere with the beliefs of any religious individual or group.[8]

Once Justice Black had identified Virginia as the principal battleground over church-state relations during the Period of Formulation, his historical argument flowed smoothly: If the Virginian experience was key, then the landmarks of that experience became the critical materials from which to derive the meaning of the constitutional text. Three documents became the "legislative history" of the First Amendment's religion clauses: the Virginia Declaration of Rights of 1776 (written by George Mason with important amendments by James Madison), Madison's 1785 "Memorial and Remonstrance against Religious Assessments," and the 1786 Virginia Statute for Religious Freedom (drafted by Thomas Jefferson in 1779).

In the end, Justice Black derived from these subtexts one succinct passage that, for him, summarized the original intent and present meaning of the religion clauses:

> Neither a state nor the Federal Government can set up a church. Neither can pass laws which aid one religion, aid all religions, or prefer one religion over another. Neither can force nor influence a person to go to or to remain away from church against his will or force him to profess a belief or disbelief in

any religion. No person can be punished for entertaining or professing religious beliefs or disbeliefs, for church attendance or nonattendance. No tax in any amount, large or small, can be levied to support any religious activities or institutions, whatever they may be called, or whatever form they may adopt to teach or practice religion. Neither a state nor the Federal Government can, openly or secretly, participate in the affairs of any religious organizations or groups and *vice versa*. In the words of Jefferson, the clause against establishment of religion by law was intended to erect "a wall of separation between church and state."[9]

In this grand passage, Justice Black married his understanding of the clauses and Jefferson's metaphorical "wall of separation," thereby generating a theory (strict separation) that would dominate the Court's thinking about church-state relations for decades to come.

Perhaps surprisingly, after providing this uncompromisingly separationist account of church-state relations in America, Justice Black concluded that the bus-fare reimbursement plan before the Court in *Everson* was constitutional. In his view, the New Jersey program was an appropriate public-welfare measure designed to provide safe transportation for school children.

Justice Rutledge, the author of the principal dissent in *Everson*, merely restated Justice Black's account of the Period of Formulation with different emphasis. Thus, like Justice Black, he saw Virginia as the laboratory in which the basic elements of the religion clauses were isolated; but for him, James Madison clearly designed and conducted the experiment. As he put it:

All the great instruments of the Virginia struggle for religious liberty thus became warp and woof of our constitutional tradition, not simply by the course of history, but by the common unifying force of Madison's life, thought and sponsorship. He epitomized the whole of that tradition in the Amendment's compact, but nonetheless comprehensive, phrasing.[10]

Because he viewed Madison as the personification of the religion clauses,[11] Justice Rutledge felt untroubled by the virtual absence of historical evidence concerning the First Congress's understanding of those clauses. Indeed, he took that lack of evidence as support for his position: the "sparse discussion" merely indicated "that the essential issue had been settled" by Madison's triumph in the Virginia disestablishment struggle and that the Constitution's provisions on church-state relations enacted Madison's views.

As he analyzed the statute before him in the *Everson* case, Justice Rutledge cited Madison's "Memorial and Remonstrance" as other judges would cite the Internal Revenue Code or a judicial precedent directly on point—effectively identifying the evils Madison associated with the 1784 Virginia religious assessments bill with the 1947 New Jersey bus-fare reimbursement measure. Of course, this led him to conclude that the law was unconstitutional.

Whatever their differences over the result in the *Everson* case, however, Justices Black and Rutledge agreed that the history of the Period of Formulation provided the basis for understanding the religion clauses. Over the next thirty years, a majority of the justices and most scholars embraced their view. *Everson* became not only the law of the land but the prevailing historiographical view of the First Amendment.[12]

AN ALTERNATIVE HISTORY

Even in its own time, the *Everson* Court's account of the generative history of the religion clauses did not go unchallenged. One year after *Everson* was decided, Justice Stanley Reed, dissenting in the very next religion case to come to the Court, argued that the Framers may have intended the establishment clause "to be aimed only at a state church."[13] And Justice Reed was not the only justice to challenge the orthodox view that the religion clauses were designed to implement a doctrine of strict separation of church and state. In *Zorach v. Clauson* (the "released time" case),[14] Justice Douglas described our American tradition in terms strangely at odds with Justice Black's stirring invocation of Jefferson:

> We are a religious people whose institutions presuppose a Supreme Being. . . . We sponsor an attitude on the part of government that shows no partiality to any one group and that lets each flourish according to the zeal of its adherents and the appeal of its dogma. When the state encourages religious instruction or cooperates with religious authorities by adjusting the schedule of public events to sectarian needs, it follows the best of our traditions. For it then respects the religious nature

of our people and accommodates the public service to their spiritual needs. To hold that it may not would be to find in the Constitution a requirement that the government show a callous indifference to religious groups. That would be preferring those who believe in no religion over those who do believe. . . . We cannot read into the Bill of Rights such a philosophy of hostility to religion.[15]

These counterorthodox views were not without support in academe. Even as Justice Reed wrote his dissent in *McCollum*, a few scholars were suggesting that the religion clauses required only that government treat religions even-handedly, not that government separate itself altogether from them.[16] To support their position, these "nonpreferentialists" advanced an account of the generative history of the religion clauses sharply at odds with the one offered by the *Everson* Court. This alternative history made two points: first, the Virginia disestablishment struggle was not typical of church-state relations in colonial and revolutionary America; second, even in Virginia, the strict separationists did not win the total victory portrayed by Justices Black and Rutledge (indeed, not even Jefferson and Madison favored the kind of strict separation embraced by the *Everson* Court).

In making their first point, nonpreferentialist scholars observed that in the Period of Formulation religion was understood to be the prop of government, instilling morality and public spirit in the citizenry. They argued that the Jeffersonian-Madisonian theory of church-state relations was not the only—or even the dominant—theory of church-state relations extant. For example, there was the "pietist" or "religious" tradition, beginning with Roger Williams and continuing through Isaac Backus and the Baptists of the late eighteenth century—a tradition that embraced separation of church and state to protect religion from government, not vice versa.[17] Indeed, the revisionists argued, when the religion clauses were adopted several states still maintained religious establishments of various sorts. Thus, they concluded, in framing the religion clauses, Congress sought only to deprive the federal government of power to tamper with these establishments, either by setting up an established religion of its own or by prohibiting all religious establishments at the state and local levels.[18]

The nonpreferentialists advanced their second point more to buttress the general view posited in their first point than to add something to it. In making their second point, they argued in the style of rebuttal by example—the citation of specific incidents taken from the Period of Formulation that are inconsistent with a commitment to strict separation of church and state. Thus, the nonpreferentialists noted that Presidents Washington, Adams, and Madison issued proclamations of national days of prayer; that a committee (including among its members James Madison) of the House of Representatives of the First Congress (the Congress that wrote the First Amendment and sent it to the states) wrote legislation (later adopted by both houses) providing for paid legislative chaplains; that, when president, both Jefferson and Madison signed treaties with Indian tribes obligating the federal government to subsidize Catholic missionaries and hospitals ministering to the needs of the tribes; and that, while serving in retirement as Rector of the University of Virginia, Jefferson permitted religious education at the school (and that Madison, as a Visitor, approved the practice). Given these practices "inconsistent" with a commitment to strict separation of church and state, the nonpreferentialists argued, the Framers could not have intended the religion clauses to require it. They concluded that Justice Black's reading of the religion clauses must be wrong.

Over the last decade, as the political and social strength of evangelical conservatism has grown, the nonpreferentialist position has gained more and more adherents, both on the bench and in the academic community. Indeed, in one 1983 case,[19] a federal district judge in Alabama, invoking the alternative history (and, in particular, relying on *Separation of Church and State: Historical Fact and Current Fiction*, a 1982 monograph by Robert Cord, a professor of political science at Northeastern University),[20] determined that the Supreme Court's decisions on school prayer had been wrongly decided because they were premised upon a misreading of history. He went on to reverse the Supreme Court's school-prayer decisions and rule that official vocal prayers in public schools were constitutionally acceptable.[21] Of course, the United States Court of Appeals for the Eleventh Circuit reversed the maverick judge's decision.[22] Nonetheless, it is significant that, in later stages of the same case (dealing with the validity of officially reserving moments during the school day for silent prayer), the Reagan administration submitted an amicus brief relying heavily on the history of the religion clauses offered by the district judge and by Cord—and that, writing in dissent from the Supreme

Court's decision in that case, Justice Rehnquist recapitulated that interpretation.[23]

Clearly, the alternative history has significant support. Yet it is striking that, from the earliest rounds of the debate over the meaning of the religion clauses, the critics of the history of those provisions offered by Justices Black and Rutledge—from Justice Reed, to the early nonpreferentialists, to the Reagan administration and Justice Rehnquist—have conceded the *Everson* Court's major premise: that the history of the period of formulation is the key to interpreting the religion clauses. Indeed, present critics of the history developed by the *Everson* Court and the doctrines it has produced typically affirm that major premise with vigor and *insist* that our reading of the religion clauses today must not deviate from the prevailing understanding of them in 1791.[24] Thus, just as the struggle between Justices Black and Rutledge in the first major religion case of the modern era was waged on relatively narrow intellectual ground, so also the debate between adherents of the orthodox view they generated and the major critics of that view has retained a narrow compass.

THE STAKES

The dispute over the history of the First Amendment's religion clauses is more than an academic squabble. As posited, it is a war to determine which camp wins the right to call the past to the bar as a "trump" witness—for both camps see the "correct" understanding of the Period of Formulation as determining the "correct" application of the religion clauses to given church-state controversies.

No single case better illustrates the stakes in the debate—or the present impasse in the constitutional law of church and state—than the Supreme Court's 1983 decision in *Marsh v. Chambers*.[25] For years, the Nebraska legislature had retained a minister to open its sessions with prayer; indeed, the legislature had used public funds to compile and publish the minister's prayers as a book. Finally, a taxpayer sued to have these payments declared unconstitutional.

Nebraska's practice seemed clearly to violate the well-settled doctrine of strict separation;[26] yet a historical argument, based upon facts drawn from the Period of Formulation, seemed to indicate that hiring legislative chaplains did not violate the religion clauses. The argument proceeded: Justices Black and Rutledge identify Madison as the principal author of the First Amendment; Madison was a member of the committee in the First Congress that successfully recommended hiring chaplains for the House and Senate; therefore, the Framers clearly did *not* understand the religion clauses to bar paying legislative chaplains from public funds.

In *Marsh*, the justices faced a dilemma. The doctrines generated by *Everson* commanded one result; the historiography unleashed by the case (employed in *Marsh* by nonpreferentialists rather than by separationists) commanded another. Six justices, led by Chief Justice Burger, decided that history (that is, history seen only through the lens of the Period of Formulation) could "trump" doctrine. Thus, while emphasizing that a "historical trump" of doctrine would be appropriate only in a case where the "original intent" of the Framers was clear, they upheld Nebraska's legislative chaplain scheme. Not since *Everson* had the justices focused so intently and exclusively on the Period of Formulation in order to decide a case. And their commitment to a historiography that viewed the framing period as dispositive led them to disregard thirty years of doctrinal development in reaching their result.

III. *Difficulties—Some Special and Some Fundamental*

THE SPECIAL DIFFICULTIES WITH LAWYERS' HISTORY

Good historians deal with currents and crosscurrents as they build pictures of the past. Good lawyers are zealous advocates in service of a cause (with the desirable result always set *ex ante*), and to that end, they seize upon data favorable to their argument, exaggerate its importance, and extrapolate the conclusions they seek from the distorted picture they have created. Given this reality, it is not surprising that good lawyers often make bad historians—or that when lawyers use history to make arguments, they often use it one-sidedly.

Even the brief account of the religion clauses debate I offered in the last section reveals that each side has available to it data from the Period of Formulation. The results have been what you would expect from lawyer-historians. Each group tugs and hauls at the evidence to paint a picture of that time consistent with its preconceived views. Each group charges that the other fails to account for "crucial" evidence, yet each ignores equally "crucial" evidence against its own position. And neither camp produces a balanced picture of the Period of Formulation.

I offer, just to give a sense of the problem, one of what could be dozens of examples: the dispute between separationists and nonpreferentialists over the meaning and importance of Thomas Jefferson's letter of January 1, 1802, to the Baptists of Danbury, Connecticut (the letter containing the famous "wall of separation" metaphor). For Justice Black, Jefferson's metaphor captured, as no phrase might capture, the commitment of the Framers to the doctrine of strict separation of church and state. Yet, in *Religion and Education under the Constitution*, James L. O'Neill dismisses the Danbury letter as "Jefferson's little letter of courtesy,"[27] savaging as "an almost pathetic example of judicial ineptitude"[28] Justice Black's reliance on this letter and its "wall of separation" metaphor. Which, if either, position is correct?

Jefferson's principal biographer, the late Dumas Malone (a scholar who carried no brief in the debate over the framing of the religion clauses), tells the story this way.[29] The Baptists of Connecticut were being persecuted by the state's Congregationalist majority, which dominated Connecticut's government as well as its religious life. The Danbury Baptist Association appealed to the new president to support its religious liberty against a state government that viewed the free exercise of religion as a favor granted, and not as an inalienable right. Indeed, the Baptists appealed to Jefferson in terms pointedly echoing his Virginia Statute for Religious Freedom. Meanwhile, the newly elected President himself was being attacked by the conservative clergy of New England, who denounced him most loudly for his "irreligion."[30] When he received the letter from the Danbury Baptists, Jefferson decided to make his reply a public declaration of his administration's support for religious dissenters. He went so far as to submit his letter for review to his in-house experts on New England, Postmaster General Gideon Granger and Attorney General Levi Lincoln. Granger thought that the letter might touch off "a temporary spasm among the Established Religionists" but endorsed the draft as written. Lincoln recommended only the deletion of language explaining as conformity with the First Amendment Jefferson's refusal to issue proclamations of days of thanksgiving or other "occasional performances of devotion." The

Attorney General based his recommendation, which Jefferson accepted, on political considerations only, not on any disagreement with Jefferson's understanding of the First Amendment.[31]

Does all this mean that Justice Black had it right all along? No. Whereas critics of the "orthodox" history of the Period of Formulation unduly minimize the significance of Jefferson's letter to the Danbury Baptists, Justice Black and other advocates exaggerate its importance when they offer it as critical evidence that the Framers meant the religion clauses to implement a policy of strict separation of church and state. First, from 1785 through 1790, Jefferson was in Paris as American minister plenipotentiary; he was not in Virginia, or even in the United States. In his correspondence with Madison and other friends and colleagues, Jefferson did criticize the Federal Convention for not including a declaration of rights in the Constitution, and he did propose several ways in which advocates might manipulate the ratification campaign in order to add amendments (including a declaration of rights) to the new charter. Indeed, Jefferson persuaded Madison to abandon his opposition to a bill of rights and to become the principal spokesman in Congress for amendments. Yet Jefferson had—and sought—*no* influence on the substance of Madison's proposed amendments, including the First Amendment and its religion clauses. Second, although the Danbury Baptists letter *was* a formal statement of Jefferson's policy, it postdated by more than a decade the framing and ratification of the Bill of Rights and, therefore, is not dispositive proof of even Jefferson's (let alone the framers') understanding of the religion clauses in 1789. And, third, because in 1802 most authorities believed that the Bill of Rights restricted only the federal government (and not the states),[32] a statement (even a presidential statement) on church-state affairs in Connecticut likely was viewed by all as based upon general policy considerations—and not upon the First Amendment.

The problems associated with lawyers' history can be avoided, of course. By employing the traditional tools of historians and by avoiding the temptation to slip into the more familiar lawyer's role of advocate, constitutional scholars can produce a more accurate picture of the Period of Formulation than those provided by the two major interpretative camps. But even the most dispassionate scholar who seeks to understand the Period of Formulation will face profound historiographical problems. For example, there are few records of the deliberations at any of the relevant layers, and the network of relevant layers (including as it does both the deliberations in the First Congress *and* the deliberations in *each* state legislature) is complex.

THE FUNDAMENTAL DIFFICULTY WITH
THE DEBATE'S MAJOR PREMISE

A second, and more fundamental, flaw flows from the shared premise that the key to interpreting the religion clauses is understanding the history of the Period of Formulation. By obsessively focusing on the Period of Formulation, both sides of the present debate engage in a profoundly antihistorical exercise: They fail to acknowledge the evolution of both religion and American society, and they fail to credit the concomitant changes in the relationship of religion and other institutions in American life.

History is the story of change over time. True, historians write histories of "periods"—indeed, I have suggested that we might write a better history of the Period of Formulation. But, even if it were available, the "perfect" history of the Period of Formulation would not alone provide the "perfect" interpretation of the religion clauses—for, in the interpretation of a constitutional text, it is not appropriate to "freeze" the moving picture of history at one frame, treating the snapshot thus produced as though it captured the whole story.

The first problem associated with using freeze-frame history to guide contemporary interpretation and application of the religion clauses is that, even if the chosen frame (here, the Period of Formulation) could be brought into perfect focus, it is not clear how it could be used to decide a case. Both groups in the interpretative debate I have described tend to reason by analogy from the Period of Formulation to the present, almost willfully ignoring the vast and remarkable currents of change separating that time from our own. But the changes create differences between the Period of Formulation and our own time that cast into doubt any attempt to establish analogies between them.

The second—and more basic—problem associated with using freeze-frame history to inform our interpretation of the religion clauses is that the very attempt to freeze the frame challenges the essence of the religion clauses as *constitutional* texts. The Constitution is not a statute, written to capture the position of a particular legislature at a particular time on a matter of public policy; the

Constitution is the core charter of relationships in our body politic, designed to endure even as circumstances and institutions change. The history of a constitutional provision only begins with its formulation and ratification, for the formulators and ratifiers only begin the task of transferring the basic governing principle into law.[33] The Framers merely set a course by establishing, in a vague and inchoate way, basic principles. Only over time—over a "period of elaboration"—is the full meaning of the text developed. Freeze-frame history is antithetical to this essential feature of constitutional (as opposed to statutory) texts and thus is fundamentally inappropriate as a guide for interpreting them.

Moreover, freeze-frame history is singularly inappropriate when the constitutional text being interpreted is the religion clauses. In no area of constitutional law has there been such dramatic evolution—evolution that, in some ways, has completely transformed the terms of discussion and the institutions to which they apply. Consider just some of the many examples:

There has been an explosion of religious diversity in America unparalleled anywhere else in the world, and certainly unanticipated in the eighteenth century.[34] What was "unthinkable" to many in 1791 has occurred, as citizens worship without regard to the Bible—indeed, as some worship no God at all.[35]

Major new institutions have emerged, and old ones have changed dramatically. Education is a clear case in point. In the eighteenth century, there was no public school system. In the nineteenth century, as public school systems developed, Roman Catholics struggled to establish their own systems of schools because they perceived that the "public" school systems placed Protestant Christianity at the heart of their curriculum; on the other hand, the majority of Americans feared and resisted the creation of parochial schools as a threat to democracy.[36] Then, in the twentieth century, though the relationship of the parallel school systems normalized, parents of children in sectarian schools continued to press for state aid,[37] and some parents of children in public schools launched a purge of "godlessness" from the schools.[38]

Perhaps most important, the scope of application of the religion clauses was expanded dramatically—indeed, fundamentally altered—by the Fourteenth Amendment. It is now beyond cavil that the Fourteenth Amendment "applies" the proscriptions of the religion clauses to state and local governments.[39] The scope

of application of other rights also has expanded by "incorporation," of course, but no other part of the Bill of Rights has seen
its very purpose fundamentally altered by incorporation, as is
arguably the case with the religion clauses. It is evident that, at
least for some of the framers of the First Amendment and for
some of its supporters during ratification, the purpose of the
religion clauses was to protect state establishments from super-
session by a federally established church.[40] To the extent that
these framers represent the "original intent" of all those who
drafted and adopted the religion clauses, incorporation meant
that, through the subsequent and superseding "intent" of the
framers of the Fourteenth Amendment, the religion clauses
came to forbid that which they were at first designed to protect.

For the religion clauses, more than for any other provision of
the Constitution, the case is clear: freeze-frame history is inappropriate. If Clio is to be enlisted as the presiding muse of constitutional interpretation, at least with regard to the religion clauses,
the history of those provisions must be appreciated as change over
time. Theologians refer to the difference between "substance" and
"accident";[41] others refer to the difference between "concepts"
and "conceptions."[42] Whatever the nomenclature, if history is to
guide constitutional interpretation in this area, it must highlight
the core principles (the "substance" or essential "concepts") revealed in the story of our nation's evolving understanding of the
text over the Period of Elaboration that has followed the Period of
Formulation.

IV. Some New Lines of Inquiry

We can approach issues of church-state relations in a way that
respects the integrity of the past yet makes use of that record to
establish a coherent jurisprudence of church and state for the
present. To that end, I propose that we abandon the interpretative
framework employed by both sides in the debate I have described,
with its exclusive reliance on the Period of Formulation. In its
place, I propose that we put an interpretative framework sensitive
to the interrelationship of the Period of Formulation and the
Period of Elaboration. In short, I suggest that the history of the
religion clauses be seen as something more than an attempt to pull
church-state controversies through the needle's eye of the Fram-

ers' intent, and that it be seen instead as an ongoing judicial and political effort to apply overarching principles, or "metaprinciples," of church-state relations in the face of ever-changing circumstances.

I believe that one enduring metaprinciple that will emerge from an appropriate review of the historical record is a principle of equality. In the Period of Formulation, Americans embraced the principle that their new government should not favor one religion over another, that it should treat all religions equally. Of course, at that time most Americans thought that the spectrum of religious belief encompassed little more than the fractious and contending Protestant sects—the Episcopalians, Presbyterians, Congregationalists, Baptists, Methodists, Quakers, and the like. Catholics and Jews numbered less than five percent of the population, and they certainly were politically insignificant. But the nineteenth century witnessed a remarkable growth in America's Catholic population—a growth that demanded, even in the face of continuing social bigotry and persecution against Catholics, an adaptation of the basic theme of equality among religious sects. Thus, the notion of religious equality expanded to embrace all Christian sects. At the same time, and even more markedly at the dawn of the twentieth century, the size and prominence of the nation's Jewish population grew, and the idea of religious equality expanded concomitantly to subsume all branches and denominations of the Judeo-Christian tradition. Most recently, the dramatic influx of "new religions" has transformed the principle of equality yet again, making it impossible to treat traditional monotheistic religions and nontheistic (or even atheistic) religions unequally.

I believe that a second enduring metaprinciple that will emerge from an appropriate review of the historical record is a principle of separation. This concept also has passed through several stages. In the early days of our nation, when the federal government's role in most aspects of social life was limited, churches and the federal government rarely interacted—and, when they did interact, they did so within the context of religious homogeneity that I have described. As our nation grew, and especially as the role of government in education and the provision of necessary social services expanded dramatically, our sensitivity to the identification of religion and government became more pronounced.

Though I offer these two metaprinciples with confidence that the historical record will reveal their enduring presence in our nation's understanding of the religion clauses, I offer them only tentatively. Much work must be done if the interpretative framework I propose is to be employed. I suggest only a few areas of possible inquiry.

First, we must set the Period of Formulation in its historical context—between the colonial history of British North America and the evolution of religion, politics, and society in the new republic following adoption of the Constitution and the Bill of Rights. For example, we must address the curious fact that the revolutionary era coincided with an abrupt and noticeable decline of formal religious observance in America, or, viewed differently, with a brief pause between two religious revivals, or "Great Awakenings" (that of the late colonial period and that of the first decades of the nineteenth century). Superficially, it could be argued that a movement to separate church and state was part of a general decline in interest in religion. It may be, however, that, although formal religious observances and outward manifestations of belief, such as church attendance and membership, declined in the revolutionary period, there was no comparable decline in the depth or sincerity of belief itself. It may be that this movement from institutional to more individual religion is linked to the revolutionary generation's rejection of religion as an essential prop of government in the national sphere and to the gradual, parallel disestablishment taking place in the American states between the 1770s and the 1830s.

Second, we must devote attention to the period between the dismantling of the state establishments in the early nineteenth century and the 1870s, when the Supreme Court first heard cases invoking the First Amendment's religion clauses. It has been suggested that during the nineteenth century there emerged a de facto religious consensus that obviated any formal structures or requirements linking religion to government.[43] This assertion must be tested. Beyond this, we must seek an exact understanding of whatever dominant religious consensus existed in the United States and what effect it might have had on relations between church and state in this period, including its effects on religious or unbelieving minorities.[44]

Third, we must explore the relations between the emergence in the nineteenth century of government institutions (hospitals, schools, relief agencies, and the like)[45] designed to minister to the needs of the people and competing institutions maintained by religious organizations. We must determine how changing views of governmental responsibilities in this period affected prevailing understandings of the proper relation between religion and government.[46]

Fourth, we must examine carefully what I call the "Period of Articulation"—the four decades from 1947 through 1987, during which the Supreme Court made its first assiduous and determined effort to define the meaning of the religion clauses. And, as we examine this period, we must do more than simply chronicle the landmarks of doctrinal development. We must examine the evolving doctrines in the context of the political, social, and religious history of the times.[47]

SCHOLARS OFTEN HAVE SOUGHT to capture the history of the religion clauses in metaphors—whether Jefferson's metaphor of "a wall" or Roger Williams's metaphor of "the garden and the wilderness." I could capture what I have argued here in a metaphor as well—one drawn from the language of musical composition. I believe that the principles that animate the First Amendment abide not only in the basic themes given expression during the Period of Formulation, but also in the variations, transpositions, and orchestrations of those themes that social, technological, and intellectual developments during the Period of Elaboration demanded or made possible. To understand the religion clauses, we must hear the entire composition—not just its first notes.

Notes

This essay presages a book I am writing on the history and theory of church-state jurisprudence in the United States—viewed from the perspectives of both constitutional law and the history of American religion. I am indebted to Richard B. Bernstein, who has provided valuable comments on each draft of this essay. I am also grateful for the extensive and extraordinarily helpful comments of David D. Drueding, Lisa E. Goldberg, and William E. Nelson and for the assistance of Thomas Viles of the class of 1987 at New York University School of Law. Finally, I thank the Filomen D'Agostino and Max E. Greenberg Research Fund of New York University School of Law for its generous financial assistance.

1. U.S. Constitution, Amendment 1.

2. William E. Nelson and John Phillip Reid, *The Literature of American Legal History* (Dobbs Ferry, N.Y.: Oceana, 1985), pp. 235–42 (citing Morton J. Horwitz, "The Conservative Tradition in the Writing of American Legal History," *American Journal of Legal History* 17 [1973]: 275, 276, as the origin of the term).

3. In a thoughtful article, my colleague William E. Nelson examines the usefulness of history in constitutional adjudication. William E. Nelson, "History and Neutrality in Constitutional Adjudication," *Virginia Law Review* 72 (1986): 1237–96. Nelson identifies two basic approaches to history: the *descriptivist*, which seeks to recover a more or less "true" picture of the past on its own terms, and the *contextualist*, which assumes that a fact from the past, taken by itself, is without significance unless placed in some context with meaning in the present. Nelson then examines these two historical methods by reference to three models of constitutional adjudication—*interpretivism*, which emphasizes a close reading and application of the constitutional text and the intent of its framers; *neutral principles*, which seeks to discern principles of constitutional jurisprudence inherent in American society and shared by most if not all Americans; and *antitheoretical realism*, which approaches legal and constitutional disputes as unique and which rejects attempts to determine such disputes by reference to judicial precedent or historical evidence.

This essay addresses issues distinct from those raised by Nelson. I start from the premise, which I take Nelson to have demonstrated, that history can play an important role in constitutional interpretation. On that assumption, I define what I see as the appropriate historical "database." Having identified this database, I do not ask what kind of history (contextualist or descriptivist) is best suited to the enterprise, or whether the interpretation of history, once derived, binds (interpretivism), guides (neutral principles), or otherwise informs (antitheoretical realism) the constitutional decisionmaker.

4. *Everson v. Board of Education*, 330 U.S. 1, 33 (1947) (Rutledge, J., dissenting). Compare Justice Black's opinion for the Court, Everson, p. 8:

> These words of the First Amendment reflected in the minds of early Americans a vivid mental picture of conditions and practices which they fervently wished to stamp out in order to preserve liberty for themselves and for their posterity. Doubtless their goal has not been entirely reached; but so far has the Nation moved toward it that the expression "law respecting an establishment of religion," probably does not so vividly remind present-day Americans of the evils, fears, and political problems that caused that expression to be written into our Bill of Rights. Whether this New Jersey law is one respecting an "establishment of religion" requires an understanding of the meaning of that language, particularly with respect to the imposition of taxes. Once again, therefore, it is not inappropriate briefly to review the background and environment of the period in which that constitutional language was framed and adopted.

5. 330 U.S. 1 (1947).

6. Though by its terms the First Amendment applies only to Congress, the Supreme Court has held that it applies with equal force to state and local governments through the due-process clause of the Fourteenth Amendment. Though now beyond dispute, the proposition that portions of the Bill of Rights apply to all

levels of government still generates some controversy. This controversy—known as the "incorporation" controversy—has inspired a vast and contentious literature, which is beyond the scope of this essay. See, e.g., *Adamson v. California*, 332 U.S. 46, 96–123 (1947) (Black, J., dissenting); Charles Fairman, "Does the Fourteenth Amendment Incorporate the Bill of Rights? The Original Understanding," *Stanford Law Review* 2 (1949): 5; Howard N. Meyer, *XIV: The Amendment that Refused to Die* (1975; reprint, Boston: Beacon Press, 1981); Howard Jay Graham, *Everyman's Constitution* (Madison: State Historical Society of Wisconsin, 1968); Raoul Berger, *Government by Judiciary: The Transformation of the Fourteenth Amendment* (Cambridge, Mass.: Harvard University Press, 1977); Michael Kent Curtis, *No State Shall Abridge* (Durham, N.C.: Duke University Press, 1986).

7. *Everson*, p. 9.

8. *Everson*, p. 11 (emphasis added).

9. *Everson*, pp. 11–12.

10. *Everson*, p. 39. See also note 11.

11. Rutledge went even further than Black in identifying Madison as "the First Amendment's author" and in regarding the "Memorial and Remonstrance" as "the most concise and the most accurate statement of [Madison's] views concerning what is an 'establishment of religion'" (*Everson*, p. 37). He even reprinted the full texts of both the "Memorial and Remonstrance" and the Virginia bill for religious assessments that it attacked as a "Supplemental Appendix" to his opinion (*Everson*, pp. 63–74).

12. Cases applying *Everson* and its history of the Period of Formulation include *McCollum v. Board of Education*, 333 U.S. 203 (1948); *McGowan v. Maryland*, 366 U.S. 420 (1961); *Engel v. Vitale*, 370 U.S. 421 (1962); *Abington Township School District v. Schempp*, 372 U.S. 203 (1963); *Board of Education v. Allen*, 392 U.S. 236 (1968); *Walz v. Tax Commission*, 397 U.S. 664 (1970); *Lemon v. Kurtzman*, 403 U.S. 602 (1971); and *Wallace v. Jaffree*, 472 U.S. 38 (1985). Historical works echoing the *Everson* account of that period include Anson Phelps Stokes and Leo Pfeffer, *Church and State in the United States*, rev. ed. (New York: Viking, 1964); Leo Pfeffer, *Church, State and Freedom*, rev. ed. (Boston: Beacon Press, 1967); Leo Pfeffer, *Religion, State, and the Burger Court* (Buffalo: Prometheus Books, 1985); Philip B. Kurland, *Religion and the Law* (Chicago: Aldine Publishing, 1962); Irving N. Brant, *The Bill of Rights: Its Origins and Meaning* (Indianapolis: Bobbs-Merrill, 1965); Leonard W. Levy, *Judgments: Essays on American Constitutional History* (Chicago: Quadrangle, 1972); Leonard W. Levy, *The Establishment Clause: Religion and the First Amendment* (New York: Macmillan, 1986); William Lee Miller, *The First Liberty: Religion and the American Republic* (New York: Knopf, 1986). See also Sidney E. Mead, *The Old Religion in the Brave New World: Reflections on the Relation between Christendom and the Republic* (Berkeley: University of California Press, 1977); Sidney E. Mead, *The Nation with the Soul of a Church* (New York: Harper & Row, 1975). E. R. Norman, *The Conscience of the State in North America* (Cambridge: Cambridge University Press, 1968), provides a useful comparative perspective. But see the works cited in note 16.

13. *McCollum v. Board of Education*, 333 U.S. 203, 238–56 (1948) (Reed, J., dissenting).

14. *Zorach v. Clauson*, 343 U.S. 306 (1952).

15. *Zorach*, pp. 313–15. The dissenters in *Zorach*—Justices Black, Frankfurter, and Jackson—bitterly attacked the Court's opinion:

It was precisely because Eighteenth Century Americans were a religious people divided into many fighting sects that we were given the constitutional mandate to keep Church and State completely separate. Colonial history had already shown that, here as elsewhere zealous sectarians entrusted with governmental power to further their causes would sometimes torture, maim and kill those they branded "heretics," "atheists," or "agnostics." The First Amendment was therefore to insure that no one powerful sect or combination of sects could use political or governmental power to punish dissenters whom they could not convert to their faith. Now as then, it is only by wholly isolating the state from the religious sphere and compelling it to be completely neutral, that the freedom of each and every denomination and of all nonbelievers can be maintained. It is this neutrality the Court abandons today . . . .

Zorach, pp. 318–19 (Black, J., dissenting).

Compare *Zorach*, pp. 324–25 (Jackson, J., dissenting):

As one whose children, as a matter of free choice, have been sent to privately supported Church schools, I may challenge the Court's suggestion that opposition to this plan can only be antireligious, atheistic, or agnostic. My evangelistic brethren confuse an objection to compulsion with an objection to religion. It is possible to hold a faith with enough confidence to believe that what should be rendered to God does not need to be decided and collected by Caesar.

The day that this country ceases to be free for irreligion it will cease to be free for religion—except for the sect that can win political power. The same epithetical jurisprudence used by the Court today to beat down those who oppose pressuring children into some religion can devise as good epithets tomorrow against those who object to pressuring them into a favored religion. . . . We start down a rough road when we begin to mix compulsory public education with compulsory godliness.

See also *Zorach*, pp. 320–23 (Frankfurter, J., dissenting).

16. The principal works advocating the "no preference" understanding of the religion clauses and the Period of Formulation are James M. O'Neill, *Religion and Education under the Constitution* (1949; reprint, New York: Da Capo, 1972); Mark De Wolfe Howe, *The Garden and the Wilderness: Religion and Government in American Constitutional History* (Chicago: University of Chicago Press, 1965); Chester James Antieau, Arthur T. Downey, and Edward C. Roberts, *Freedom from Federal Establishment: Formation and Early History of the First Amendment's Religion Clauses* (Milwaukee: Bruce Publishing, 1964); Walter Berns, *The First Amendment and the Future of American Democracy* (New York: Basic Books, 1976); Jay Mechling, ed., *Church, State, and Public Policy: The New Shape of the Church-State Debate* (Washington, D.C.: American Enterprise Institute, 1978); and Robert L. Cord, *Separation of Church and State: Historical Fact and Current Fiction* (New York: Lambeth Press, 1982). See also, among polemical works, Richard John Neuhaus, *The Naked Public Square: Religion and Democracy in America*, 2d ed. (Grand Rapids, Mich.: Eerdmans Publishing, 1986), and Rockne M. McCarthy, James W. Skillen, and William A. Harper, *Disestablishment a Second Time:*

Genuine Pluralism for American Schools (Grand Rapids, Mich.: Christian University Press, 1982).

17. The best statements of this view are Howe, passim, and Berns, chs. 2, 3. But see also, for a separationist concurrence, William Lee Miller, passim.

18. Some nonpreferentialists also argue that after the Civil War, when the Fourteenth Amendment was proposed and ratified, the dominant national view of church-state relations was the same as that which prevailed in the Period of Formulation, and thus that the adoption of the Fourteenth Amendment did not fundamentally alter or limit the states' powers in church-state relations. Even if the Fourteenth Amendment does "apply" the religion clauses to the states, they claim, it does so only to the extent that they prevent the states, like the federal government, from establishing an official church. See, e.g., O'Neill, pp. 162–63; Cord, pp. 84–101.

19. *Jaffree v. Board of School Comm'rs of Mobile County*, 554 F. Supp. 1104 (S.D.Ala. 1983). The companion case is *Jaffree v. James*, 554 F. Supp. 1130 (S.D.Ala. 1983). These two cases were consolidated on appeal.

20. Cord's study bears the endorsements of several eminent figures in the movement challenging the "strict separationist" interpretation of the religion clauses, among them Senator Daniel P. Moynihan and William F. Buckley, Jr., who contributed an admiring foreword to Cord's volume.

21. 554 F. Supp. at 1113–1118.

22. *Jaffree v. Wallace*, 705 F.2d 1526 (11th Cir. 1983), aff'd, *Wallace v. Jaffree*, 466 U.S. 924 (1984).

23. *Wallace v. Jaffree*, 472 U.S. 38, 91–114 (1985) (Rehnquist, J., dissenting).

24. See, e.g., Edwin Meese, "Interpreting the Constitution," *USA Today*, Sept. 1986, pp. 36–39; Meese, "The Law of the Constitution," Bicentennial Lecture, Tulane University Citizens' Forum on the Bicentennial of the Constitution (Oct. 21, 1986) (copy available from U.S. Department of Justice); Meese, Address to Annual Convention of American Bar Association, Washington, D.C., July 9, 1985 (copy available from U.S. Department of Justice); Robert H. Bork, "Original Intent and the Constitution," *Humanities*, Feb. 1986, p. 22.

25. *Marsh v. Chambers*, 463 U.S. 783 (1983).

26. See, e.g., *Lemon v. Kurtzman*, 403 U.S. 602, 612–13 (1973) (governmental action violates the establishment clause unless its purpose is secular, its primary effect is secular, and it avoids entangling government and religion).

27. O'Neill, p. 79; see also pp. 81, 83. Justice Rehnquist echoed O'Neill's characterization of this letter in his dissent in *Wallace v. Jaffree*, 472 U.S. at 92.

28. O'Neill, p. 80.

29. Dumas Malone, *Jefferson the President: First Term, 1801–1805* (Boston: Little, Brown, 1970), pp. 108–09.

30. Address of Danbury Baptist Association, 7 Oct. 1801, quoted in Malone, p. 109. See generally Malone, ch. 11, "The Religion of a Reasonable Man," and ch. 12, "Torrent of Slander."

31. See Malone, p. 109 n. 51, for citations of Jefferson's original draft of the Danbury letter and for his correspondence with Granger and Lincoln; these documents, now in the Jefferson Papers at the Library of Congress, will eventually be published in Julian Boyd, Charles Cullen, et al., eds., *The Papers of Thomas Jefferson*, 24 vols. to date (Princeton: Princeton University Press, 1950-).

32. But see, e.g., *Gardner v. Village of Newburgh*, 2 Johnson's Chancery Cases 162

(N.Y. 1816) (opinion of Chancellor James Kent) (construing and applying, in the absence of N.Y. constitutional provision governing takings of private property, the writings of jurists and natural-law theorists, other state constitutional provisions, and especially Fifth Amendment to U.S. Constitution); Petition of Prisoners, Suffolk Gen. Sess. (May 1809), cited in William E. Nelson, *Americanization of the Common Law* (Cambridge, Mass.: Harvard University Press, 1975), p. 131 n. 155. William W. Crosskey, *Politics and the Constitution in the History of the United States*, 3 vols. (vol. 3 with William Jeffery) (Chicago: University of Chicago Press, 1953–80), 2:1056–82, rejects the holding of the U.S. Supreme Court in *Barron v. Baltimore*, 32 U.S. 243 (1833), that the federal Bill of Rights did not bind the states, but Crosskey concedes that the First Amendment, which was expressed as a limitation on the powers of Congress, was *not* intended to bind the states. I am indebted to my colleague Bill Nelson for these references.

33. See generally Charles A. Miller, *The Supreme Court and the Uses of History* (Cambridge, Mass.: Harvard University Press, 1969); Archibald Cox, *The Role of the Supreme Court in American Government* (New York: Oxford University Press, 1976); Thomas Grey, "Do We Have an Unwritten Constitution?" *Stanford Law Review* 27 (1975): 703; Stephen R. Munzer and James W. Nickel, "Does the Constitution Mean What It Always Meant?" *Columbia Law Review* 77 (1977): 1029. The most recent statement of this view is a speech by Justice William J. Brennan, Jr., to the Text and Teaching Symposium, Georgetown University (Washington, D.C., Oct. 12, 1985) (available from U.S. Supreme Court Press Office), reprinted in *The Great Debate: Interpreting Our Written Constitution* (Washington, D.C.: Federalist Society, 1986), pp. 11–25.

H. Jefferson Powell's article "The Original Understanding of Original Intent," *Harvard Law Review* 98 (1985): 885, casts additional light on this issue. After examining the hermeneutical theories prevailing during the Period of Formulation and after analyzing the writings of principal delegates to the Federal Convention and supporters of the Constitution during the ratification controversy, Powell concludes that the Framers did not intend their views on the meaning of constitutional provisions to bind future generations.

34. Sydney E. Ahlstrom, *A Religious History of the American People* (New Haven: Yale University Press, 1972), pp. 3–4; Martin E. Marty, *Pilgrims in Their Own Land: 500 Years of Religion in America* (New York: Viking, 1985), pp. 403–70; Jacob Needleman, *The New Religions* (Garden City, N.Y.: Doubleday, 1970); Harvey Cox, *Turning East* (New York: Simon & Schuster, 1977); Robert N. Bellah, Richard Madsen, William M. Sullivan, Ann Swidler, and Steven M. Tipton, *Habits of the Heart: Individualism and Commitment in American Life* (1985; reprint, New York: Perennial Library-Harper & Row, 1986), pp. 219–50. See also "Toward a Constitutional Definition of Religion," *Harvard Law Review* 91 (1978): 1056, 1066–72.

35. A pathbreaking recent study of the history of atheism and unbelief in the United States is James Turner, *Without God, Without Creed: The Origins of Unbelief in America* (Baltimore: Johns Hopkins University Press, 1985).

36. See Lawrence M. Cremin, *American Education: The National Experience, 1783–1876* (New York: Harper & Row, 1980); Ray A. Billington, *The Protestant Crusade, 1800–1860* (1938; reprint, Chicago: Quadrangle, 1965); Diane Ravitch, *The Great School Wars* (New York: Basic Books, 1973).

37. Diane Ravitch, *The Troubled Crusade: American Education, 1940–1980* (New York: Basic Books, 1983), pp. 3–42.

38. Of particular note are two similar, though distinguishable, cases that are still being litigated. In one, the "Tennessee secular humanism case," a federal district judge ruled that, because certain texts used in the English curriculum of the public schools of Hawkins County, Tennessee, were offensive to the plaintiffs' religion, the school board had to permit the plaintiffs' children to "opt out" of their English classes so long as the parents agreed to arrange for the provision of comparable education at home. *Mozert v. Hawkins County Public Schools*, 647 F. Supp. 1194 (E.D. Tenn. 1986), *rev'd*, 827 F.2d 1058 (6th Cir. 1987). In the other, the "Alabama secular humanism case," taking place before the federal judge who was reversed by both the Eleventh Circuit and the Supreme Court in the *Jaffree* cases, the plaintiffs are claiming that secular humanism is a religion pervading public-school texts, that Christianity has been excluded systematically from the public schools, and that therefore wholesale revision of the public school system and its curriculum is constitutionally required. The Alabama secular humanism case is still at the pretrial stage. See also *Roman v. Appleby*, 558 F. Supp. 449 (E.D.Pa. 1983) (counseling sessions with student on matters of religion, sex, and family relationships violated neither parents' nor students' free exercise rights); *Cornwell v. State Board of Education*, 314 F. Supp. 340 (D.Md. 1969), *aff'd*, 428 F.2d 471 (5th Cir.), *cert. denied*, 400 U.S. 942 (1970) (sex-education programs upheld over paternal religious objections on grounds of state's compelling interest in public health); *Williams v. Board of Education*, 388 F. Supp. 93 (S.D.W.Va.), *aff'd*, 530 F.2d 972 (4th Cir. 1975) (dismissal of parents' complaint seeking to enjoin use of textbooks allegedly offensive to Christian morals); *Moody v. Cronin*, 484 F. Supp. 270 (C.D. Ill. 1979) (compulsory coeducational physical educational classes in which "immodest" clothing was worn violated free exercise rights of some students where state could not show compelling interest or that less restrictive means could not be employed). McCarthy, Skillen, and Harper present the historical, religious, and legal arguments of this "crusade."

39. *Cantwell v. Connecticut*, 310 U.S. 296 (1940); *Everson v. Board of Education*, 330 U.S. 1 (1947); *Board of Education v. Allen*, 392 U.S. 236 (1968). See note 6.

40. See the colloquy between Representative Samuel Huntington of Connecticut and Representative James Madison of Virginia, in Joseph Gales and W. W. Seaton, eds., *Debates and Proceedings in the Congress of the United States, Compiled from Authentic Materials* [*Annals of Congress*], 42 vols. (Washington, D.C., 1834–56), 1:757–59 (H.R., Aug. 15, 1789). On the paucity of evidence of the intent of the framers of the Bill of Rights, see the discussion by Levy, pp. 187–89.

41. Council of Trent, session 13, canon 2; reproduced in H. Denzinger, *Enchiridion Symbolorum, Definitionum et Declarationum de Rebus Fidei et Morum*, 31st ed. (New York: Herder & Herder, 1957), p. 884. See also Karl Rahner, *Theological Investigations* (New York: Doubleday, 1966), 4:296–311; Edward Schillebeeckx, *The Eucharist* (New York: Doubleday, 1968).

42. Ronald Dworkin, *Taking Rights Seriously* (Cambridge, Mass.: Harvard University Press, 1977), pp. 131–36. For a critique, see Munzer and Nickel, pp. 1037–41.

43.

The vast majority of Americans [in the Period of Formulation] assumed that theirs was a Christian, i.e. Protestant, country, and they automatically expected that government would uphold the commonly agreed on Protestant ethos and morality. In many instances, they had not come to grips with the implications their belief in the powerlessness of government in religious matters held for a society in which the values, customs, and forms of Protestant Christianity thoroughly permeated civil and political life. The contradiction between their theory and their practice came only later, with the advent of a more religiously pluralistic society, when it became the subject of a disputation that continues into the present.

Thomas J. Curry, *The First Freedoms: Church and State in America to the Passage of the First Amendment* (New York: Oxford University Press, 1986), p. 219. See also Howe, pp. 11–12, 31, 97–98, 154; Wade Clark Roof, "America's Voluntary Establishment: Mainline Religion in Transition," in Mary Douglas and Steven M. Tipton, eds., *Religion and America: Spirituality in a Secular Age* (Boston: Beacon Press, 1983), pp. 130–49.

44. See, e.g., Ahlstrom; Marty, *Pilgrims in Their Own Land*; Martin E. Marty, *A Nation of Behavers* (Chicago: University of Chicago Press, 1977); Martin E. Marty, "Religion in America since Mid-Century," in Douglas and Tipton, pp. 273–87; Mark A. Noll, Nathan D. Hatch, and George M. Marsden, *The Search for Christian America* (Westchester, Ill.: Crossway Books, 1983); Robert T. Handy, *A History of the Churches in the United States and Canada* (New York: Oxford University Press, 1976); Morton Borden, *Jews, Turks, and Infidels* (Chapel Hill: University of North Carolina Press, 1985); Catherine Albanese, *Sons of the Fathers: The Civil Religion of the American Revolution* (Philadelphia: Temple University Press, 1976).

Patricia U. Bonomi, *Under the Cape of Heaven: Religion, Society, and Politics in Colonial America* (New York: Oxford University Press, 1986), presents a challenging and persuasive argument against the conventional wisdom that the late eighteenth century witnessed a significant decline not only in formal church affiliation and attendance but also in religious feeling. Bonomi's work is especially important for two reasons: First, she examines the actual practice of religion throughout colonial America, instead of focusing on New England, as most of her predecessors have done. Second, she identifies as principal causes of the American Revolution (1) the American colonists' resistance to the English campaign to found a bishopric of the Church of England for British North America and (2) the destabilizing effects of the Great Awakening on the internal organization of American denominations, which stimulated the Americans' growing willingness to question institutional and hierarchical authority in the secular as well as in the religious sphere. An excellent study that exemplifies the earlier literature's emphasis on New England is Nathan O. Hatch, *The Sacred Cause of Liberty: Republican Thought and the Millenium in Revolutionary New England* (New Haven: Yale University Press, 1977).

45. On hospitals, see, e.g., Paul Starr, *The Social Transformation of American Medicine* (New York: Basic Books, 1983). On education, see, e.g., Cremin; Ravitch, *The Great School Wars*.

46. See generally Morton Keller, *Affairs of State: Public Life in Late Nineteenth-Century America* (Cambridge, Mass.: Harvard University Press, 1977); William E. Nelson, *The Roots of American Bureaucracy* (Cambridge, Mass.: Harvard University Press, 1982); Eric F. Goldman, *Rendezvous with Destiny* (New York: Knopf, 1942); Richard Hofstadter, *The Age of Reform: From Bryan to FDR* (New York: Knopf, 1955); Henry Steele Commager, *The American Mind* (New Haven: Yale University Press,

1950); Robert H. Wiebe, *The Search for Order, 1877–1920* (New York: Hill & Wang, 1967).

47. One of the several factors to be examined would have to be the growing respectability of atheism and unbelief in American culture. See generally Turner. Another would be the challenge to traditional religion presented by science. A good example of the burgeoning recent literature exploring the contradictions between religious faith and a scientific worldview is A. R. Peacocke, *Creation and the World of Science* (Oxford: Clarendon Press, 1979). See also Robert Jastrow, *God and the Astronomers* (New York: Warner, 1978). Science fiction abounds with explorations of these issues. Among the best are Walter M. Miller, Jr., *A Canticle for Leibowitz* (reprint, New York: Bantam, 1985), and Carl Sagan, *Contact* (New York: Simon & Schuster, 1985). The starkest clash between science and religion is the "creationism" dispute, which has repeatedly found its way into the courts. See, e.g., Niles Eldredge, *The Monkey Business: A Scientist Looks at Creationism* (New York: Washington Square Press, 1982); *McLean v. Arkansas Board of Education*, 529 F. Supp. 1253 (E.D. Ark. 1982); and *Edwards v. Aguillard*, 107 S.Ct. 2573 (1987). Douglas J. Futuyma, *Science on Trial: The Case for Evolution* (New York: Pantheon, 1983), pp. 228–31, presents a short but useful bibliography of literature on both sides of the issue.

＠ℓ＠ℓ＠ℓ

Gender Equality and Constitutional Traditions

DEBORAH L. RHODE

For over two and a half centuries, understandings about gender have played a substantial role in shaping American legal institutions. Yet only in the last two and a half decades has discrimination on the basis of gender given rise to significant legal remedies. Until quite recently, American constitutional traditions excluded concerns about women, just as women themselves were largely excluded from the processes of constitutional decisionmaking. Although subject to the Constitution's mandates, women were unacknowledged in its text, uninvited in its formulation, unsolicited for its ratification, and, before the last quarter-century, largely uninvolved in its official interpretation.

When the framers of America's founding documents spoke of men—of men "created equal and endowed with certain inalienable rights"—they were not using the term generically. Thomas Jefferson, author of that celebrated phrase in the Declaration of Independence, did not believe that women should participate in political governance. In his view, in order to prevent "depravation of morals and ambiguity of issues, [women] should not mix promiscuously in gatherings of men."[1] On becoming president, Jefferson accordingly rejected a proposal to appoint female candidates to the public service as an "innovation" for which neither he nor the public was prepared.[2]

Similar sentiments were apparent in *The Federalist Papers*, which provided the intellectual justifications for the nation's constitutional structure. The *Papers* mentioned women only once; the reference, by Alexander Hamilton, was a warning about the perils to the state from the intrigues of courtesans and mistresses.[3] Efforts to secure more favorable attitudes toward women's political role had no apparent success. The most celebrated example was Abigail Adams's request that her husband and his colleagues "Remember the Ladies" and grant them more favorable treatment in the country's new legal codes. "Depend upon it," John Adams responded, "[w]e know better than to repeal our Masculine systems."[4]

Among those well acquainted with women's studies, this is familiar history. Yet among the public generally, this legacy has most often been ignored. Our celebration of the framers' vision, our reverence for their original intent, and our deference to a shared constitutional tradition rarely acknowledge in more than footnote fashion what all of this leaves out.

The omissions do not, of course, involve only women and gender. Our constitutional heritage has been skewed by race, class, and ethnicity as well as sex. Moreover, the limitations imposed by this legacy are not simply of historical interest; they continue to shape our sense of national identity, legal possibilities, and social priorities. The following analysis seeks to explore such limitations from the perspective of gender. By focusing on women's efforts to gain constitutional protections, first suffrage and then an Equal Rights Amendment, we may gain a clearer sense of the capacities and constraints of our dominant ideological traditions. A better understanding of how law functions as a social text may illumine, as well as influence, our cultural construction of gender.

I.

The two constitutional campaigns launched by the American women's-rights movement, although a century apart, reflect certain striking parallels. Both emerged at a time when the legal ideology surrounding women's roles had grown increasingly out of step with social and economic realities. Moreover, both were outgrowths of civil-rights struggles that in some measure defined and delimited feminist objectives.

The suffrage campaign and the broader women's movement of which it was a part were responses to a regime in which the sexes were more separate than equal. Throughout the eighteenth and nineteenth centuries, the dominant ideological assumption was that men should occupy the public and women the private sphere and that law should reinforce that boundary. The "cult of domesticity" that was particularly pronounced in the antebellum era was equally apparent in legal ideology for a much longer period. Early common law and statutory mandates imposed a wide range of disabilities; married women, for example, generally could not enter contracts, hold or convey property, retain their own wages, stand for public office, serve on juries, or engage in licensed occupations.[5]

There were, to be sure, exceptions to these prohibitions, based on special equitable principles or social custom.[6] And, during the mid-nineteenth century, state legislatures began passing married women's property acts that removed many common-law disabilities.[7] However, sex-based discrimination continued in a broad range of governmental policies concerning education, employment, military service, family life, and related matters. What bears emphasis here is the absence of successful constitutional challenges to such discrimination for almost two centuries after ratification. Despite broad language in the post–Civil War Fourteenth Amendment guaranteeing equal protection of the laws to all citizens, it was not until 1970 that the Supreme Court found any sex-based constraints in violation of this principle.

That was not for lack of opportunities. In the century after passage of the Fourteenth Amendment, a majority of justices upheld an array of gender classifications in protective labor legislation, educational admission policies, jury selection procedures, and eligibility requirements for certain occupations and professions.[8] The reasons varied, but many reflected the attitudes apparent in a celebrated 1873 decision upholding women's exclusion from legal practice. According to the concurring opinion, the "law of the Creator" as well as the Constitution decreed that the "paramount destiny and mission of women [were] to fulfill the noble and benign offices of wife and mother."[9] Although the precise method of divine communication was never elaborated, the message was apparent to other nineteenth- and early twentieth-century jurists as well. For the next century, federal courts viewed women's role at the "center of home and family life" as justification for a broad range of gender restrictions.[10]

Yet these restrictions, built on the assumption that women's nature was solely to nurture, became increasingly difficult to reconcile with broader social trends. During the late nineteenth and early twentieth centuries, the growing opportunities for female education, the decline in birth rates, the rise in industrialization and urbanization, and the demand for female labor all helped expand the boundaries of women's "separate sphere." So too, women's involvement in the abolitionist movement, and the disparity they experienced between the rhetoric of rights and the constraints of role, helped lay the foundations for a feminist consciousness. Sex-based discrimination in antislavery activities helped inspire the first American women's-rights conference (Seneca Falls, 1848) as well as demands that women obtain the same constitutional guarantees as blacks.[11]

This focus on individual rights remained the dominant organizing principle for the early American women's movement. The Declaration of Sentiments, adopted at the Seneca Falls Conference, borrowed from Jefferson's language if not his intent, and resolved that women were "created equal" with "certain inalienable rights," including the right to occupy any "station in society as [their] conscience shall dictate."[12] Elaborating this theme, Elizabeth Cady Stanton subsequently made clear that "[i]n discussing the rights of women, we are to consider what belongs to her as an individual . . . [and] as the arbiter of her own destiny."[13]

Critical among those rights was self-governance. Judicial tolerance for gender discrimination encouraged women to place increased emphasis on legislative reform and access to political power. By the close of the nineteenth century, the constitutional campaign for suffrage dominated the feminist agenda. Among many proponents, the ballot emerged as an all-purpose prescription for social ills. Suffrage, it was variously claimed, would secure woman's "equal place and equal wages in the world of work"; it would open to her all the schools, colleges, professions, and "advantages of life"; and it would "purify politics."[14]

Given these expectations, many suffragists found victory "hardly less demoralizing than defeat"; the Nineteenth Amendment secured the vote in 1920, but for the next four decades women neither voted as a block on women's issues nor won substantial protection against discrimination.[15] During that period, gender roles grew less separate, but remained far from equal. Although women were entering the workplace in increasing numbers, they were securing neither an "equal place" nor equal wages within it. During the early 1960s, the vast majority of female employees were clustered in a small number of relatively low-status, low-paying jobs, and only a tiny percentage obtained access to the most prestigious professions. Full-time women workers earned only about sixty percent of the average man's salary, a gap that did not substantially narrow when corrected for factors such as age, education, experience, hours worked, and so forth.[16] Women had difficulty gaining access to credit, to educational and vocational training, and to public office; the only governmental level at which they were significantly visible was local school and library boards.[17]

II.

The struggle for an equal rights amendment, like the struggle for the vote, was a response to these inequalities, and an outgrowth of the growing disparity between legal traditions and social trends. The stereotypical assumptions about women's place that had dominated judicial attitudes were out of phase with contemporary demographic patterns. By the 1960s, birth rates had fallen and female labor force participation had risen to the point where ninety percent of women could expect paid employment at some point in their lives, and the average mother could anticipate spending about two-thirds of her adult life without children under 18.[18] By the end of the 1970s, a majority of American families had a working wife or mother, and only sixteen percent conformed to the traditional model of male breadwinner and full-time female homemaker.[19]

The absence of adequate legal guarantees for these changing gender roles fueled feminist organization. Moreover, as was true a century earlier, a major catalyst for such activity was the discrimination women experienced within groups ostensibly dedicated to a more egalitarian social order. Many leaders of the contemporary women's movement began their political involvement in civil-rights organizations that failed to extend their liberal principles to issues involving gender.[20]

Like their nineteenth-century predecessors, women activists have relied heavily on such principles in building their campaign for sexual equality. For example, the statement of purpose of the National Organization for Women (NOW), the largest and most prominent representative of the contemporary women's movement, reflects the same focus on individual rights as the Declaration of Sentiments. NOW has emphasized eliminating conditions that prevent women from "enjoying equality of opportunity and freedom of choice, which is their right as individual Americans and human beings."[21] Consistent with that objective, most law-related activities of the women's movement have centered on securing equal treatment between the sexes.

The most significant of those activities focused on passage of an Equal Rights Amendment (ERA) to the Constitution. Some version of such an amendment was introduced in every congressional term between 1923 and 1972. Finally, after a half-century's struggle, both the House and Senate endorsed a requirement that "equality of rights under the law shall not be denied or abridged by the United States or any state on account of sex." This text was then submitted to the states for ratification, and the dispute it sparked consumed much of the energy of the women's movement over the next decade.

In 1982, the period for ratification expired without the necessary endorsements by two-thirds of the states. Proponents immediately reintroduced the text in Congress, and the NOW leadership subsequently declared the amendment its highest priority. Yet before embarking on a full-blown ERA revival campaign, we should reconsider its limitations. The liberal legalism that has traditionally dominated the feminist agenda, with its emphasis on individual rights and equality of opportunity, has been of enormous significance in challenging sex-based discrimination. But at this historical juncture, such an approach offers an inadequate theoretical and practical framework for the contemporary women's movement.

On a theoretical level, the traditional focus is both too broad and too narrow. Its vision is too sweeping in that it offers no way of mediating between two ultimately irreconcilable ideals: individual choice and equality of opportunity. Yet the conventional approach is also too limited in that it fails to challenge the terms of the choices currently available and the egoistic paradigm within which they are presented.

As feminists have increasingly noted, the most fundamental barriers confronting contemporary American women do not spring from the kinds of formal unequal treatment that a constitutional amendment would address. Over the last quarter-century, courts and legislatures have struck down most of the overt vestiges of sex-based discrimination. Many constraints on opportunity that persist, especially for women of color and women from lower-class backgrounds, stem from socialization processes and socioeconomic disparities that are rooted in family structures. Yet equalizing life chances would require equalizing life circumstances in ways that are flatly inconsistent with individual liberty. To attempt to provide the material and psychological resources for all persons to realize their full potential would require collectivizing childrearing functions and dramatically narrowing the scope for autonomy in intimate relationships. The traditional liberal feminist emphasis on individual choice ultimately fails to raise or resolve our most fundamental policy questions. We cannot maximize some choices without constraining others. The central question is what choices to encourage, and on that point conventional frameworks have too often remained agnostic.

Yet if the implications of this individual-rights, equal-opportunity approach are in one sense too sweeping to be useful, they are, in another sense, too limited to be empowering. America's excessive preoccupation with individual entitlement at the expense of collective needs has generated an extended critical tradition that need not be summarized here.[22] Moreover, as feminist theorists such as Carol Gilligan have increasingly argued, the focus on protecting rights has too often obscured the significance of preserving relationships.[23] Concern for caretaking values historically associated with women demands not simply access to, but alteration of, existing institutions. It is not enough, for example, to grant individual women the right to enter current educational and employment structures and seek success under the same standards applicable to men. The point rather is to rethink the standards and refashion the structures in ways that more adequately respond to human relationships. At a minimum, that will entail public and private policies that encourage more cooperative organizational environments and that allow for fuller accommodation of work and family responsibilities.

The rhetoric of rights is limiting in still another sense. Equality in formal entitlements cannot begin to secure equality in social experience as long as rights remain restricted to those that predominately white, upper-middle-class male policymakers have regarded as fundamental. Absent from the list are rights necessary to secure most women a meaningful degree of equality or liberty, such as rights to adequate welfare assistance, birth-control services, pregnancy and parental leave policies, and child-care programs.

Not only is the rhetoric of individual rights an inadequate vehicle for attaining such objectives, so too is the discourse of equal opportunity. Equal treatment is of limited value in contexts where the sexes are not equally situated. And as statistics from the mid-1980s make evident, women remain disproportionately disadvantaged in a broad array of circumstances.

To take only the most obvious examples, women are still dramatically overrepresented at the lower end of the socioeconomic spectrum and dramatically underrepresented at the upper end. When paid and unpaid labor are combined, female employers work significantly longer hours for significantly less financial security than males. Despite two decades of equal-pay and equal-opportunity legislation, the work force remains highly gender-segregated and gender-stratified; the average full-time female worker in the mid-eighties still earns slightly over two-thirds of the salary of the average male worker.[24] Half of all current marriages will end in divorce, and, despite statutory guarantees of equal or equitable division of marital property, most wives end up with neither equality nor equity. Rather, most are left with far greater parental responsibilities and far fewer resources for performing them.[25] Ninety percent of all single parents are women, and over a third of the households they head are below the poverty line. Two out of every three poor adults are female.[26] Women also constitute the vast majority of victims of sexual violence and are often victimized twice, once by the experience of injury and once by the process of proving it.[27] In these contexts, mandates of equal treatment are not sufficient to secure men's and women's treatment as equals.

It has been, in part, these concerns about the value of formal equality in circumstances of social inequality that have fueled opposition to a constitutional equal rights amendment. For the first half-century after the amendment's introduction in the

twenties, much of that opposition centered on concerns about
the fate of sex-based policies purportedly favoring women, especially protective labor legislation. To many early opponents, it
made no sense to purchase abstract constitutional entitlements at
the expense of concrete protections, such as minimum wages,
maximum hours, or regulation of working conditions.[28] Yet as
ERA supporters often noted, these protective measures, by making women more expensive employees, often "protected" them
out of jobs desirable to men.

For that reason, by the time Congress endorsed the ERA in
1972, courts had already struck down such legislation as a violation of equal-employment laws. So too, during the decade of
ratification campaign, judges and legislators were mandating gender neutrality in other statutes that had previously favored
women, such as sex-based alimony, custody, and marital-support
provisions.[29] But despite considerable efforts, contemporary ERA
supporters were unable to clarify how few preferential policies
(outside the area of military service) were actually at risk from the
amendment. Indeed, the problems these supporters faced during
the 1970s ratification campaign reflect more fundamental political
difficulties with constitutional entitlements as an agenda for social
change.

Part of those difficulties arose from the substantive limitations in equal rights frameworks noted above. As the deadline for
ratification drew nearer, it became increasingly apparent that
many of women's most pressing problems could not be solved by
equal entitlements, and those that could were already the subject
of increasing judicial and legislative initiatives. Yet while these
reforms reduced the substantive need for constitutional intervention, they also reduced the substantive grounds for opposing it.
What remains of interest is why so many women organized
against equal rights and provided political justifications—or ra-
tionalizations—for state legislative opposition.

That question is particularly significant in light of anti-ERA
groups' influence over the terms of constitutional debate. As was
true in the suffrage campaign, opponents' activity was sporadic,
but their ideology was crucial. In both contexts, the "antis defined
the context within which [feminists'] ideas developed, posed the
problems [they] had to solve and asked the questions they had to
answer."[30] Those problems and questions had less to do with the
legal than with the symbolic implications of constitutional change.

From opponents' perspective, such change signaled an assault on gender difference, not gender disadvantage.

To anti-ERA leaders, like their antisuffragist predecessors, equality threatened sexual roles that appeared biologically destined and culturally appropriate. Phyllis Schlafly, the architect of the contemporary campaign against equal rights, invoked the same "separate spheres" arguments that had inspired antifeminists a century earlier. The basic position, as she once summarized it, was that "women have babies so men should support them."[31] To conservatives in both generations, a constitutional amendment came to symbolize an assault against traditional understandings of masculinity and femininity, and an invitation to an unpalatable "unisex" society.[32] The perceived significance of this assault was apparent in the titles of groups that organized against the ERA: "Feminine Anti-Feminists," "Winsome Wives and Homemakers," and "Women Who Want to Be Women."[33]

In both constitutional campaigns, opponents viewed equal rights as a symbolic stand-in for a broader set of feminist priorities. For women who had organized their lives in accordance with traditional values, particularly full-time homemakers and occupants of low-status jobs, these priorities appeared elitist and unsettling. The women's-rights movement, with its perceived emphasis on political and professional advancement, appeared to devalue other choices. Ironically enough, it was the rhetoric of antifeminists rather than feminists that seemed to confer stature and dignity on caretaking roles that society as a whole had undervalued.

Feminists' responses to these concerns left something to be desired in both constitutional campaigns. All too often, suffragists attempted to broaden their base of support by narrowing their social vision. Some attempted to placate antifeminist concerns by overstating and oversimplifying—i.e., by sentimentalizing women's distinctive role and exaggerating their capacity to "purify" political life. Other suffrage proponents appealed to prejudices of class and caste and emphasized the desirability of allowing educated white female voters to outnumber "unlettered and unwashed" laborers fresh from the slave plantations of the South and ghettos of Eastern Europe.[34]

In the contemporary constitutional campaigns, feminists avoided these difficulties but adopted political strategies that were self-defeating in other respects. One approach, more inspired in theory than in practice, was to meet opponents on their own terrain and show that homemakers as well as professional women supported equal rights. So, for example, when ERA opponents began distributing home-baked gifts to state legislators, ERA advocates responded in kind and began matching their enemies muffin for muffin. Yet these gestures, particularly as caricatured by the press, often trivialized the issues. According to standard journalistic accounts of "Rights Battle Boom[ing] from Kitchens," the campaign became a contest between rival hausfraus.[35]

An additional difficulty was that ERA supporters who pursued this domesticated lobbying strategy were often upstaged by their more provocative colleagues. The radical wing of the women's movement was unconvinced that the most direct route to politicians' votes was through their stomachs. Rather, these supporters offered tokens to legislative opponents such as animal manure and children's potties.[36] Such gestures were unlikely to persuade those most in need of persuasion. Moreover, the proponents' tendency to become mired in mindless debates over legal technicalities, or issues such as the fate of single-sex restrooms under egalitarian mandates, deflected attention from critical social problems.

That is not, of course, to overstate the significance of feminists' political miscalculations, nor to undervalue the importance of their political achievements. As was true in the struggle for suffrage, equal rights advocates became increasingly adept at legislative lobbying and mass organization as the campaign wore on. In the long run, those political skills are likely to prove as critical as the constitutional results they were designed to secure.

Yet the political as well as theoretical difficulties in feminist strategies over the last decade raise questions about the appropriate priorities for the next one. At this juncture, it makes sense to place primary emphasis on issues that can unite rather than divide women and to pause in the struggle for symbolic entitlements. A constitutional mandate of equal rights is likely to be more a catalyst than a source of change. Without a fundamental reordering of American institutions and values, we cannot hope to secure significant progress toward gender equality. Such a reconstruction will require sustained political commitments and a substantive agenda that extends beyond equal rights. That agenda will, at a minimum, entail initiatives that respond to women's unequal circumstances, such as strategies concerning pay equity, affirmative action, adequate child care, welfare reform, reproductive freedom, and sexual violence.

One redeeming aspect of the unsuccessful ratification struggle is that it may have brought these points home and helped equip women with the political experience to make their perceptions felt. If so, then the process may have been more significant than the immediate objective feminists sought to attain. It is not simply the abstract guarantee of equal rights, but the consciousness with which they are exercised, and the recognition of their limitations, that can bring us closer to true equality between the sexes. Had either the suffrage or the equal rights amendment sailed quickly through state capitals, supporters would have missed valuable instruction in the mechanics of *realpolitik* and the limits of their own vision. If there is a further encouraging lesson to learn from the difficulties of both constitutional campaigns, it is that the vast majority of American women on both sides of the debates wanted equality in some sense: equality in economic security and social status. The challenge that remains is to draw from those common aspirations the basis for a common struggle.

Notes

1. Martin Gruberg, *Women in American Politics* (Oshkosh, Wis.: Academia Press, 1968), p. 4.

2. Richard B. Morris, *The Forging of the Unions* (New York: Harper & Row, 1987), excerpted in *Columbia*, April 1987, p. 40.

3. *Federalist*, no. 6 (Hamilton); *The Federalist Papers* (1788; reprint, New York: New American Library, 1961), pp. 54–55. See also Morris, p. 41.

4. Alice S. Rossi, ed., *The Feminist Papers: From Adams to de Beauvoir* (New York: Bantam Press, 1973), pp. 10–11.

5. See generally Barbara Welter, "The Cult of True Womanhood, 1820–1860," *American Quarterly* 18 (1966): 151–74; William Blackstone, *Commentaries on the Laws of England*, 15th ed. (1756; reprint, Oxfordshire: Professional Books, 1982), 1:442–45; Leo Kanowitz, *Women and the Law* (Albuquerque: University of New Mexico Press, 1970), pp. 35–37.

6. Given the limitations of existing research, the extent to which formal disabilities constrained women's alternatives is difficult to assess. For different views on the frequency of exceptions to common law restrictions, see, e.g., Mary R. Beard, *Women as a Force in History* (New York: Macmillan, 1946), pp. 158–66; Norma Basch, *In the Eyes of the Law* (Ithaca: Cornell University Press, 1982), pp. 30–35; Linda Kerber, *Women of the Republic: Intellect and Ideology in Revolutionary America* (Chapel Hill: University of North Carolina Press, 1980), pp. 149–53; Marylynn

Salmon, "The Legal Status of Women in Early America: A Reappraisal," *Law & History Review* 1 (Spring 1983): 129-51.

7. Linda E. Speth, "The Married Women's Property Acts, 1839-1865: Reform, Reaction, or Revolution?" in D. Kelly Weisberg, ed., *Women and the Law* (Cambridge, Mass.: Schenkman, 1982), 2:69, 70; Basch, *In the Eyes of the Law*.

8. See e.g., *Bradwell v. State*, 83 U.S. 130 (1872) (legal practice); *Muller v. Oregon*, 208 U.S. 412 (1908) (protective labor); *Goesaert v. Cleary*, 335 U.S. 464 (1948) (bartending); *Williams v. McNair*, 316 F. Supp. 134 (D.S.C. 1970), aff'd mem., 401 U.S. 951 (1971) (education); *Hoyt v. Florida*, 368 U.S. 57 (1961) (jury service).

9. *Bradwell v. State*, 83 U.S. 130, 141-42 (1872).

10. *Hoyt v. Florida*, 368 U.S. 57, 61-62 (1961) (jury service). See also In the Matter of Goodell, 39 Wis. 232, 244 (1875) (legal practice); *Heaton v. Bristol*, 317 S.W. 2d 86, 100 (Tex. Civ. App. 1958), cert. den. 359 U.S. 230 (1959) (education); *United States v. St. Clair*, 291 F. Supp. 122, 125 (S.D.N.Y. 1968), (military); *United States v. Cook*, 311 F. Supp. 618, 622 (W.D. Pa. 1970) (military). See Kanowitz and "Sex, Discrimination, and the Constitution," *Stanford Law Review* 2 (1950): 691, 713.

11. See generally Carl Degler, *At Odds* (New York: Oxford University Press, 1980), p. 345; William O'Neill, *Everyone Was Brave: A History of Feminism in America* (Chicago: Quadrangle, 1969), p. 7; Mary Ryan, *Womanhood in America*, 3d ed. (New York: F. Watts, 1983); Aileen Kraditor, *The Ideas of the Woman Suffrage Movement: 1890-1920* (New York: Norton, 1971), p. 40; Carol Hymowitz and Michaele Weissman, *A History of American Women* (New York: Bantam, 1978), p. 80.

12. Declaration of Sentiments (1848), reprinted in Rossi, p. 419.

13. Elizabeth Cady Stanton, "The Solitude of Self" (1892), quoted in Kraditor, p. 40.

14. Elizabeth Cady Stanton, "The Ballot—Bread, Virtue, Power," *Revolution*, Jan. 8, 1968, p. 1. See also Anna Howard Shaw, passages from Speeches, quoted in Kraditor, p. 50, n. 28; Susan B. Anthony and Ida Husted Harper, eds., *History of Woman Suffrage* (Indianapolis: Hallenback Press, 1902), 4:39, 308-09.

15. O'Neill, p. 266. See William Henry Chafe, *The American Woman: Her Changing Social, Economic and Political Roles, 1920-1970* (New York: Oxford University Press, 1972), p. 27; Nancy Woloch, *Women and the American Experience* (New York: Knopf, 1984), pp. 355-56; Andrew Sinclair, *The Better Half: The Emancipation of the American Woman* (New York: Harper & Row, 1965), pp. 93, 343; Ethel Klein, *Gender Politics* (Cambridge, Mass.: Harvard University Press, 1984), pp. 142-43.

16. U.S. Women's Bureau, *Fact Sheet on the Earnings Gap*, Feb. 1971, p. 1; Larry E. Suter and Herman P. Miller, "Income Differences between Men and Career Women," *American Journal of Sociology* 78 (Jan. 1973): 962-74.

17. See generally the introduction to President's Commission on the Status of Women, *American Women: Report of the President's Commission on the Status of Women* (New York: Scribner's, 1965); Barbara Babcock et al., *Sex Discrimination and the Law: Causes and Remedies* (Boston: Little, Brown, 1975); Barbara Brown et al., "The Equal Rights Amendment: A Constitutional Basis for Equal Rights for Women," *Yale Law Journal* 80 (1971): 871.

18. President's Commission; Caroline Bird, "The Androgynous Life," in Mary Lou Thompson, ed., *Voices of the New Feminism* (Boston: Beacon Press, 1970), pp. 178-98; Caroline Bird and the National Women's Conference, *What Women Want: From the Official Report to the President, the Congress and the People of the United States* (New York:

Simon & Schuster, 1972); Alice Rossi, "Family Development in a Changing World" (1971), quoted in Gayle Graham Yates, *What Women Want: The Ideas of the Movement* (Cambridge, Mass.: Harvard University Press, 1975), p. 155.

19. U. S. Department of Labor, *Manpower Report of the President, 1973* (Washington, D.C.: Government Printing Office, 1973), p. 168; Ryan, p. 222; Klein, pp. 38–39; Barrie Thorne, "Feminist Reckoning of the Family: An Overview," in Barrie Thorne with Marilyn Yalom, eds., *Rethinking the Family: Some Feminist Questions* (New York: Longman, 1982), pp. 1–24.

20. See generally Maren Lockwood Carden, *The New Feminist Movement* (New York: Russell Sage Foundation, 1974), pp. 154–55; Judith Hole and Ellen Levine, *Rebirth of Feminism* (New York: Quadrangle, 1971), pp. 253–59, and sources cited therein.

21. Zillah R. Eisenstein, *The Radical Future of Liberal Feminism* (New York: Longman, 1981); see generally Carden, pp. 3, 135–36.

22. See, e.g., C. B. MacPherson, *The Political Theory of Possessive Individualism* (Oxford: Clarendon Press, 1962), p. 3.

23. See, e.g., Carol Gilligan, *In a Different Voice* (Cambridge, Mass.: Harvard University Press, 1982).

24. U. S. Bureau of the Census, Current Population Reports, *Money Income of Households, Families and Persons in the United States: 1984* (Washington, D.C.: Bureau of the Census, 1986); Heidi H. Hartmann, Patricia P. Roos, and Donald J. Trieman, "An Agenda for Basic Research on Comparable Worth," in Heidi Hartmann, ed., *Comparable Worth: New Directions for Research* (Washington, D.C.: National Academy Press, 1985), p. 3.

25. Lenore Weitzman, *The Divorce Revolution* (New York: Free Press, 1985); Ruth Sidel, *Women and Children Last* (New York: Viking, 1986).

26. U. S. Commission on Civil Rights, *A Growing Crisis: Disadvantaged Women and Their Children*, Clearinghouse Publication 78 (Washington, D.C.: U. S. Commission on Civil Rights, 1983); Sidel; Janice Peterson, "The Feminization of Poverty," *Journal of Economic Issues* 21 (1987): 329.

27. See, e.g., Catharine MacKinnon, *Feminism Unmodified* (Cambridge, Mass.: Harvard University Press, 1987). Rosemary Tong, *Women, Sex and the Law* (Totowa, N.J.: Rowman and Allenheld, 1984).

28. See, e.g., Susan D. Becker, *The Origins of the Equal Rights Amendment* (Westport, Conn.: Greenwood Press, 1981); Alice Kessler-Harris, *Out to Work* (New York: Oxford University Press, 1982), p. 188; Sheila Rothman, *Woman's Proper Place* (New York: Basic Books, 1978), p. 57.

29. See *Rosenfeld v. Southern Pacific Company*, 444 F.2d 1219 (9th Cir. 1971); EEOC Guidelines, 29 C.F.R. §1604 (1986) (protective labor); *Orr v. Orr*, 440 U.S. 268 (1979) (alimony); Deborah Rhode, "Equal Rights in Retrospect," *Law and Inequality: A Journal of Theory and Practice* 1 (1983): 1.

30. Kraditor, p. 12.

31. Diana Loercher, "Equality for Women Stalled?" *Christian Science Monitor*, Feb. 15, 1973, p. 6, col. 2 (quoting Phyllis Schlafly). For comparable antisuffragist arguments, see Nancy F. Cott, ed., *Root of Bitterness: Documents of the Social History of American Women* (New York: Dutton, 1972), p. 141.

32. See George Whittenberg, *The ERA and You* (New York: Vantage Press, 1975), p. 54; Nick Timmesch, "The Sexual Equality Amendment," *New York Times Magazine*, June 24, 1973, p. 54.

33. Janet Boles, *The Politics of the Equal Rights Amendment: Conflict and the Decision Process* (New York: Longman, 1979), pp. 200–02.

34. Olympia Brown, "Foreign Rule," NAWSA Convention, Washington, D.C. (Jan. 21–23, 1889), in Anthony and Harper, 4:148; Elizabeth Cady Stanton, "Address to the National Woman Suffrage Convention," Washington, D.C. (Jan. 19, 1869), in Stanton, Susan B. Anthony, and Matilda Joslyn Gage, eds., *History of Woman Suffrage* (Rochester, N.Y., 1881), 2:348–55; Elizabeth Cady Stanton, "Educated Suffrage," NAWSA Convention, Washington, D.C. (Feb. 12–18, 1902), in Anthony and Harper, 4:15.

35. Joan Hurling, "ERA Capitol Conflict," *Kanakee Daily Journal*, March 15, 1973, p. 25; "Rights Battle Booms from Kitchens," *Chicago Daily News*, March 15, 1973, p. 34; "Women Try to Cook Up Votes," *Chicago Tribune*, March 15, 1973. See also Sheila Wolfe, "ERA Given Boost at State Breakfast," *Chicago Tribune*, March 15, 1973, sec. 2, p. 9.

36. See Boles, p. 125.

Race Relations, History, and Public Policy: The Alabama Vote Fraud Cases of 1985

NELL IRVIN PAINTER

Black Americans, unlike voluntary immigrants to the United States, have not been allowed the choice of embracing or rejecting the myths of this country's origins. They do not see themselves as the spiritual descendants of the Puritans and seldom believe the promises of the last, best hope of man. Afro-Americans were brought here against their will, enslaved, degraded, and sealed into a heredity status as the poorest segment of the American working class. This history has given black Americans an identity that, while overtly racial, is also economic, a multilayered status whose complexities have emerged since the mid-1960s. Discerning observers such as the historian Edmund S. Morgan trace the enduring ambiguities of race and class to the colonial period, when Afro-Americans inherited the negative stereotypes that the English elite had attached to their own poor.[1] To this day, race carries economic connotations, so that to speak of blacks is to speak of the poor in the United States. The congruence of race and class in the revolutionary United States meant that Afro-Americans inherited an ambiguous legacy from the Founding Fathers, who, like Thomas Jefferson, owned human beings while composing a Declaration of Independence that proclaimed the equality and liberty of all men. For two generations in this nation's early life the spirit of Jefferson the slaveowner triumphed over that of Jefferson the spokesman for human rights where Afro-Americans were concerned.

A. Leon Higginbotham points out the paradox of a Declaration that allowed slavery in the eighteenth century but supplied the phrases that (in the nineteenth century) undermined the legitimacy of holding people as property.[2] In the late eighteenth and early nineteenth centuries, there was little question that the Constitution, the foundation of American law, continued to protect the peculiar institution, a fact made clear with the strengthening of the fugitive-slave clause in 1850. The antebellum Constitution also denigrated the status of free blacks. According to Chief Justice of the United States Roger Taney in the Dred Scott decision of 1857, "it is impossible to believe" that the rights and privileges of citizens were intended to be extended to blacks, who therefore possessed no rights that whites needed to respect.[3]

During the antebellum period, state laws defined enslaved blacks as personal property, making it a crime for anyone to teach them to read or write. Free blacks were less fettered, but in most places they could not fully exercise the rights of citizens. Subject to statutory limitations and physical abuse, free blacks were treated, as the abolitionists used to say, as a hissing and a byword. Speaking for the enslaved in 1852, Frederick Douglass called the Fourth of July a whites-only holiday: "The rich inheritance of justice, liberty, prosperity and independence, bequeathed by your fathers, is shared by you, not by me. . . . This Fourth [of] July is *yours*, not *mine*. To drag a man in fetters into the grand illuminated temple of liberty, and call upon him to join you in joyous anthems, were inhuman mockery and sacrilegious irony."[4]

But Douglass changed his view of the relation between federal public policy and blacks when Union victory in the Civil War added the Reconstruction Amendments to the United States Constitution. The Thirteenth (1865), Fourteenth (1868), and Fifteenth (1870) Amendments abolished slavery and promised blacks citizenship, equal protection under law, and suffrage, thereby extending the sentiments of the Declaration of Independence and the Constitution to Afro-Americans—in theory, at least.

The substitution of multiracial democracy for white-supremacist oligarchy in the South during Reconstruction proved more demanding than Washington politicians had expected, and after a few years the federal government gave up on protecting black and white Reconstructionists against violent whites seeking to overturn the biracial regimes. During the 1870s, white supremacist redeemers came to power in all the former Confederate states, disfranchising blacks and creating a society and economy that oppressed the poor, black and white.

The downfall of democracy in the South and the disfranchisement, segregation, and lynching that followed left blacks with a sobering realization: the most promising political innovations in their regard might be subverted. Since the end of Reconstruction, faith in government and optimism in politics have been, for Afro-Americans, signs of unpardonable naïveté, and those who let down their guard against white treachery are sooner or later liable to the charge of forgetting the lessons of history. Blacks who cooperate with whites—for whatever greater gains—run the risk of being seen by other blacks as fools as well as traitors.

৶৶

CONSIDERING THESE VERY DIFFERENT juristic statuses—first as denizens, then as citizens, then as de jure citizens who occupied a distinctly second class de facto—Afro-Americans have thought and acted as the symbolic descendants both of Jefferson and of Jefferson's slaves. They have resented slavery, the institution that assured Mr. Jefferson his livelihood and standing, and prized freedom, the greatest civic good according to the planter revolutionaries.

During the era of segregation, roughly 1877–1960, blacks considered the southern states their oppressors and federal policy their only potential avenue of relief. Even so, federal concessions to black civil rights came one by one, each after prolonged struggle. Between the two world wars, civil-rights organizations, notably the National Association for the Advancement of Colored People (NAACP), lobbied (fruitlessly) for the passage of federal antilynching legislation and brought cases (successfully) before the Supreme Court that would strike down the degrading and hypocritical white-supremacist formula of "separate but equal."

The *Brown* decision of 1954 and the civil-rights movement that produced the federal Civil Rights Acts of 1957 and 1964 and the Voting Rights Act of 1965 inaugurated a new tradition in federal policy and race relations.

After 1965, blacks began gingerly to consider the federal government, in particular the Civil Rights Division of the Justice Department, an ally in the struggle for civil rights. The alliance had never been completely public for blacks, nor, given the nineteenth-century precedents, very secure. But the hardening of federal policy toward blacks that occurred after 1981 has served to highlight the contrast between the two traditions—the long-standing distrust and the newer partnership—by tending toward a restoration of the older pattern.

⚬⚬⚬

THE REAGAN ADMINISTRATION has advocated a series of policies that disregard black concerns: tax-exempt status for private academies that discriminate, the dismantling of affirmative-action plans, indifferent enforcement and reluctant support for the renewal of the Voting Rights Act. The Republican party also undertook a controversial policy of voter purges that affected black voters disproportionately. Republicans denied that the "ballot integrity program"—which targeted precincts in three states in which less than twenty percent of the votes had been cast for President Reagan in 1984—was aimed specifically at blacks.[5]

While these initiatives were under way, five cases originating in the Alabama Black Belt illustrate the degree to which the Reagan administration has broken with recent federal history. In southwestern Alabama in 1985 the Criminal Division of the United States Justice Department suspected of vote fraud men and women who had been prominent civil-rights activists and leaders in the expansion of suffrage to people who, before the passage of the Voting Rights Act in 1965, had been disfranchised. The national news media covered the trials of the most prominent defendants: Albert Turner, head of the Perry County Civic League (PCCL), and Spiver Gordon, Jr., head of the Greene County Civic League (GCCL). Turner had been a close associate of the Reverend Martin Luther King, Jr., in the 1960s, and both he and Gordon were leaders of the Southern Christian Leadership Convention (SCLC) in Alabama. Turner had marched in King's cortege in 1968, and a photo of him leading one of the mules drawing King's casket appeared often in 1985. A review of the trials will explain if not clarify where these events belong in the history of American race relations.

Before the passage of the Voting Rights Act in 1965, the ten counties of the poor, majority-black southwestern Alabama Black Belt were all dominated economically and politically by the descendants of antebellum planters, a small number of landowning white families who were extremely conservative politically.[6] After 1965, however, effective political organization yielded black control in five of the ten counties (including Greene and Perry). By 1982 there were more than 70,000 blacks registered to vote in the area, compared to 62,700 whites.[7] Absentee balloting allowed the conversion of a numerical black majority into political power.

"Do you know why the roads to white folks' cemeteries are paved in the Black Belt?" asked a black voting activist rhetorically. "It's so people won't get their feet wet if it rains on election day."[8] Absentee ballots, known as being easy to fiddle and steal, had raised suspicion for years, and until recently white elites had controlled the votes of the dead and of people who lived elsewhere but voted in the Black Belt. During the 1960s and 1970s, the PCCL and GCCL would apparently win elections only to find the next day that absentee ballots had overturned their victories. The Civic Leagues complained of absentee-ballot fraud to the Justice Department, but Justice said the cases were too narrow to pursue. The Civic Leagues then learned to work the absentee-ballot system, tapping large numbers of potential voters among the elderly and illiterate who preferred voting at home, where they might avail themselves of assistance in private. Today hundreds of absentee ballots are routinely cast in Black Belt elections, by old people, illiterates, and working people whose jobs make it impossible to vote during the narrowly proscribed hours during which the polls remain open. The United States Justice Department found that more than seven hundred absentee ballots—roughly fifteen percent of the whole—were cast in the Perry County Alabama primary election in 1984.[9]

By this time two local groups, the White Citizens' Council and the Concerned Citizens of Perry County, began seeking ways to undercut the power of Albert Turner and the PCCL. In Greene County in 1984 a "Political Action Committee" (PAC) or "Coalition" movement got under way in opposition to Spiver Gordon and the GCCL. In both counties the two sides are called the Civic

League and the Coalition. Most of the black leadership and black voters support the Civic Leagues. On the side of the Coalitions are representatives of the white elites and black minorities. In black-dominated counties like Perry and Greene, white candidates no longer win elections, so the Coalitions as well as the Civic Leagues run black candidates.

In the 1984 elections in Greene County the Civic League candidates spoke of people-oriented policies and black empowerment. Pledging themselves to the majority of people in the county, the GCCL advocated an increase in the tax that the county levied on parimutuel betting at the privately owned but county-licensed Greene County greyhound racing track and the reallocation of these revenues toward organizations serving the poor. The Civic League also supported the annexation to the town of Eutaw one multiracial and three black subdivisions, which would have tended to weaken elite white control of the county seat. (Although half the southwestern Black Belt counties are run by blacks, wealthy whites retain control of all ten county seats.) And finally the GCCL promised to increase property-tax rates to benefit the public schools. Since whites send their children to segregated private schools, the public schools are virtually all black.

The Coalition's candidates opposed these initiatives, promising fiscal responsibility and the ability better to attract industry and handle the county's revenues.[10] The Coalition tended to speak of responsible government and improvement of the climate for business, citing the Black Belt's enormous need for economic development. Greene County tax assessor John Kennard, a Coalition candidate, said that "black people in this state cannot liberate themselves by themselves. It has to be some kind of cooperative venture with the power structure, the economic interests. We have to work with the people we marched against."[11] Warren Kynard, tax assessor of Perry County, told me that he saw himself as a pragmatist, a long-range planner who realized that running as a Coalition candidate was simply good strategy, considering that whites own eighty-six percent of the land and pay ninety-two percent of the property taxes.[12]

The United States Justice Department became involved in these differences in local politics in 1984, but on whose initiative is not clear. Civic League supporters (and even some of their opponents) maintain that the initiative came from Washington. Opponents point to Republican Senator Jeremiah Denton of Alabama, who had gained office in 1980 by a very narrow margin and whose opposition to black civil rights and support of military spending over domestic spending would deny him black support in 1986. United States attorneys in Alabama contend that black candidates in the Black Belt demanded an investigation by a local district attorney who subsequently approached the Justice Department. In any event, the Justice Department became involved in local politics in the Alabama Black Belt after a change in federal policy.

Before the Justice Department altered its procedures in the fall of 1984, the federal government refrained from investigating cases that concerned only a small number of votes, that were purely local elections, or that were elections in which fraud would not have affected the outcome. (Hence the complaints of absentee ballot abuse brought earlier by the Civic Leagues had not been investigated.) But the 1984 policy targeted possible abuse of "the elderly, the socially disadvantaged, or the illiterate" even in local elections in which the outcome of the election was not in question.[13]

Prior to the 1984 Alabama primary election, local white officeholders and federal officials secretly marked black ballots and after the election undertook an intensive investigation of absentee ballots. The Justice Department examined hundreds of absentee ballots in five Black Belt counties, finding from fifteen to two dozen per county with alterations that the Justice Department considered fraudulent. Agents of the Federal Bureau of Investigation and the Justice Department questioned one thousand black voters, mostly elderly or illiterate, producing ballots thought secret and asking whether these were, in fact, the ballots the voters had intended to cast. In the Perry County investigation more than one hundred elderly voters were bussed out of the Black Belt to Mobile to testify before a grand jury.

The proceedings frightened and confused voters and resulted in a reduction of about fifteen percent in the numbers of votes cast in the 1986 election. In the five vote-fraud trials, only one defendant, Spiver Gordon, was convicted of any charges whatever. Not surprisingly, the Justice Department's prosecution of the Greene County trial raised a good deal of suspicion.

While Justice Department lawyers maintained that race was not a factor in the inquiry, they used all six of their peremptory challenges to eliminate the six blacks in the pool of prospective jurors. Thus an all-white jury found Gordon guilty of some of the charges brought against him. One of Gordon's lawyers found it "remarkable that the Justice Department is coming in to defend the rights of blacks but won't permit blacks to sit on these juries." He revealed that the Justice Department investigation had focused only on the five black-dominated Black Belt counties and that within those counties it had failed to question whites who had cast absentee ballots. The defense showed that some of the absentee ballots that the defendants had supposedly tampered with had been changed from votes for Civic League candidates to votes for Coalition candidates.[14]

The cases became so controversial that the Subcommittee on Civil and Constitutional Rights of the House Judiciary Committee held a one-day hearing, which produced wide newspaper coverage. News stories featured the views of the defendants and their supporters, and editorial opinion overwhelmingly condemned the Justice Department for intimidating blacks in an area with a long history of black disfranchisement. The *Atlanta Constitution* doubted the wisdom of the Justice Department's having spent hundreds of thousands of dollars and an entire year interrogating thousands of blacks over a handful of ballots that seemed more to indicate procedural casualness than outright fraud. The *Constitution* concluded that "the charges are not nearly as serious as the long-term damage the inquiry poses for black political participation in Alabama." The *Washington Post* noted that the Justice Department had taken the white side of local controversies and warned of the "chilling effect" of "intervening too clumsily in local political struggles" in a region where blacks "remember all too well the days of disenfranchisement and intimidation."[15]

The *Post*'s mention of race indicated the defendants' success in influencing public opinion. As if to recall the ambiguity of the relationship between blacks and the political process in this country, both the Justice Department and the defendants cited historical precedent in the vote-fraud cases. The defendants and their supporters defined the issues in racial terms and situated the events within the history of the civil-rights movement. Albert Turner's impeccable civil-rights credentials gained his side enormous moral prestige. With a record of more than twenty years of support of black civil rights to his credit, Turner became a symbol of the struggle for the vote, while his prosecution represented an assault on black suffrage. In January 1985 Alabama State Senator Hank Sanders, one of Turner's lawyers, said that the federal government was "attacking us with sledge-hammer blows, to try to kill the few hard earned gains we have made. . . . [T]his is purely a political trial to weaken the voting strength of Black people. It has nothing to do with a criminal act." He termed the investigation of the voting-rights activists "a sophisticated re-enactment of post-Reconstruction activities intended to reduce black participation in the political process."[16]

Just as the Perry County defendants went on trial, civil-rights supporters celebrated the twentieth anniversary of the Selma-to-Montgomery march for voting rights, which Martin Luther King, Jr., had led and which had encouraged the passage of the Voting Rights Act. The Reverend Joseph E. Lowery, president of SCLC, warned the crowd at the anniversary march "to be ready to go to jail again" in 1985 as in 1965. A white participant from Nashville said she had come to celebrate the anniversary and "to lend my support to the black people here in the Black Belt who have been indicted on voting fraud."[17]

In August 1985, supporters of the defendants mounted a "freedom caravan"—a 1960s-style flatbed truck featuring a dummy of a black lynch victim—that visited seven county seats in the Black Belt. One of the speakers in the freedom caravan was Maryland State Senator Clarence Mitchell III, president of the National Black Caucus of State Legislators. Mitchell told a crowd at the Wilcox County courthouse that "the civil rights movement started here in the Black Belt" and that "individuals aren't on trial here. The whole movement for civil rights is on trial, and we will not be intimidated."[18]

The Department of Justice denied that race had played any part in the prosecution. United States attorneys spoke of criminal (rather than civil) wrongdoing and portrayed the defendants as perverters of the legacy of the civil-rights movement. Federal prosecutors also cited the march that had occurred twenty years before. In closing arguments in the Perry County trial, one of the federal prosecutors told the jury that the people marching from Selma to Montgomery in 1965 "didn't go across the [Edmund Pettus] bridge so Albert Turner could vote more than once in an election. . . . No man is above the law—no matter who his friends are or who he has marched with."[19] Justice Department officials argued that blacks, not whites, had filed the complaints that had led to the investigations and to federal indictments. United States Attorney Jefferson Sessions III of the southern district of Alabama told me repeatedly that this was a criminal trial with no racial significance whatever.[20]

Even though it never gained very wide support, the Justice Department contention needed to be addressed, because black witnesses testified for the prosecution. It was one thing to portray the trials as a white-versus-black struggle in which the Justice Department was supporting whites. But it was another to come to terms with blacks' taking what was called the white side in the battle.

Clarence Mitchell summed up an argument that supporters of the defendants made when pressed: "Don't let anyone fool you into thinking this is black-on-black. . . . There are some who are the same color as us, but they're not our kind." He called blacks supporting the prosecution "black Judases." A cochair of the Alabama Black Belt Defense Committee spoke of black Coalition candidates as having been "manipulated" by whites. "To call them Uncle Toms is to be nice to them," he said, for they were characters of far more sinister intent. On the other side Jefferson Sessions complained that one of the defendants' lawyers drew the color line in these cases, played on black sensibilities, and made "vicious, personal attacks" on black witnesses for the prosecution.[21] Perry County Commissioner Reese Billingslea believes that he and Warren Kynard became targets of black criticism "because we don't do the things that favor one race."[22]

Sessions and Billingslea might have gained more support if the Alabama Black Belt had not had a crushing history of white supremacy, black disfranchisement, and a long-standing hierarchy in which race, wealth, and power (and their lack) coincided. The Black Belt's income distribution intensifies the traditional American association of poverty with blackness and of wealth with whiteness. If "black" is explicitly interpreted as poor black, the Civic Leagues' claim of vindicating black interests makes perfect sense in the light of history, beginning with the seventeenth-century identification of blackness with slavery and following up to the twentieth-century civil-rights movement. The civil-rights activists of the 1950s and 1960s found a broad area of compassion for the poor that extended beyond race. The public career of the Reverend Martin Luther King, Jr., exemplifies this pattern and reveals an agenda of economic reform within the ideals of the campaign for black civil rights.

The movement with which King is associated began with racial issues in the South and ended in the advocacy of a "reconstruction of the entire society."[23] Activists like Albert Turner and Spiver Gordon extended their commitment to black rights to a wider political and economic agenda: the empowerment of the poor and disadvantaged of any race. In the 1980s, therefore, civil-rights supporters combat both racism and the powerlessness that accompanies poverty. Such goals demand political and economic change, which accommodation with the powers that be would limit or stymie. Hence the conflict with black Coalition supporters.

While the PCCL- and GCCL-led black majorities support what they call people-oriented politics, Greene County tax assessor John Kennard, a Coalition member, advocates policies that are probusiness (low taxes, minimal support of public services such as schools). His kind of conciliation of elites is to be found in conservative circles throughout the country, for what he calls "cooperation with the power structure" is a hallmark of probusiness Reaganism. The connection between black civil rights and economic reform would automatically have cost Coalition candidates (whose allies were white elites) much black support and made it difficult for blacks to follow a political route established in the mid–nineteenth century.

One innovation of nineteenth-century politics was the political machine, in which poor men without education could make a personally remunerative career in politics. Distributing jobs and handouts, many machine politicos served the individual but not the class needs of their poor constituents by refraining from pursuing fundamental political or economic change. The main motive in seeking a career in politics was personal gain, not fundamental economic reform. If, as has been charged, the black adherents to the Coalitions in the Alabama Black Belt were acting as self-serving individualists lacking any sense of larger responsibilities, they belong to a long-standing tradition in American politics. But the history of civil rights and the persistence of white racism obstruct this path. Blacks playing the politics of personal gain must ally themselves with the powerful, who are and were invariably white. Accommodationists, therefore, risk a far worse stigma than economic opportunism. They are called traitors to the race, a concern that evidently figured on both sides of the vote-fraud cases.

In the Blac,s in national politics, the Reagan administration's espousal of "traditional values" extends to one of the oldest: racism. The Black Belt vote-fraud prosecutions not only served the business priorities of local elites but also seem to have been intended to teach a lesson to blacks who had gotten out of place. John Russell, assistant director of the Justice Department's Office of Public Affairs, said that "arrogance on the part of blacks" had indicated a need for investigation.[24] Similarly, the regional director of the Republican National Committee wrote a memo about the party's ballot-integrity program in Louisiana that predicted that the program "could keep the black vote down considerably."[25] Other policies of the Reagan administration buttress the contention that it keeps racial as well as political and economic hierarchies in mind.

Given the relationship they see between race and class, voting-rights activists would probably not be surprised if the Justice Department's intimidation of vulnerable black voters refocused national attention on poverty as well as racism, for in the 1960s a focus on racism led to a war on poverty. The outbreak of acts of racial violence and confrontation continues, and a renewed discussion of racism seems about to begin. If matters of race lead to considerations of the injuries of class in the South, such an outcome would instruct this administration's Justice Department, which, at best, betrays an incredible ignorance of southern history.

Notes

I would like to thank Allen Tullos, Carlos Williams, Peyton McCrary, Jefferson Sessions III, Frank Donaldson, John C. Bell, Ira Burnim, Warren Kynard, John Zippert, Bill Cobey, Tom Gordon, and David Garrow for sharing valuable information.

1. Edmund S. Morgan, *American Slavery, American Freedom: The Ordeal of Colonial Virginia* (New York: W. W. Norton & Co., 1975), pp. 363–87.

2. A. Leon Higginbotham, Jr., *In the Matter of Color: Race and the American Legal Process—The Colonial Period* (New York: Oxford University Press, 1978), pp. 372–73.

3. 60 U.S. (19 How.) 393 (1856), quoted in Derrick A. Bell, Jr., *Race, Racism and American Law* (Boston: Little, Brown & Co., 1973), p. 10.

4. John W. Blassingame, ed., *The Frederick Douglass Papers*, ser. 1 (New Haven: Yale University Press, 1977), 2:368.

5. Phyllis Crockett, "GOP Voter Purge," *All Things Considered*, National Public Radio, 30 Oct. 1986.

6. The counties are Pickens, Greene, Sumter, Chocktaw, Marengo, Hale, Perry, Dallas (in which the city of Selma is located), Wilcox, and Lowndes. The current average family income in the southwestern Alabama Black Belt is $7,619

for blacks, $18,663 for whites (Thulani Davis, "Whose Black Power? Turf Battles in the New South," *Village Voice*, 2 Sept. 1986, p. 24). In 1981 the state of Alabama prosecuted two elderly black women, Maggie Bozeman and Julia Wilder of Pickens County, for absentee-vote fraud, although the case was finally overturned in federal court. Despite the reversal of the convictions, the cochairs of the Alabama Black Belt Defense Committee believe that the prosecution has continued to reduce black voting in Pickens County (Wendell H. Paris and John Zippert, "Fact Sheet on Federal Grand Jury Investigations and Indictments of Black Leaders in Alabama Vote Fraud" [unpublished, 1985]).

7. Allen Tullos, "Crackdown in the Black Belt: Not-So-Simple Justice," *Southern Changes*, 7.2 (May–June 1985): 4.

8. Wilcox County Commissioner Bobby Joe Johnson in Tullos, "Not-So-Simple Justice," pp. 6–7.

9. Telephone interview with Tom Gordon, 23 Sept. 1986; John C. Keeney, Deputy Assistant Attorney General, Criminal Division, Department of Justice, in "Civil Rights Implications of Federal Voting Fraud Prosecutions," Hearing before the Subcommittee on Civil and Constitutional Rights of the Committee on the Judiciary, House of Representatives, 99th Congress, 1st session, 25 Sept. 1985, p. 99 (cited hereafter as Congressional Hearing).

10. Allen Tullos, "Crackdown in the Black Belt: On to Greene County," *Southern Changes*, 7.3–4 (July–Sept. 1985): 2–3, and telephone interview with John Zippert, publisher of the *Greene County Democrat*, 21 Jan. 1987.

11. In Davis, pp. 23–24.

12. Telephone interview with Warren Kynard, 21 Jan. 1987.

13. U.S. Justice Department memo, 22 Oct. 1984, in Congressional Hearing, app. 1, p. 154.

14. Ira Burnim in Congressional Hearing, p. 126, and telephone interview with Ira Burnim, 15 Dec. 1986.

15. *Atlanta Constitution*, 3 Sept. 1985, *Washington Post*, 7 Sept. 1985.

16. *Greene County Democrat*, 30 Jan. 1985, *New York Times*, 26 Aug. 1985.

17. *Birmingham News*, 8 March 1985, and Marty Collier in *Birmingham News*, 6 March 1985. See also *Birmingham News*, 3 March 1985, and *New York Times*, 4 March 1985.

18. *New York Times*, 26 Aug. 1985.

19. Assistant United States Attorney E. T. Rolison in *New York Times*, 6 July 1985.

20. Telephone interview with Jefferson Sessions III, 23 Sept. 1986.

21. *Birmingham News*, 3 June 1985, telephone interview with John Zippert, 21 Jan. 1987; and telephone interview with Jefferson Sessions III, 23 Sept. 1986.

22. *Orlando Sentinel*, 8 Sept. 1985.

23. In David Levering Lewis, "Martin Luther King, Jr., and the Promise of Nonviolent Populism," in John Hope Franklin and August Meier, eds., *Black Leaders of the Twentieth Century* (Urbana: University of Illinois Press, 1982), p. 297.

24. John Russell in Tullos, "Not-So-Simple Justice," p. 4.

25. Chris Wolff in Crockett, "GOP Voter Purge."

Rights in Theory, Rights in Practice

NORMAN DORSEN

Rights are not theoretical. They are practical, usable, and enforceable. They are meant to protect and fulfill people. If they are not exercised, they atrophy and may be lost. At the same time, rights are grounded in theory, nurtured in theory, and often lost in theory. Those whose very practical job it is to secure rights—whether individual lawyers or institutions such as the ACLU and the NAACP—are well advised to learn the history of the doctrines and principles that they urge on courts and legislatures.

Americans possess different kinds of rights, each traceable to a different source. Common-law rights, such as those governing contractual relations and tortious behavior (civil wrongs such as assault, negligence, defamation) are the product of judicial action occurring over centuries; through a gradual process of inclusion and exclusion, the judiciary clarifies the definition of these rights. Rights are also created in statutes enacted by the Congress and by state and local legislative bodies. Environmental protection laws, securities laws, civil-rights laws, housing regulations, and countless other enactments enable persons to assert rights before courts and administrative agencies. There are also international "human rights," still in their germinal stage, that are the joint product of international bodies such as the United Nations, "customary" behavior by nations, and the decisions of international judicial tribunals.

The constitutional right is yet another type of right. Its source is of course the Constitution of the United States, ratified in 1787 and put into effect in 1789. These rights have a special bite: they trump all other kinds of rights. A common-law or statutory or international right cannot be implemented if it runs afoul of a provision of the Constitution. In such cases it is, as we say, "invalid." Constitutional rights are also of special importance because they determine the authority of government and the legal relationship of the state to individuals.

Although the Constitution, as a test, is the source of constitutional rights, some liberties in the United States are traceable to a natural-law tradition that long antedated the Constitution. For example, the Virginia Declaration of Rights (1776) asserted that "all men are by nature equally free and independent, and have certain inherent rights . . . namely, the enjoyment of life and liberty, with the means of acquiring and possessing property, and pursuing and obtaining happiness and safety."[1] This sentiment was reflected in the Declaration of Independence (1776), which spoke of "inalienable rights," and in the Constitution itself, which embodied these principles, most conspicuously in the Ninth Amendment. Accordingly, the Supreme Court over the years has recognized a number of rights not explicitly grounded in the text of the Constitution, including, for a season, freedom of contract, and, in recent years, the right to travel, freedom of association, and rights of personal privacy and autonomy.

There is another sense in which the Constitution, while authoritative, is not the end of the tale. It was recognized from the beginning that the Constitution was not frozen in time. In an often-quoted passage, Chief Justice John Marshall said in *McCulloch v. Maryland* (1819), for a unanimous Court, that the Constitution is an instrument "intended to endure for ages to come and, consequently, to be adapted to the various crises of human affairs."[2] This insight has been almost universally accepted. For example, in 1910 the Court discussed the meaning of the clause that prohibits "cruel and unusual punishments":

Time works changes, brings into existence new conditions and purposes. Therefore, a principle to be vital must be capable of wider application than the mischief which gave it birth. This is peculiarly true of constitutions. They are not ephemeral enactments, designed to meet passing occasions.[3]

And more recently, Justice Benjamin Cardozo observed: "The great generalities of the Constitution have a content and a significance that vary from age to age."[4]

Whatever the differences in philosophy among judges and commentators, this understanding of the Constitution was virtually common ground until Attorney General Edwin Meese, in a series of speeches, expressed what he called a "jurisprudence of original intention," which would "endeavor to resurrect the original meaning of constitutional provisions and statutes as the *only* reliable guide for judgment."[5]

The torrent of reply explained why Meese's approach to the Constitution was simplistic and unhelpful. In many if not most controversies in which "the great generalities of the Constitution"—freedom of speech and religion, due process, equal protection of the laws—are open to interpretation, it is not possible to ascertain the "original meaning." Some issues arising under those headings could not have been foreseen, others were never discussed, and still others were the objects of conflicting "intentions." Moreover, it is not easy to decipher the eighteenth-century mind in relation to twentieth-century problems, especially when it is a group "intention" that is being sought, and further when it is several groups whose intentions are of concern—the members of the Constitutional Convention, the First Congress (which proposed the Bill of Rights), and the ratifying conventions of the several states that approved the original document and amendments.[6]

As David Richards convincingly explains in these pages,[7] it is useless to treat the Constitution and the rights that hinge on it as fundamentalist holy writ, divinely created (not merely so inspired) and immutable in their edicts. An exclusive inquiry into "original intention" is neither practicable as a matter of interpretation nor consistent with the underlying philosophy of a document evolving to meet the exigencies of future generations.

I do not mean to suggest that text and history are unimportant to constitutional interpretation. To the contrary, they must be the starting points of analysis. But in the effort to apply the great principles embodied in generalized language to the problems of our time, text and history must be supplemented by an understanding of the purposes of particular constitutional provisions, by the values that underlie them, and by the judicial interpretation that the Constitution has received over two centuries. Supporters of Meese, such as Solicitor General Charles Fried, often claim that Meese's detractors want us to "cut ourselves loose from past meanings" in order to be "free to create and innovate."[8] This is a straw-man opponent: Meese's critics do not ignore the constitutional text and its "original intention"; they simply employ them in a manner of interpretation that is at once more sophisticated and more traditional than Meese would allow.

Here are three current issues in which determining the rights involved requires a kind of interpretation that the Meesean doctrine does not allow but that is nevertheless entirely consistent with the tradition of constitutional interpretation in American judicial history.

1. *The application of the Bill of Rights to the states.* Meese first enunciated his "jurisprudence of original intention" in a speech before the American Bar Association. The chief burden of his speech was that the Bill of Rights was not intended to and should not apply to the states—even though numerous Supreme Court decisions have so ruled.

Meese was correct on one point, which, as we shall see, happens to be irrelevant to the current debate. He accurately stated that the Bill of Rights was not applicable to the states when it was ratified in 1791. The Supreme Court so held in 1833,[9] concluding that the purpose of the Bill of Rights was to protect citizens against the new, rather scary and untested national government. So far so good. But in his speech Meese blithely skipped all the way to 1925, when, he said, the Court first improperly "incorporated" one of the provisions of the Bill of Rights against the states. In making this leap, Meese ignored the central question of whether the Fourteenth Amendment, ratified in 1868, accomplished some form of incorporation when it provided that no state may "abridge the privileges or immunities of citizens of the United States" or "deprive any person of life, liberty, or property, without due process of law." The critical question, debated by judges and scholars for a century, is whether these clauses, plainly designed to limit *state* power in the wake of a Civil War fought largely on this issue, applied the Bill of Rights to the states, or, if it did not, just how it subjected the states to federal constitutional norms in its relations with its citizens. Meese simply avoided these questions.

But the Supreme Court had to grapple with the problem, and it did so over a period of thirty years, in which the combatting forces relied on history, precedent, and the role of the judiciary in support of their respective views. In the end, the Court in the 1960s and 1970s settled on a theory—"selective incorporation"—that has resulted in the application of most of the Bill of Rights, one by one, to the states, including Miranda's privilege against self-incrimination, Gideon's right to counsel, and all the elements of the First Amendment relating to freedom of speech and religion. In reaching this result, the Court did not confine itself to Meese's limiting formula of "original intention"; instead, it used the diverse tools of constitutional interpretation that judges have employed from the beginning of the Republic.[10]

2. *Racial affirmative action.* Although the word "slavery" does not appear in it, three provisions of the Constitution countenanced the bondage of blacks. After the Civil War, the newly ratified Fourteenth Amendment barred states from "deny[ing] to any person within [their] jurisdiction the equal protection of the laws." For almost one hundred years, this provision was underenforced by the executive branch and its application restricted by the courts. Not until 1954, when *Brown v. Board of Education*[11] invalidated the state-imposed separation of the races, was a second beginning made to admit blacks to civil equality. The effort, which was measurably aided by congressionally enacted civil-rights laws in the 1960s, took many forms and encountered considerable resistance, resistance that persists to this day. But it nevertheless made genuine progress in establishing the rights of blacks and in mitigating the second-class citizenship under which they had labored for so long.

A special aspect of the struggle for racial equality—affirmative action—illustrates both the theoretical and the practical difficulties involved in establishing genuine racial equality under law. The question is whether the equal-protection clause requires government to be color-blind, thus prohibiting discrimination in *favor* of blacks (or other nonwhites). For example, is it constitutionally permissible for a state university to prefer racial minority candidates in its admissions policy, even to the extent of imposing a minimum numerical quota? With regard to employment, is it permissible for a governmental unit, such as a police or fire department, to impose a hiring quota for minorities if there has been a finding that the unit previously discriminated against minority applicants? if there has been no such finding? Is it permissible to discharge whites from their jobs to ensure better racial balance, with or without a finding of prior discrimination?

There are no simple answers to these questions, and certainly none that flow ineluctably from the constitutional text or the "original intention" of the framers of the Fourteenth Amendment. Traditional legal doctrine requires us to read the words "equal protection" in light of their "pervading purpose," as the Supreme Court said soon after the Civil War, to secure "the freedom of the slave race . . . and [to protect] the newly-made freeman and citizen from the oppressions of those who had formerly exercised unlimited dominion over him."[12] In this light, government favoritism for blacks, especially when designed by members of the majority white race to rectify past wrongs, is consistent with the constitutional scheme.

The Supreme Court has not reached a consensus in this difficult field, but it has generally agreed that affirmative action is a strong remedy that should be used in a flexible and sensitive manner that falls as lightly as possible on the majority groups whose interests it impairs. Thus, the Court has rejected racial quotas for admission to universities but has upheld consideration of race in efforts to enhance diversity in student bodies.[13] It has rejected the firing of whites in violation of bona fide seniority systems to achieve a racially balanced work force,[14] but in several contexts it has upheld the use of race in hiring and promotion decisions.[15] The difficult questions—of what the theory of rights demands and what practicality allows—spawned by affirmative action will not disappear but will assume new forms as America continues to strive toward a racially integrated and just society.

3. *Abortion.* The Supreme Court's most controversial decision in recent years is *Roe v. Wade* (1973), which held that the right of privacy embraced by the due-process clause of the Fourteenth Amendment encompasses "a woman's decision whether or not to terminate the pregnancy."[16] The Court ruled that the decision to abort must be left to the woman and her attending physician, although it permitted a state, if it chose, to regulate abortion in the second trimester in the interests of maternal health, and in the third trimester to regulate or proscribe abortion except where necessary to preserve the life or health of the mother.

The Supreme Court's holding, while welcomed by many, was assailed by others as "not inferable from the language of the Constitution, the framers' thinking respecting the specific problem in issue, any general value derivable from the provisions they included, or the nation's governmental structure."[17] A massive campaign was begun to reverse *Roe v. Wade* by constitutional amendment or legislative action. The Reagan administration has urged the Supreme Court to overrule its own decision.[18]

Once again, in order to come to grips with the issue it is necessary to clarify the theory. Thus, the absence of the word "privacy" in the Constitution cannot be dispositive in view of the Court's willingness, sometimes unanimously, to hold that the Constitution protects fundamental values, such as the right to travel and the freedom of association, neither of which is mentioned in the document.[19] In fact, privacy is well grounded in the Constitution: the Supreme Court referred to it as basic more than a century ago in a case protecting the privacy of personal papers,[20] and in a long series of decisions it has upheld, with specific reference to family and sexual privacy, the right of an individual to choose whom to marry, to procreate, whether to use contraceptives, and how to direct the upbringing of his or her children.[21]

In opposing *Roe v. Wade*, the Reagan administration made a misdirected appeal to history. It asserted that "those who drafted and voted for the Fourteenth Amendment would have been surprised indeed to learn"[22] that they were protecting the right to abortion. Perhaps—but certainly no more than they would have been surprised to learn that they were ensuring the rights of women, aliens, or nonmarital children—all now constitutionally protected. As we have noted, the Constitution was not frozen in time. If the right to decide whether to give birth and raise a family is consistent with precedent and with the overriding purpose of ensuring liberty to Americans, there is no warrant for accepting a cramped view of individual rights.[23] It is ironic, indeed hypocritical, for an administration that trumpets its intention to free Americans from government control and meddling oversight to try to bring the heel of government down on women who wish to live their lives according to their own, and not someone else's, moral beliefs.

Nor is the claim that the fetus is "human" or a "person" a basis for a different result. American law has never accorded constitutional personhood to the unborn. More fundamentally, deciding whether or not human life begins before birth is essentially a matter of religious belief, and no group should be allowed to impose its views on those with different convictions. In a free and diverse society, people have varied conscientious opinions on this question, which is not subject to empirical resolution. There is no basis in religious or philosophical debate on the nature of the fetus for overturning *Roe v. Wade*.

THERE IS NO more important function for courts, indeed for all of government, than to define the rights of its citizens. But courts cannot and do not rely, as on a Rosetta Stone, on a single theory of constitutional interpretation, whether it is textual literalism, original intention, or some other holistic vision. For solutions, the judge must look to these sources—but also to analogy in judicial precedent, to the purposes of constitutional provisions, to the mores of the people, to institutional functions and restraints, and to the probable consequences of legal decisions on an ongoing society and on the lives of its people. It is not easy to work subtle constitutional issues through a matrix as complex as this, but there is no escape from the task in the unending quest to achieve a just society, in theory and in fact.

Notes

1. Virginia Declaration of Rights (1776), in B. Schwartz, ed., *The Bill of Rights: A Documentary History* (New York: Chelsea House, 1971), 1:234.

2. *McCulloch v. Maryland*, 17 U.S. (4 Wheat.) 316, 415 (1819).

3. *Weems v. United States*, 217 U.S. 349, 373 (1911).

4. B. Cardozo, *The Nature of the Judicial Process* (New Haven: Yale University Press, 1921), p. 17.

5. Meese, Speech before the American Bar Association, July 9, 1985, printed in *The Great Debate: Interpreting Our Written Constitution* (Washington, D.C.: Federalist Society, 1986), p. 10.

6. See, e.g., Powell, "The Original Understanding of Original Intent," *Harvard Law Review* 98 (1985): 885; Sandalow, "Constitutional Interpretation," *Michigan Law Review* 79 (1981): 1033.

7. Richards, "Founders' Intent and Constitutional Interpretation," in this volume.

8. Fried, "Sonnet LXV and the 'Black Ink' of the Framers' Intention," *Harvard Law Review* 100 (1987): 751, 758.

9. *Barron v. Mayor of Baltimore*, 32 U.S. (7 Pet.) 243 (1833).

10. The evolution is traced in G. Gunther, *Constitutional Law* 11th ed. (Mineola, N.Y.: Foundation Press, 1985), pp. 419–40; G. R. Stone, L. M. Seidman, C. R. Sunstein, and M. V. Tushnet, *Constitutional Law* (Boston: Little, Brown & Co., 1986), pp. 707–24.

11. 347 U.S. 483 (1954).

12. *Slaughterhouse Cases*, 83 U.S. (16 Wall.) 36, 71 (1973).

13. *Regents of the University of California v. Bakke*, 438 U.S. 265 (1978).

14. *Firefighters Local Union No. 1784 v. Stotts*, 467 U.S. 561 (1984) (layoffs of whites in violation of seniority system invalid); *Wygant v. Jackson Board of Education*, 106 S. Ct. 1842 (1986) (school board's policy of preferential protection against layoffs to black employees invalid).

15. *Local 28 of Sheet Metal Workers v. Equal Employment Opportunity Commission*, 106 S. Ct. 3019 (1986) (affirmative action plan to govern employment practices after finding of discrimination by union's membership policies upheld); see also *Johnson v. Transportation Agency, Santa Clara County*, 107 S. Ct. 1442 (1987) (affirmative action plan for hiring and promoting women in traditionally segregated job classification in which women have been significantly underrepresented upheld despite proof of prior sex discrimination).

16. 410 U.S. 113, 153 (1973).

17. Ely, "The Wages of Crying Wolf: A Comment on Roe v. Wade," *Yale Law Journal* 82 (1973): 920, 930.

18. Brief of the United States, amicus curiae, in *City of Akron v. Akron Center for Reproductive Health, Inc.*, 462 U.S. 416 (1983).

19. See, e.g., *Shapiro v. Thompson*, 394 U.S. 618 (1969) (right to travel); *Aptheker v. Secretary of State*, 378 U.S. 500 (1964) (same); *NAACP v. Alabama*, 357 U.S. 449 (1958) (freedom of association).

20. *Boyd v. United States*, 116 U.S. 616 (1886).

21. *Zablocki v. Redhail*, 434 U.S. 374 (1978) (right to marry); *Loving v. Virginia*, 388 U.S. 1 (1967) (same); *Skinner v. Oklahoma*, 316 U.S. 535 (1942) (right to procreate); *Griswold v. Connecticut*, 381 U.S. 479 (1965) (right of married couple to use contraceptives); *Eisenstadt v. Baird*, 405 U.S. 438 (1972) (same for unmarried persons); *Meyer v. Nebraska*, 262 U.S. 390 (1923) (right to establish a home and bring up children); *Pierce v. Society of Sisters*, 268 U.S. 510 (1925) (same). But see *Bowers v. Hardwick*, 106 S. Ct. 2841 (1986) (state law prohibiting sodomy does not violate the fundamental rights of homosexuals).

22. Brief of the United States, amicus curiae.

23. See L. Tribe, *Constitutional Law* 2d ed. (Boston: Little, Brown, 1988), p. 1308: the "judiciary has thus reached into the Constitution's spirit and structure, and has elaborated from the spare text an idea of 'human' and a concept of 'being' not merely contemplated but required."

III

❧❧❧

DOMESTIC POLICIES

⁂⁂⁂

Jefferson, Science, and National Destiny

GERALD HOLTON

The explicit reference to "science" in the American Constitution is deceptively slim and narrow: only to the expressed power Congress shall have "to promote the progress of science and useful arts, by securing for limited times to authors and inventors the exclusive right to their respective writings and discoveries" (art. 1, sec. 8). But one can trace two sets of richly tangled lines to and from this locus. One reaches back into the intellectual history of colonial America, where science, in the sense of systematic knowledge, played a large role in the imagination of the nation's founders. The other set runs forward to this day, when that seemingly chaste constitutional reference to the promotion of science has burgeoned into the president's $65 billion budget proposal to Congress for the "conduct of research and development" during the bicentennial year—most of it for projects far removed from "science" as understood either in the eighteenth century or in modern times, and ironically leaving many good science projects underfunded.

In such fields as statescraft we constantly find that we can still learn much from the originators of our nation's practices and myths. Might they also have something to teach us about the modes of scientific research proper for our time? I believe so.

Focusing for this purpose on Thomas Jefferson will be appropriate if only because he was never quite comfortable with his role as one of the foremost political figures. He saw himself chiefly as philosopher, educator, scholar, planter, and student of the sciences, and he arranged that even on his gravestone no reference would be made to his presidency or to any of his other political offices. His service in the administration was as often as not a reluctant one. He did not like his appointment as the first secretary of state in 1789 and resigned it at the end of 1793 in order to return to farming at Monticello. He told Edward Rutledge that he had no passion to govern men, and on hearing of his election as vice-president, he wrote to James Madison (Jan. 1, 1797), "I am unable to decide in my own mind whether I had rather have it or not have it."[1]

Nor did he hold earlier political leaders in highest esteem; rather, it was of Francis Bacon, John Locke, and Isaac Newton that he wrote, "I consider them as the three greatest men that have ever lived, without any exception."[2] It was therefore appropriate that, after four years of retirement at Monticello, on arriving in the nation's capital, then at Philadelphia, he was first installed as the newly elected president of the American Philosophical Society on March 3, 1797—calling this (in a letter to the Secretaries of the Society) "the most flattering incident of my life"[3]—and only on the following day proceeded to be inaugurated as vice-president of the United States. Moreover, he returned a few days later to the American Philosophical Society to give a scientific paper, of which we shall hear more below. A passage he wrote some years later to John Adams catches the spirit: "I have given up newspapers in exchange for Tacitus and Thucydides, for Newton and Euclid, and I find myself much the happier."[4]

About science, Jefferson was never reluctant or regretful. In his early years, he came under the influence of Professor William Small at the College of William and Mary, under whom he studied mathematics and Newton's *Principia*. That contact, he said later, "probably fixed the destinies of my life."[5] His correspondence from beginning to end shows him never more relaxed or enthusiastic than when discussing scientific matters. "Nature," he said, "intended me for the tranquil pursuit of science, by rendering them my supreme delight." His curiosity and persistence seemed infinite. Thus he kept his garden book for fifty-eight years continuously, noting when trees flowered and how his experimental plantings fared. He recorded the weather daily several times for years on end, even on the greatest day in American history, on July 4, 1776—at 6 a.m., 9 a.m., 1 p.m., and 9 p.m. His exuberance and wide range have given historians of science the opportunity to study "Jefferson as a naturalist," "Jefferson as a vaccinator," "Thomas Jefferson as meteorologist," Jefferson on prehistoric Americans, on ethnology, geography, botany, paleontology, mathematics, weights and measures, eugenics, agriculture, archeology, astronomy, medical theory and practice, and on and on.[6]

There is a danger, however, that Jefferson's wide interests, similar to those of other major figures of the eighteenth century, cause him to be labeled and discussed as chiefly involved in the accumulation of findings—an "encyclopedic" fascination. To be sure, in Jefferson's collected papers there are well over a hundred references to various encyclopedias, and he owned and evidently studied many of these.[7] He even became, if only anonymously, a contributor to the new *Encyclopédie méthodique*, through his collaboration in 1786 with Démeunier on an article on the United States. Moreover, Jefferson's *Notes on the State of Virginia*, his early work written in 1781–82 (and itself excerpted in the early American reprint edition of the *Encyclopedia Britannica*),[8] was an encyclopedic survey of his home state, with such systematic headings as Boundaries, Rivers, Ports, Climates, Populations, Aborigines, Laws, and Weights and Measures.

But reading it, one sees at once that it is not a work in the service of mere accretion. Silvio Bedini correctly commented that it "received wide acclaim as the first comprehensive study of any part of the United States, and as one of the most important works derived from America to that time."[9] Nor is Jefferson's aim chiefly to dramatize and encourage the pursuit of the sciences—though he did so as no high public official in American history has done since, and sometimes at political risk to himself. (His opponents seized on his interest in natural history, one of them saying Jefferson should resign his presidency because he must surely be deranged, in view of his passion for collecting and exhibiting new animals and searching for the bones of the extinct mastodon.)

What, then, was Jefferson's most basic motivation for his abiding interest in scientific matters? To what degree he may be considered to have been a practicing scientist himself, and how good his science was, are questions that have recently been raised again, thanks to John C. Greene's fine book *American Science in the*

Age of Jefferson.[10] Greene sees Jefferson as an inveterate connoisseur of science but not as a serious scientist when measured against what was happening in Europe at that time—one thinks here of Laplace, Lavoisier, Thomas Young, Humphry Davy, and others. In such discussions an apologetic note is bound to enter. And to be sure, Jefferson contributed directly to science much less than did Benjamin Franklin.

Yet the least one must grant Jefferson is that he had a good understanding of the heart of the scientific method. Illustrations for this statement are not difficult to find. Thus, in early 1796, Jefferson heard of the finding, in his own state of Virginia, of the fossilized remains of a huge-clawed animal. He obtained the bones, and speculated with delight that they might be those of a hitherto unknown, monstrous American lion. He named it *Megalonyx* (big claw), studied the bones, arranged that they be sent to the American Philosophical Society, and wrote a memoir describing them. Thus it came about that on March 10, 1797, having just been made vice-president of the United States, Jefferson had his paper read to the members of the Society while presiding over the meeting.

Here the essential point for us is this: Toward the end of his paper,[11] Jefferson referred to the unfortunate idea, which was then current among French scientists, that the climate in America was so disadvantageous that it tended to produce stunted and degenerated life forms. Jefferson had long been annoyed by this slight on his country. He had tried to shake Count de Buffon by sending him the skeleton of an enormous American elk, three times the bulk of the European kind. In his new paper, Jefferson now took the opportunity both to contribute to science and to answer Buffon's challenge. To Jefferson, the discovery of the bones of a giant animal was evidence against the European theory of degeneracy. This must have been very satisfying to the patriot in him. Yet, at the end of the paper, where he sums up the lesson of his new find, the scientific impulse tells him how to draw the right balance. He writes: "Are we then from all this to draw a conclusion, the reverse of that of Monsieur de Buffon. That nature has formed the larger animals of America, like its lakes, its rivers, and mountains, on a greater and prouder scale than in the other hemisphere? Not at all; we are to conclude that she has formed some things large and some things small, on both sides of the earth for reasons which she has not enabled us to penetrate;

and that we ought not to shut our eyes upon one half of her facts, and build systems on the other half."[12]

Jefferson was no less a patriot for being comfortable with scientific thinking. Again and again, he hoped to conquer superficial variety and differences by embracing two themata fundamental to science, namely, generalization and unification. In the Declaration of Independence, he had written that all men are created equal; now he was saying that on the whole all animals are created equal, regardless of location on the globe—just as elsewhere he wrote that the Indians of North America, save for the accident of opportunity and circumstance, were on a par with the rest of mankind; just as in his bill of 1777 for the Establishing of Religious Freedom, he provided for freedom of the profession of any religion whatever; and just as he dared to propose universal education, one of the first to do so.

One can easily multiply examples of Jefferson's sound scientific instinct. Nevertheless, by the standards of the times, the previously noted, somewhat apologetic evaluations of Jefferson's science are defensible. He was not a significant scientist any more than he was a mere encyclopedist.

But far from forcing us now to dismiss him with such evaluations, they allow us to focus on a significant fact: Jefferson's main contribution in this area was that he pointed toward a specific way of *doing* science, a science-policy model fundamentally different from the two standard ones against which he has habitually been measured—a third model, one that is still struggling to come to prominence in our time.

For consider the first of the two standard models of our era: what might be called the "Newtonian Research Program," named thus because Newton, while not the first to pursue it, was so explicit about this motivation. In the preface to his *Principia*, Newton described his ambition. The observable phenomena (such as the fall of objects to earth, and some celestial motions) led him to postulate the existence of one general force of gravity by which all bodies attract one another, and from this in turn he had been able to deduce in detail "the motion of the planets, the comets, the moon, and the sea." But what everyone else took to be a stupendous achievement was for Newton only the beginning of the true program: "I wish we could derive the rest of the phenomena of Nature by the same kind of reasoning from mechanical principles."[13] All the other phenomena of Nature also—optics, chemistry, the operation of the human senses—nothing less than the mastery of the entire world of experience, subsuming it ultimately under one unified theoretical structure! To this day, that motivation emerges from the writings and confessions of our foremost scientists, and it is not inappropriate to term it the "Newtonian Research Program." In short, it is the search for *omniscience*.

By contrast, the reigning alternative vision for science may be called the "Baconian Research Program," for it was most eloquently defended by Francis Bacon and his followers. This style concentrates on science in the service of *omnipotence*, or as Bacon had put it, on "the enlarging of the bounds of Human Empire, to the effecting of all things possible."[14]

It is not our concern here to question to what degree these shorthand labels are appropriate, or to what extent these two styles—both of them reflected in Hegel's perception of the self-infinitizing tendency of man—have on occasion interpenetrated each other in practice. Rather, we should attend to what I would call the "Jeffersonian Research Program," the third policy for the pursuit of science, centrally neither Newtonian nor Baconian, but as befits the man who saw both Newton and Bacon among his chief heroes, a model that takes something from each of these two programs and combines them in a new way. To put it briefly, this third style locates the center of research in an area of basic scientific ignorance that lies at the heart of a social problem. It is therefore neither purely discipline-oriented nor purely problem-oriented (the latter being largely the application of *available* basic knowledge for meeting perceived needs). The Jeffersonian type of research project, by contrast, is positioned intentionally in an uncharted area on the map of science itself, the specific siting being motivated by a credible perception that the findings to be obtained will sooner or later have a bearing upon a persistent national or international program. This policy, attentive both to the drive to new knowledge and to the amelioration of mankind's needs, reflects the fact that Jefferson himself saw a combined-mode goal for science—the fuller understanding of nature as well as what he called simply "the freedom and happiness of man."

We can illustrate this Jeffersonian policy for undertaking and structuring scientific investigations by examining one of the chief scientific episodes in Jefferson's life: his plans for the exploration of the North American continent, culminating eventually in his commissioning the Lewis and Clark expedition of 1803–06. On that enterprise, an exemplar of organizing the physical and intellectual resources of a nation, a great deal has been written, but not, it seems to me, with the proper recognition of Jefferson's twofold policy aim that is the focus of attention here. Jefferson himself pointed to it when he wrote that the aim of the project was "to extend for [the citizens of this nation] the boundaries of science, and to present to their knowledge that vast and fertile country which their sons are destined to fill with arts, with science, with freedom and happiness."[15]

The plan for launching such an expedition was of course nourished generally by the intense interest, at least among the literati, even in earlier, colonial America, in all aspects of that vast, promising, and largely unknown continent, and in all subjects from its topography to its native inhabitants. We see this in the charters and activities of such organizations as the American Philosophical Society and the American Academy of Arts and Sciences, both founded before the achievement of statehood. Jefferson was a child of the frontier, the son of a surveyor and explorer who in 1751 had helped to make the first good map of Virginia. Even as a boy, Jefferson would have heard of plans to explore the continent, the beckoning land he later called "terra incognita."

The sequence of Jefferson's early, failed attempts at exploration, leading to the Lewis and Clark expedition, is well known: for example, the plans made with the adventurous John Ledyard in Paris in 1786. Even before that, on December 4, 1783,[16] still as a private citizen, Jefferson proposed to General George Rogers Clark that he lead an expedition "for exploring the country from the Mississippi to California." Nothing came of that either. But the urgency of such a project was greatly increased in 1792 by the achievement of Captain Robert Gray of Boston, whose ship, the *Columbia Rediviva*, had recently been the first American vessel to circumnavigate the globe. Gray reached the mouth of "Columbia's River" in Oregon on May 12. He entered it, went some thirty-six miles upstream, named the river, and in accordance with a tradition widely respected internationally, thus set claim for the United States for sovereignty over the valley, the watershed of the river, and the adjacent coast.

Gray's achievement did not become known in the eastern United States until the end of July 1793. By April of that year, Jefferson had been able to launch yet another attempt at a first expedition to explore what later came to be called the Territory of Louisiana, that vast and largely unmapped territory between the Mississippi River and the Rocky Mountains of the West, then all still owned by Spain. It was supposed to be a small exploring party. This time, Jefferson was planning it in his capacity as vice-president of the American Philosophical Society, arranging with the French botanist André Michaux to launch the transcontinental exploration. The budget was not to exceed $400, to be raised by subscription.

It was very much a plan of a learned society, and it, too, failed. But the most important component, one that survived for later service, was Jefferson's set of instructions of April 1793 to Michaux:

> . . . the chief objects of your journey are to find the shortest and most convenient route of communication between the United States and the Pacific ocean, within the temperate latitudes, and to learn such particulars as can be obtained of the country through which it passes, its productions, inhabitants, and other interesting circumstances. . . . You will, in the course of your journey, take notice of the country you pass through, its general face, soil, rivers, mountains, its productions animal, vegetable, and mineral so far as they may be new to us and may also be useful or very curious; the latitudes of places or materials for calculating it by such simple methods as your situation may admit you to practice; the names, numbers, and dwellings of the inhabitants, and such particularities as you can learn of their history, connection with each other, languages, manners, state of society and of the arts and commerce among them. Under the head of Animal history, that of the Mammoth is particularly recommended to your enquiries . . . .[17]

We recognize again the pen of the author of the *Notes on Virginia* of a dozen years earlier, including his preoccupation there with the fossil remains of the mammoth that had been found in Ohio, and the tradition among Indians, in which Jefferson hopefully believed, that a gigantic creature of this sort was still roaming in the northern part of the continent.

In 1801, eight years after Michaux's failure, all these pieces—Jefferson's early, indiscriminate love for science, his fascination with the frontier, his encyclopedic study of his own state, the gaining by the young Republic of a foothold at the mouth of the

Columbia River, and so on—at last came together when Jefferson assumed the presidency of the United States. He had appointed as his private secretary Meriwether Lewis, who earlier, when not yet twenty, had begged him to be allowed to go on Michaux's ill-fated journey. The itch to explore the continent was in the blood of both men. But Jefferson now had a double role: he was the chief of state of a vigorous young nation with a growing population, and he was also the man who wrote that the studies of science had fixed the destinies of his life and were his supreme delight.

By the end of 1802, before the great opportunity of the Louisiana Purchase offered itself, Jefferson wrote to the British and Spanish ministers in Washington to find out what their government's reaction would be if a party of explorers were sent up the Missouri River and across the mountains to the Pacific. The British minister informed his government as follows:

> The President has for some years past had it in view to set on foot an expedition entirely of a scientific nature for exploring the Western Continent of America by the route of the Great River Missouri. . . . He supposes this to be the most natural and direct water-communication between the two Oceans, and he is ambitious in his character of a man of letters and of science, of distinguishing his Presidency by a discovery, now the only one left to his enterprise. . . .[18]

John Greene has commented on this plan and its characterization:[19] "Such indeed was Jefferson's purpose, although he was careful to express the commercial, military and diplomatic benefits that would accrue from the expedition in his message to Congress requesting funds for the enterprise." On this view, Jefferson's purpose was indeed "an expedition entirely of a scientific nature." But others have urged a very different view. In his essay "The Purpose of the Lewis and Clark Expedition," Ralph B. Guinness called it a "politico-commercial" venture for which fur trade was "the primary concern";[20] and Bernard DeVoto, in the book significantly entitled *The Course of Empire*, identified the expedition as "an act of imperial policy."[21]

The debate here is between those who see the exploration essentially in the service of the Newtonian Program, part of the pursuit of omniscience, versus those who see it as a Baconian Program of enlarging the bounds of human powers, part of the search for omnipotence. But here, as so often, Jefferson was neither destined nor content to follow the models of others. He was capable of his own originality and of seeing the possibility of a marriage between the Newtonian and Baconian Programs.

In April 1803, to everyone's surprise, Napoleon offered to sell the Americans the whole Louisiana Territory, chiefly to obtain resources for his war on Great Britain. The transaction went quickly, and almost doubled the territory of the United States. But three months before Napoleon's offer, in a confidential address, Jefferson had already asked Congress, taking advantage of the expiration of an act establishing trading houses with Indians in border areas, for authority and funds for yet another of his attempts at crosscontinental exploration. On January 18, 1803, he proposed that "an intelligent officer, with ten or twelve chosen men . . . might explore the whole line, even to the Western ocean."[22] He assured Congress that the nation claiming sovereignty over those territories would regard this "as a literary pursuit, which it is in the habit of permitting within its dominions." He asked Congress to provide $2,500 and to label the venture so as to "cover the undertaking from notice" as an attempt of "extending the external commerce of the United States."[23]

Congress complied on February 28, 1803. But Jefferson had already appointed Lewis to lead the expedition and had begun to arrange with scientific friends that they give instruction to Lewis. For example, writing on February 27, 1803, to Benjamin S. Barton of the American Philosophical Society, Jefferson asked him to teach Lewis how to identify rapidly new objects "in the lines of botany, zoology, or of Indian history." He adds, "I make no apology for this trouble, because I know that the same wish to promote science which has induced me to bring forward this proposition, will induce you to aid in promoting it."[24]

Jefferson's directives to what became known as the Lewis and Clark expedition overlap substantially with those he had given years earlier to Michaux. As Jefferson spells it out in detail over many pages,[25] it is the dream of a naturalist, encyclopedist, and surveyor, but merged with the vision of the statesman: "The object of your mission is to explore the Missouri river, and such principal stream of it, as . . . may offer the most direct and practicable water communication across this continent for the purposes of commerce. . . . You will take careful observations of latitude and longitude, at all remarkable points on the river. . . . The variations of the compass too, in different places, should be noticed."²⁶ There follows a long section on knowledge to be acquired about the native inhabitants, including their languages, traditions, monuments, food, clothing, diseases and remedies, the state of morality, religion, and information among them; orders to observe "the soil and face of the country, its growth and vegetable productions, especially those not of the United States; the animals of the country generally, and especially those not known in the United States; the remains or accounts of any which may be deemed rare or extinct [again, the hope to find a mammoth?]. . . . [The] climate, as characterised by the thermometer . . . the dates at which particular plants put forth or lose their flowers or leaf. . . ."²⁷ (We are back in Jefferson's garden.)

About two weeks after signing his instructions to Lewis, the news reached Jefferson that the treaty transferring the Louisiana Territories to the United States had been executed. This development, Jefferson said, "increased infinitely the interest we felt in the expedition, and lessened the apprehensions of interruptions from other powers."²⁸ But in fact Captain Lewis had already been packing his bags, and left Washington on July 5, 1803, on his journey, not to return for more than three years. There is little doubt such an expedition would have been attempted, whether the transfer by treaty had succeeded or not.

While awaiting the return of the explorer, Jefferson did what one would expect of him. He began to educate Congress. In November 1803, he submitted an "Account of Louisiana," based on whatever information he had been able to get from knowledgeable Westerners. By February 1806, Jefferson had received enough news from Lewis to prepare another message to Congress, stressing the new observations on Indians and on geography. To complement this educational purpose, he also sent to each senator and representative five reports by scholars and explorers concerning the tribes, geography, and meteorological observations of areas west of the Mississippi.

Jefferson enthusiastically received in 1805 the first shipment of samples from the expedition, containing skins and skeletons of animals, live animals, and specimen of minerals and plants. He kept a few for display at Monticello, but arranged to distribute most of them, to the American Philosophical Society in Philadelphia to be studied there, to Charles W. Peale's museum, and to expert gardeners who would grow the seeds. When Lewis and Clark returned, bearing quantities of unknown flora and fauna, maps, and other trophies, Jefferson constantly helped to make the results known and to speed the publication process. He treasured particularly the vocabularies of Indian languages that Lewis had collected and given to him, and it was one of Jefferson's most heartrending losses when these, together with Jefferson's notes on them, were stolen, and thrown by thieves into a river.

In a letter to one of his scientific friends, Benjamin Rush, Jefferson had shared his joy of obtaining authority from Congress in February 1803, "to undertake the long desired object of exploring the Missouri and whatever river, heading with that, leads into the Western ocean."[29] That, and not the fur trade or the "course of empire," was foremost in his mind as he was fashioning his program of exploration and research, which symbolized the joint claims of his science and his country: a research program designed to serve simultaneously the search for truth and the national interest. It is a policy that, despite its appropriateness and its successes in occasional adoptions, is still struggling for recognition, for its rightful place in the necessary spectrum of contemporary scientific activity.[30]

Notes

1. Albert Ellery Bergh, ed., *The Writings of Thomas Jefferson*, v. 9 (Washington, D.C., 1907), p. 358.

2. Jefferson to John Trumbull, Feb. 15, 1789, in Julian P. Boyd et al., eds., *The Papers of Thomas Jefferson*, v. 14 (Princeton: Princeton University Press, 1958), p. 561.

3. Jefferson to the Society, Jan. 28, 1797, *Transactions of the American Philosophical Society* 4 (1799): xii–xiii; in *Proceedings of the American Philosophical Society* 87 (1943–44): 263–76.

4. Jefferson to Adams, Jan. 12, 1812, in Bergh, v. 13, p. 124.

5. Autobiography, dated Jan. 6, 1821, Bergh, v. 1, p. 3.

6. See, for example, the collection of essays *Thomas Jefferson and the Sciences*, ed. I. Bernard Cohen (New York: Arno Press, 1980).

7. Among these were the *Chambers Cyclopedia* of 1751–52, the *New and Complete Dictionary of Arts and Sciences* of 1763–64, and the American reprint edition of the *Encyclopedia Britannica* (see note 8). He also wrote often to obtain copies for himself and for others (e.g., Jefferson to William Short, April 27, 1790, in Boyd et al., v. 16, pp. 387–89), and he advised James Madison to include the *Encyclopédie méthodique* on a

"list of books proper for the use of Congress" (Report of Jan. 24, 1783, in Boyd et al., v. 6, p. 216). In fact, he ordered a copy of the *Encyclopédie méthodique* for public use in early 1781 and apparently became so engrossed in it that in July 1782 a resolution had to be passed "to take measures for getting from Mr. Jefferson the Encyclopaedia belonging to the public" (Boyd et al., v. 6, p. 258).

8. Third edition, 1788–97; see Boyd et al., v. 14, p. 412.

9. Silvio A. Bedini, "Thomas Jefferson," in *Dictionary of Scientific Biography*, ed. C. C. Gillispie (New York: Scribner's, 1973), 7:88–89.

10. John C. Greene, *American Science in the Age of Jefferson* (Ames: Iowa State University Press, 1984).

11. Jefferson, "A Memoir on the Discovery of Certain Bones of an Unknown Quadruped, of the Clawed Kind, in the Western Part of Virginia," in *Transactions of the American Philosophical Society*, 4 (1799):246–60. The animal was soon identified as an extinct giant ground sloth.

12. Jefferson, "Memoir," p. 258.

13. *Sir Isaac Newton's Mathematical Principles*, rev. Florian Cajori, original (1729) trans. Andrew Motte (Berkeley: University of California Press, 1960), p. xviii.

14. Francis Bacon, *The New Atlantis*, in *The Works of Francis Bacon*, ed. J. Spedding, R. L. Ellis, and D. D. Heath (London, 1857–59), 3:156.

15. Bergh, v. 18, p. 160.

16. Boyd et al., v. 6, p. 371.

17. Donald Jackson, ed., *The Letters of the Lewis and Clark Expedition with Related Documents, 1783–1854* (Urbana: University of Illinois Press, 1962), pp. 669–70.

18. Greene, p. 196.

19. Greene, p. 196.

20. Ralph B. Guinness, "The Purpose of the Lewis and Clark Expedition," *Missouri Valley Historical Review*, 20 (1933):90–100.

21. Bernard DeVoto, *The Course of Empire* (Boston: Houghton Mifflin, 1952), p. 411.

22. *The Debates and Proceedings in the Congress of the United States, Seventh Congress, Second Session* (Washington, D.C., 1851), p. 26.

23. *Debates*, p. 26.

24. Jackson, pp. 16–17.

25. Draft of 1803; final letter to Lewis signed on June 20, 1803. Jackson, pp. 61–62.

26. Jackson, pp. 61–62.

27. Jackson, p. 63.

28. Bergh, v. 18, p. 157.

29. Jackson, pp. 18–19.

30. Examples from the history of twentieth-century science show that such attempts continue and of course that there is now an international dimension to them as well as a national one. I have discussed two recent examples of this Jeffersonian Program (or, as it may also be called, "combined-mode" research): (a) Orso Mario Corbino's description in 1929 of the need for research on nuclear physics in Italy under Fermi, both because it was the major research frontier and because success might allow Italy to "regain with honor its lost eminence" in physics, as well as eventually making nuclear-power generation likely. See G. Holton, *The Scientific Imagination: Case Studies* (New York: Cambridge University

Press, 1978), pp. 164–65, and references cited therein. (b) President Jimmy Carter's and his science adviser's initiatives in 1978 to identify important questions of basic research that, if answered, would also have the promise of early national and international utility. See G. Holton, *The Advancement of Science, and Its Burdens: The Jefferson Lecture, and Other Essays* (New York: Cambridge University Press, 1986), pp. 188–94.

The New Discontinuity
in Health Policy

DANIEL M. FOX

Early in this century, a small group of physicians, convinced that a new era in the history of medicine had recently begun, began to formulate a new theory of health policy. This theory shaped the institutions of the health sector and determined the allocation of resources among them until the mid-1970s. The success of this theory, which I call hierarchical regionalism, was made possible by two other beliefs that most Americans regarded as self-evident for much of this century. The first was the conviction that improved health would be financed by economic growth rather than by the redistribution or rationing of resources. The second was the belief that health care was special, that preventing and treating illness took precedence over other social goals. In the past decade, however, the unexpected consequences of the theory of hierarchical regionalism, reinforced by a sense of the limits of economic growth and by an anticollectivist ideology, have stimulated a new sense of discontinuity between past and present.

These statements may bewilder people who are not immersed in health affairs and even some of those who are. The history of health policy has been studied systematically by only a relative handful of historians, political scientists, and members of the health professions.[1] I introduce that history here to an imaginary reader, who I assume is generally familiar with the history of American politics, economic life, and science in this century, but whose experience of health affairs has been acquired as a consumer of medical care and of stories in the press and on television.

Consider what this reader would have known about health policy in 1976. She or he would have been pleased that most Americans had most of their medical care paid for by somebody else—as a result of benefits provided through employment, Social Security, private purchases of insurance, and appropriations by the federal government and the states. For half a century, moreover, reports of astonishing advances in medical science and technology had been routine. The problems of diagnosing and treating infectious disease seemed to be solved; the biology underlying chronic diseases was becoming better understood.

Moreover, authority in health affairs was increasingly centralized. The federal government paid for most research and was the largest single source of funds for care and for the construction of hospitals and other facilities. In 1972 people with disabilities and victims of end-stage renal disease had become the first Americans to have their medical care nationalized since the elderly in 1965. Most people believed that other groups would soon be included. Many journalists and some members of Congress said that national health insurance was imminent.

Centralization of authority in health affairs was also increasing within the states, which were spending more for health care and, in many cases, regulating institutions more stringently than ever before. The states were, moreover, the major source of operating and capital funds for medical and other health professional schools.

Despite this growing public responsibility for health affairs, voluntary associations still had enormous power. They dominated the hospital industry. Blue Cross and Blue Shield—nonprofit organizations—had a major share of the health-insurance market. Scandals involving proprietors of nursing homes in the mid-seventies seemed to demonstrate the wisdom of restraining the profit motive in health affairs.

My imaginary reader of 1976 was becoming aware of problems in the health sector. The costs of care, for example, were rising faster than the gross national product. The states and the federal government had established mechanisms to control costs without compromising the quality of care. A few firms offered

their employees a choice between standard insurance (which provided service or paid cash benefits up to a maximum) and health
maintenance organizations (which offered unlimited care but restricted choice of physicians and hospitals). A very attentive
reader would have known that the states and the federal government had, through Medicaid, become the largest payer for nursing-home care, the cost of which was increasing as the number of
old people grew. Such a reader might also have sensed that medical scientists were announcing new discoveries about causes and
cures of diseases less frequently than they had a few years earlier.
Few people, however, could escape the frequent exhortations to
prevent illness and reduce costs by eating better, exercising more,
and smoking, drinking, snorting, or injecting fewer substances.[2]

A decade later, these problems had intensified, and the consensus about the achievements of science and the desirability of
centralized authority had disintegrated. The epidemic of AIDS,
which was first identified in 1981, exploded the widespread belief
that medical scientists knew how to control the spread of infectious disease, especially in industrial nations. Officials of the federal government and many of the states were abdicating the
authority in health affairs they had been acquiring since the
1930s. The one exception was payment for medical care. Business
leaders and public officials were now using their purchasing
power to reduce, or at least contain, the cost of services. Calling
themselves prudent buyers, they terrified hospital managers and
physicians by requiring, for example, mandatory second opinions
and preadmission screening.

In addition, voluntarism became less important as an ideology
in health affairs. Investor-owned hospitals and nursing homes
were increasing their share of the market. Voluntary hospitals,
whose leaders had adopted the rhetoric of business corporations
some years earlier, were now establishing holding companies and
for-profit subsidiaries to compensate for their declining revenues
as the prudent buyers caused occupancy to decline. By 1986, when
federal tax reform compromised the nonprofit status of Blue
Cross and Blue Shield, many of the plans had, in effect, already
become insurance companies in everything except corporate
form.[3] Many Blue Cross plans, for example, had ceased to give
priority to open enrollment and were becoming antagonistic toward hospitals, with which they had once claimed a historic special
relationship.

These changes in health affairs were the result of declining support for the three beliefs, or theories, I introduced at the beginning of this essay. Hierarchical regionalism was a victim of its own success. A society in which improvements in health could no longer be financed by economic growth was uncertain about how much to pay for health care by explicitly rationing services or by redistributing income. Adherents of a new anticollectivist ideology had no patience with the venerable tradition that sick people had special claims on public and voluntary institutions.

The Unexpected Consequences of Hierarchical Regionalism

Most of the debates about health policy from the first decade of the century until the 1980s were disputes about how to implement the principles of hierarchical regionalism and thereby treat the sick more effectively. According to these principles, medical science and services should be organized in pyramids within geographical regions that did not necessarily coincide with political jurisdictions. The laboratories of medical schools and the wards of the teaching hospitals associated with them should be at the top of each pyramid. One level down, large general hospitals affiliated with the medical school should serve subregions. The lowest level consisted of ambulatory-care clinics, health centers, and the offices of physicians in private practice. Institutions providing convalescent care and long-term care for people with chronic illness should be coordinated with each level of the hierarchy, along with such public health services as screening, reporting, visiting nurses, prevention, and education. Within each region, the hierarchy should be composed of voluntary and public institutions and professionals, especially physicians, who practiced alone and in groups.[4]

This logic of organization seemed self-evident because hardly anybody questioned the theory on which it rested. According to this theory, the history of medicine became discontinuous with its past as the result of the scientific breakthroughs of the final decades of the nineteenth century. Bacteriology, parasitology, immunology, and pharmacology, supported by advances in physiology and chemistry, were creating a new era in which science would conquer diseases, one at a time. This new scientific knowledge was usually discovered in the laboratories of medical schools and research institutes. It was then tested and demonstrated in the wards of teaching hospitals. Next the new knowledge was disseminated down the levels of a hierarchy to physicians and other health professionals. Just as knowledge moved down the hierarchy in each region, patients moved upward as their illnesses became more severe or when they had rare diseases. The purpose of health policy was to ensure continued progress in medical science, and therefore less morbidity and mortality from disease, by encouraging the formation of regional hierarchies; by financing research, education, and the construction of facilities; and by ensuring that most people could pay for care. A policy of hierarchical regionalism was to be the means by which Americans acknowledged the special claims of the sick on society.

By the 1960s, the American variant of hierarchical regionalism was enormously successful. No country spent nearly as much for medical research. The National Institutes of Health funded scientists, most of whom worked in medical schools and teaching hospitals, to study the biology underlying chronic degenerative diseases. A massive federal program financed the construction of hospitals, nursing homes, and rehabilitation facilities on the basis of state plans that described how regional hierarchies would be created and strengthened. The medical profession was growing in size, and most physicians were now specialists. Most Americans, perhaps ninety percent according to some estimates, had some third-party coverage for medical care. In the middle and late 1960s, almost everyone concerned with health policy was euphoric, looking forward to advancing science, more sophisticated physicians and technology, and more insurance coverage for more people.

By the late 1970s, however, euphoria was replaced by despondency as a result of the unexpected consequences of hierarchical regionalism. Chronic disease did not yield as easily to the methods of laboratory and clinical science as infectious disease had. There were not as many dramatic cures, and life expectancy ceased to increase. By the early 1980s the AIDS epidemic undercut the assumption that a vaccine for any infectious disease could be routinely produced. Generous public support for hospital construction and medical education had created a surplus of beds and physicians. Moreover, many physicians who worked in community hospitals now had the skills and equipment to perform procedures that, until recently, had been possible only in the teaching hospitals at the top of regional hierarchies. Investor-owned hospital chains were establishing their own hierarchies to compete with public and voluntary institutions. For a few years in the mid-1980s, for example, an investor-owned hospital was the only institution performing heart implants. Even comprehensive health insurance caused problems: most economists agreed that insurance increased the cost of care by removing disincentives to physicians and patients to defer problematic treatment or to use cheaper methods.

Hierarchical regionalism did not have the same consequences in other countries. In the United States, it had been achieved as a result of a series of agreements, some of them tacit, negotiated in regions, the states, and nationally since the 1930s. Under these agreements, physicians had unquestioned authority over what was done to patients, third parties agreed to pay most of the costs claimed by hospitals, academic physicians accepted aid for education and research from governments but agreed that voluntary insurance should pay for most health care, and planning was defined by state and federal officials as a method of encouraging the orderly proliferation of facilities, not as a way to force hard choices. In Western Europe, where there were different social contracts among the parties with stakes in health policy, the results were very different. In contrast to the United States, health policy in these countries has given higher priority to the equitable distribution of services than to growth. Equity was achieved by strengthening centralized authority over regional hierarchies. As a result, these countries addressed their economic crises in health affairs of the 1970s and 1980s by rationing and regulating instead of by challenging the underlying assumptions of their social policy.[5]

As the unexpected consequences of hierarchical regionalism in America became evident, leaders in health policy, like their counterparts in Europe, tried first to control the problems rather than to reexamine their assumptions about proper health policy. State regulatory agencies drew up new regional plans and insisted that some hospitals close and others get smaller. Federal and state officials and medical specialty societies took steps to reduce the number of physicians in graduate training, especially for the surgical subspecialties. Employers promoted health maintenance organizations to reduce utilization of hospital services by providing a range of alternatives. Public and private insurers brought medical hierarchy to bear on physician behavior by mandating second opinions, preadmission screening, and utilization review and by requiring that new technology be assessed before its use was reimbursed.

Health Policy as a Hard Choice

Hierarchical regionalism, as Americans practiced it, was an expensive theory in a country that, for the first time since the 1930s, was wondering how much health care it could afford. The enormous increase in the percent of the national product spent for health services since World War II had mainly been financed by the proceeds of uninterrupted economic growth. Medicare, like the Social Security program in general, redistributed some income from richer to less-well-off people. But most of the growth in health personnel, facilities, and insurance had not come by taking money away from another sector of the economy.

The economic crises of the 1970s changed what most people assumed about how the growth of health services would be financed. More health services could now be provided only by reducing other expenditures that people valued: for defense, or highways, or mass transit, or environmental protection. Moreover, business leaders could no longer pass on increases in their employees' health insurance as higher prices because of heightened competition from foreign firms, whose governments usually paid most of the cost of health care for their employees.

European countries financed their regional hierarchies and controlled the growth of their health sectors by rationing services, either implicitly or explicitly. Britain, for instance, had placed an annual ceiling on the budget of its National Health Service since 1951 and created formal and informal mechanisms to ration services among and within regions.

Americans rationed health services in a different way: we simply maintained financial barriers to health care for some people. For example, state and local governments usually reimbursed voluntary and proprietary hospitals below their cost—if they paid them at all—for treating patients who were uninsured, underinsured, and ineligible for Medicaid. As a result, these institutions had incentives to transfer indigent patients to public hospitals—

where such hospitals existed—or to defer their treatment except in emergencies. Increasingly, government payers and insurance companies rationed care to people who had thought they were adequately insured—for example, by simultaneously encouraging early hospital discharge and restricting reimbursement for nursing-home and home health care.[6]

These methods of rationing were consistent with a fundamental principle underlying the provision of health services in the United States: that nobody who gains access to the institutions of the health system should be denied as much care as he or she could, in theory, receive. American rationing techniques were designed to discourage people from seeking care or to deny them access to particular institutions. Once accepted by an institution, however, a patient would usually receive all the services that were necessary to diagnose and treat disease and sustain life. Patients in public hospitals often had to wait longer for some services—CAT scans, for instance—than those in private institutions. But patients were rarely denied services just because they were old or dying. In other countries, Britain for example, services are more frequently rationed on the basis of a patient's age and likelihood of survival.[7]

The American premise that rationing should not occur after a patient is admitted to a hospital was challenged, often indirectly, in the 1980s in discussions about costs and ethics. Some critics charged that physicians drove costs up by ordering too many diagnostic tests and prescribing more medication than was strictly necessary. Many people were astonished when federal officials announced that most of each person's lifetime Medicare costs are incurred in the final months of life. But discussions of these data usually related them to the high cost of care, rather than to the refusal to withhold treatment. The media and the courts worried about when it was appropriate to remove life-sustaining respirators and feeding tubes from dying patients or severely handicapped newborns. Yet almost everyone preferred to use the euphemism "life-supporting measures" for the technology that substituted for biological processes.[8] Some experts, combining cost control and moralism, suggested that people who were at risk of diseases linked to their behavior—smoking, drinking, or overeating, for example—should pay higher insurance premiums.

Americans were groping for alternatives to two theories: their belief that increments in health services would inevitably be funded by economic growth and their commitment to providing unlimited care to everyone who achieved access to hospitals. They were asking what health services a society should provide when its members had to forgo other goods and services in order to receive them.

Is Health Still Special?

Many Americans were asking a more fundamental question: Should health still be accorded special status in social policy? By the mid-1980s, there was growing evidence of a narrowing scope of collective responsibility for the care of the sick. Health services were being transformed into commodities by an ethic of individualism that, although familiar in the history of American economic life, had hardly ever been taken seriously in health affairs. This ideological change was having a profound, if as yet unmeasurable, influence on public policy and voluntary action.

The special status of the sick and of services for them has a long history. For thousands of years caring for the sick has had high priority in Jewish and Christian theology. The earliest hospitals were established by religious orders. Beginning in the sixteenth century, hospitals were established by voluntary associations and government agencies. In the nineteenth century, when most public and philanthropic assistance to the poor required tests of both character and means, the sick needed only to demonstrate destitution to receive medical aid and hospital care.[9]

This traditional concern for the sick was reinforced and extended in the twentieth century by the same beliefs about the progress of medical science that justified hierarchical regionalism. By 1930, medicine, broadly defined, had replaced religion as the major object of philanthropy in America.[10] As a result of philanthropy, voluntary associations concerned with illness and health proliferated: hospitals, nursing and convalescent homes, and organizations to promote and provide treatment for particular diseases. Public agencies took increasing responsibility for tracking, treating, and preventing disease. Most people regarded making profits from the care of the sick as distasteful. The conventions of speech revealed the shared assumption that health services were not a commodity. For instance, physicians and hospitals were "reimbursed," not paid; pharmacists and optometrists "dispensed," rather than sold.

The special status of health affairs was rarely questioned in the thirty years after World War II. Medical research was lavishly funded. Health services for the poor, despite their inadequacies, were better financed and less demeaning than most public programs of income support, job training, and education. Moreover, if an area of social policy could cross the boundary from education or social services to health, it quickly received more resources. For example, in the 1950s, vocational rehabilitation became a health rather than a welfare policy, and it achieved large increases in funding. Since the 1960s, care for the physically and mentally disabled has increasingly been described as medical rather than educational or social, with attendant gains in resources. Counseling, originally a skill acquired by educators and psychologists, has now become a reimbursable medical expense. This so-called medicalization of social policy has had many critics, but it made good sense to many people on grounds of both economics and compassion.

The institutions that provided health services were held to higher standards than other agencies of social policy. Standards of accreditation for hospitals were more stringent and more carefully enforced than those that regulated prisons or schools or, very often, even the workplace. The media regarded stories about the mistreatment of patients in state institutions for the mentally ill or disabled as more scandalous than accounts of violence in prisons, on the streets, or in families.

Employees of organizations in the health sector jealously guarded their special status. Unfortunately, little has been written about how officials of health agencies of the federal government and the states often avoided coordinating their programs with colleagues responsible for education, social services, and housing. The aloofness of health officials, for example, was a major impediment to the implementation of several Great Society programs in the 1960s. Similarly, staff members of voluntary associations insisted that their hospitals or homes or agencies had a special claim on public and philanthropic resources because better health, not profit, was their goal. In states where they were particularly strong, voluntary associations were able to exclude investor-owned corporations from lucrative markets or place them at a serious disadvantage in competing for insurance dollars or patients.[11] In the health sector, a year-end "surplus" was morally superior to a "profit."

Around 1970, many participants in social policy believed that a peculiarly American welfare state had emerged since the 1930s. In contrast to the nations of Western Europe, the American welfare state offered its entitlements under a variety of auspices. The federal government and the states provided basic income protection and health services for the poor, the elderly, and the disabled. Voluntary associations collaborated with government agencies to care for the sick and to offer social services to the poor. Business and organized labor negotiated entitlements that were linked to employment, notably health care and supplementary retirement income, but also maternity leaves, child care, and even education. Increasingly, the federal government and the states regulated the benefits provided by voluntary associations and employers. The American welfare state seemed likely to grow and to remedy its omissions and inequities in the remaining years of the century. Health would continue to have special status in social policy.

The unexpected consequences of hierarchical regionalism and the recognition that improvements in health services must be financed by redistribution or by explicit rationing raised questions about the privileged position of health in American social policy. Many critics charged that the surplus of hospital beds and physicians was a result of excessive generosity by the federal government and the states. Others insisted that voluntary and public organizations were inherently wasteful—especially when they were indulged by philanthropists, legislators, and third-party payers. Still others complained that scientists, permitted to study the underlying biology of disease as they pleased, had lost interest in applying new knowledge to prevention and treatment.

By the late 1970s, some economists, lawyers, and entrepreneurs insisted that the problems of the health sector could be remedied by revoking its special status in social policy. They argued that health services were like any other commodity and should, therefore, be provided and regulated through the institutions of the market economy. They urged competition as a substitute for regulation. Sovereign consumers were more efficient arbiters of quality, they insisted, than the bureaucratic state. They urged changing the Internal Revenue Code to permit employees to choose between health insurance and cash or other benefits. Moreover, voluntary hospitals and nonprofit health insurance would be more efficient if they had to compete with organizations that had a profit motive. Similarly, scientists would speed the application of basic science to new technology if they could compete for grants as staff or owners of firms rather than as members of academic departments or research institutes.[12]

Entrepreneurs offered examples in point. Investor-owned hospital and nursing-home chains, they claimed, operated more efficiently than voluntary and public institutions. Their hospitals, for example, were profitable even when they were almost half empty. Competition for patients in markets with strong health maintenance organizations seemed to drive down the costs of care. New biotechnology firms, many owned by present or former academic scientists, were attracting venture capital. Universities and great teaching hospitals were establishing joint projects with manufacturers of pharmaceuticals and equipment and with hospital chains.

The advocates of market-oriented innovations hardly ever acknowledged that the apparent success of these measures was a result of the special status accorded to health in America. For instance, the investor-owned hospital chains were successful mainly because a generous government gave them a return on their equity for treating Medicare patients and permitted them to pocket the profits of economies of scale in the purchase of supplies and equipment. Similarly, the biotechnology firms and industry-university consortia benefited from the public commitment to strong funding for medical research. Thus stockbrokers told their clients that investments in the health sector would be "recession-proof."

Moreover, many voluntary associations, especially hospitals and Blue Cross/Blue Shield plans, raced to emulate the apparent success of the proponents of entrepreneurialism. In their haste, they reinforced and perhaps intensified what may be a fundamental change in Americans' assumptions about health care.

The New Discontinuity

Most people who work in health affairs have a disquieting sense of discontinuity with a past that until a decade ago seemed to be a logical progression since the beginning of the century. Theories about how to organize, pay for, and manage health services that were useful for decades now seem inadequate. The alternatives to these theories that are urged by proponents of competition are considered distasteful, even immoral, by many people who have spent their lives believing that health is special, that research in medical science is the cause of many improvements in health, and that research is best conducted and transformed into practice in regional hierarchies dominated by academic medical centers.

The practical effects of discontinuity are profoundly unsettling. Many physicians, for instance, say that they are rapidly losing control of whom they treat, at what fee, and in what setting. In order to avoid losing patients, many community-based physicians are yielding to pressure to join what are called preferred-provider organizations and independent-practice associations, in which their fees are discounted and their orders are reviewed. Academic physicians are under pressure from deans and hospital managers to treat more patients. Similarly, acting on a perception of discontinuity, hospital administrators are managing their institutions more tightly as their rates of occupancy drop in response to pressure from payers and regulators and to advances in treatment. In the same way, government officials, groping for new policies, are uncertain whether regulation or deregulation, or how much of each, will best protect the public health.

Competing remedies for the consequences of discontinuity have become a staple in professional journals, in the press, and on television. Some observers urge acceptance of an inevitable consolidation of health providers into a handful of megafirms that will sell care to everyone. Others call for public action against a destabilizing medical-industrial complex that is undoing the progress of a century. Some liberals who have regretted the "medicalization" of social welfare may be quietly enjoying the discontinuity, in the hope that it will lead to the redistribution of resources from health to education and economic development.

Discontinuity has further fragmented authority within the health sector. The consensus of the 1950s and 1960s depended on divided authority; neither government officials, nor physicians, nor hospital managers, nor insurers could achieve all of their goals. But the situation now is different: in the absence of sufficient consensus to engender compromise, no major actors in health affairs know what their authority is or what its limits are. As a result, problems are debated to frustration more often than to resolution.

Historians of social policy have no special insight into the present or the future. We use our skills at recovering the meaning of texts and images in order to clarify the relationship of past to present. In the winter of 1987–88, however, when this essay went to press, there was some evidence that the new discontinuity in health policy may turn out to have been only a temporary interruption in the history of collective responsibility for health in America. The Reagan administration and the Congress were collaborating on the first major extension of Medicare since 1972: insurance for the elderly against the catastrophic costs of illness. Moreover, by suggesting changes in the Internal Revenue Code and mandatory voluntary insurance to provide catastrophic care for other Americans, the administration had initiated the first serious discussion in more than a decade about increasing access to medical services for people who are employed. The discussion about catastrophic costs, moreover, stimulated new interest in discussing how to pay the even more severe costs of long-term care.

Another area in which recent changes have occurred is in policy toward AIDS. For the first five years of the epidemic, the federal response was evidence of the new discontinuity in health policy. The federal research budget for AIDS grew as a result of congressional initiative. There was little interest in the federal government in policy to prevent or treat the disease. Initiatives in AIDS prevention, services, and even in research was taken by state and local government, philanthropic foundations, and community groups.[13] Since late 1986, however, there have been signs that the federal government is asserting leadership: for instance, the surgeon general's endorsements of education about safe sex and the administration's request for more funds for research and drug testing.

A new centrist coalition may be forming on behalf of collective responsibility for health care. What remains to be seen is whether that coalition will withstand attacks from both the Right and the Left, how it will address the problems of Americans who lack health care because they are not employed or retired, and especially how much effect it will have in a health polity in which hierarchical regionalism, voluntarism, and the special status of the sick are no longer regarded as self-evident fundamental principles.

Notes

1. Much of this essay is based on the research I undertook for *Health Policies, Health Politics: The British and American Experience, 1911-1965* (Princeton: Princeton University Press, 1986). I describe my debt to colleagues who study policy using historical methods in the Acknowledgements and Note on Sources in that volume.

2. For a more extensive discussion of how Americans perceived health care and health policy in the late 1970s and the 1980s, see Daniel M. Fox, "AIDS and the American Health Polity: The History and Prospects of a Crisis of Authority," *Milbank Quarterly*, supp. 1 (1986): 64.

3. Some sources for these claims are cited in Fox. My generalizations about contemporary history are grounded in regular reading of the press, in medical and health policy newsletters and journals, and in my activities as an official of a university medical center and director of a health policy research center financed by public agencies and philanthropic foundations. A similar view of contemporary history is Eli Ginzberg, "The Destabilization of Health Care," *New England Journal of Medicine*, Sept. 18, 1986, pp. 757-60.

4. Readers will find the documentary basis of my discussion of hierarchical regionalism in my *Health Policies, Health Politics*.

5. For a summary of European strategies, see Brian Abel-Smith, "Who Is the Odd Man Out? The Experience of Western Europe in Containing the Costs of Health Care," *Milbank Quarterly*, 63 (1985): 1-17.

6. I have considerable documentation for the claims I make in this paper. I omit it here in order to avoid overwhelming general readers. For example, information about the rationing of intensive home health care is available in Daniel M. Fox et al., "Intensive Home Health Care in the United States: Financing a Technology," *International Journal of Technology Assessment in Health Care*, 3 (1987): 561-73.

7. For a discussion of British rationing, which has, however, been much criticized by British scholars, see Henry Aaron and William Schwartz, *The Painful Prescription* (Washington, D.C.: Brookings Institution, 1985).

8. An exception to indirect discussion is the Governor of Colorado, Richard D. Lamm. For example see his article, "Let's Address Our Taboos," *New York Times*, Oct. 13, 1986.

9. The generalizations in this paragraph rest on a rich secondary literature in the history of medicine. A place to begin is Owsei Temkin, *The Double Face of Janus and Other Essays in the History of Medicine* (Baltimore: Johns Hopkins University Press, 1977).

10. This shift was first documented by Richard Shryock, *The Unique Influence of the Johns Hopkins University on American Medicine* (Copenhagen: Ejnar Muntsgaard, 1953), p. 37.

11. New York State is a notable example.

12. There is a vast literature, scholarly and polemic, on the subjects I touch on in this paragraph. For an introduction to sophisticated advocacy of the concept that health is simply another commodity, see the papers in Jack A. Meyer, ed., *Market Reform in Health Care: Current Issues, New Directions, Strategic Decisions* (Washington, D.C.: American Enterprise Institute for Policy Research, 1983).

13. Daniel M. Fox, in Elizabeth Fee and Daniel M. Fox, eds., *AIDS: The Burdens of History* (Berkeley: University of California Press, 1988, in press).

ᏬᏝᏬ ᏬᏝᏬ ᏬᏝᏬ

The New Educational Panic

MICHAEL B. KATZ

In the late 1950s, a modest revolution began in writing about the history of American education. Early in the twentieth century, professors of education had captured the history of education as a field, divorced it from the mainstream of historical scholarship, and left it increasingly narrow, antiquated, and uninteresting. Their major purpose was to celebrate American public education by creating a mythological past that portrayed it as the capstone of democracy and the guarantor of equal opportunity.[1] Not surprisingly, this standard interpretation failed to explain the educational disasters that critics in the 1950s and 1960s began to expose: failure to teach basic skills; blackboard jungles; dull, repressive classrooms; the inability of schools to promote equality; and institutional racism. Provoked by the disparity between standard interpretations and actual conditions, historians started to reconstruct education's past to account for its present, and to inject their field into contemporary historiography.[2]

Despite the progress made in their field, these are depressing times for historians of education. Public attention has focused on the quality of education with an unmatched intensity for about twenty-five years; opinion polls locate concern with education high on the national agenda; commissions pour out commentaries on schooling at an unprecedented rate; and politicians at every level vie with each other to demonstrate their rhetorical commitment to the improvement of public schooling. Might not historians, too, seize the moment to augment their academic and popular role with explanations of America's educational decline? Indeed they have, and they will.[3]

Nevertheless, historians cannot suppress a weary sense that they are watching an old play with only a slightly revised script, which, like its predecessor, accompanies a newly intensified Cold War. I call it the new educational panic. Although the Cold War and educational panic are a familiar and recurrent duo, their last show apparently has been forgotten by almost everybody except historians.[4] Therein rest the grounds for historians' depression. It is as though the reawakening of educational history and sociology that began in the late 1950s never happened. The new educational panic ignores the links between education and its social, intellectual, economic, and political contexts, which recent educational history has explicated. In fact, this neglect of context is the new educational panic's hallmark, and its greatest danger.

Consider as a prime instance the most widely cited report of all, *A Nation at Risk: The Imperative of Educational Reform*, produced by the National Commission on Excellence in Education in May 1983.[5] In slightly more than thirty pages of military metaphors, the report blames American education for the decline in the nation's economic and military preeminence. Not only does the report lack supporting evidence, it also fails to consider how great social forces have buffeted educational institutions in the last few decades. In its pages, American schools are the products of energy, will, and competence. Smart, committed teachers motivated by merit pay can turn them around and save the country, especially if they increase the amount of homework.

Critics could point out many other faults in the work of the National Commission on Excellence in Education. It does not consider changes in the demographic composition of schools and colleges; it makes unsupported and unsupportable assumptions about the role of classroom instructional time in educational achievement; it is naively overoptimistic about technology's potential for alleviating unemployment; and it uses fear instead of reason to persuade its readers. In the end, a commission whose putative concern was intellectual excellence in American life substituted a tired metaphor, "a rising tide of mediocrity," for an analysis of what's wrong with public education. Even those who should know better—university presidents and the educational professoriat, to take the most egregious examples—have let visions of increased enrollments in education programs and a fresh supply of research dollars dull their critical abilities. Nary a one has said that the emperor, if not quite naked, is wearing very little.[6]

What accounts for the emergence of this influential document? One answer is the purposes served by a lack of context. An absence of context masks the role of the schools as "contested terrain," bypassing their part in the reproduction of power and inequality. In this way, it distracts attention from their class character and implies an artificial distinction between politics and education. Like attempts to intervene in the market, political contests over the control of education can be defined as illegitimate and destructive. At the same time, abstracting education from its social context perpetuates the myth that educational reform can serve all interests equally and facilitates the construction of a new reform coalition. Indeed, by tapping widespread, diffuse anxieties about education, the commission won support from a broad coalition: parents, rich, poor, and middling, disgusted with the failure of schools to teach their children; industrialists worried about productivity, labor discipline, and wages; Cold Warriors anxious about America's alleged decline in international stature; and university representatives concerned with declining enrollments. To all of them, the commission's simple slogans offer some hope. Whose interests the report serves best, however, is another question.

One code word, "excellence," leads straight to the report's major social implications. By definition, "excellence" implies stratification. To excel is to achieve at a level beyond the ordinary. Within schools, excellence implies the re-creation of hierarchies that give primacy of place to academic achievement and link achievement more closely to rewards in the world of work. It calls, in short, for a rigid meritocracy. For many reasons, meritocracies usually serve best those who enter them with a favored position, and it is not hard to predict who will appear most excellent and garner most rewards. A policy stressing excellence, therefore, is another way of redistributing resources upward. As usually has happened in the past, a new educational policy proposed in the interests of everyone would serve best those already privileged. In this way, the National Commission on Excellence in Education tailored reform to the national conservative political agenda.

Of course, all is not well with the schools. They do fail their students, and they fail most badly those with the least ability to look for help elsewhere and with the fewest resources to help compensate for an inadequate education. This situation is not new, although within cities it has intensified in the years since World War II. Rather, the degradation of American urban education is one product of its social history. This is the lesson that, to its detriment, *A Nation at Risk* ignores.

Consider several propositions about the historical and social context of American education. All are important implications of recent scholarship that should be incorporated into any analysis of contemporary education. I will state each briefly and then offer a few sentences (all that is possible in a short essay) of elaboration. For shorthand, I will use "education" here to refer to formal institutions both singly and organized into systems. Often, I will be referring to both public schools and higher education. Where I am not, the specification of educational level will be clear from the context of the remarks.

(1) *Education has become a form of capital, unequally distributed, and measured by credentials.* Modern universities emphasizing graduate training and research emerged in the late nineteenth century. Although the term "university revolution," usually used to describe the transition from college to university, overstates the extent and breadth of changes—many small colleges altered very little—it nonetheless captures the fundamental reorientation of the major schools. Historians still debate exactly why the great universities changed so dramatically and what those changes meant. Here, I want to emphasize only one strand: the emergence of the modern university signified a new era in the history of capital. In a dramatic new way, knowledge—advanced technical and managerial knowledge—had become a resource essential to the progress of the vast new corporations and bureaucracies. Science and technology, production and administration, coordination and marketing—all required experts and expert knowledge. By managing to capture the process through which experts were produced and to transfer the actual production of much new knowledge from outside their walls to within them, the universities staged one of the great coups in the history of capitalism. Credentials dispensed by universities became the hallmark of professional expertise, and universities, thereby, became the gatekeepers of the advanced technical-managerial society.[7]

The theory of human capital formalized a new role for knowledge. Like other forms of capital, knowledge is never equally, and rarely equitably, distributed. Even more, credentialing has become partially separated from competence. Whether formal credentials ever predicted on-the-job competence very well (or whether they always were primarily a way for occupations to regulate entry) is not clear. However, contemporary research, especially Ivar Berg's, shows that what employers purchase when they buy degrees is credentials, and little more. Indeed, Berg found remarkably little association between formal credentials and on-the-job performance. Credentials have become a form of soft money debasing and confusing the currency. They are a modern form of capital that purchases privilege, but they no longer necessarily signify the possession of the human capital in information, specialized knowledge, or skill that is their acknowledged and only valid claim to legitimacy.[8]

(2) *Education has reflected and reinforced existing patterns of social stratification and regulated social mobility.* Education's role in the reproduction of social structure follows from its emergence as a new form of capital. With tiresome consistency, historians and sociologists have shown how the demography of educational institutions has reflected structures of inequality. Early high schools had few poor children; wealthier children attended school longer; within schools, these children usually dominate the academic tracks; and so on. Universal accessibility has not meant uniform usage. Nor has education been able to promote more mobility than job markets would permit. The expansion of opportunity generated by economic growth and changing occupational structures, more than the unmediated influence of education, has promoted intergenerational social mobility.[9]

Social ecology also has reinforced educational inequality. As cities have become reservations for the very poor, they have lost the residential and industrial tax base and cultural diversity essential to educational quality. The peculiar American system of federalism, which permits small political subdivisions to guard their authority and hoard their resources, has ensured that neither integration nor fiscal equalization between cities and suburbs is a realistic aspiration.[10]

(3) *Education has been "contested terrain" in the conflicts among ethnic groups, races, classes, and genders.*[11] The great group conflicts in American life have played themselves out partly as contests for educa-

tional access and control. Examples are legion: the battles lost by Catholics in nineteenth-century America; struggles over coeducation; skirmishes over the allocation of tax dollars among different levels of education; the integration and school-busing wars; the drive for community control in the 1960s; and controversies over affirmative action. These conflicts over "contested terrain" sometimes have focused on culture or religion; in other instances, they have centered on the great walls of subordination: race, class, and gender; sometimes they have been little more than one strand in the great and continuing effort of the middle class to ensure that not too much of its money is spent on the poor. Regardless of its specific content and origin, every great national cultural and social conflict is acted out partly in the schools. This recurrent drama, incidentally, has been both widely acknowledged and deplored for a long time, as educators and affluent reformers have condemned the influence of politics on education. But their point is disingenuous, or, at best, naive. Schools affect everyone; they consume immense amounts of tax dollars. They are both profoundly political and legitimate objects of group concern. To pretend otherwise is to miss the point of democracy.[12]

(4) *For about 150 years, education has been proposed as a solution to every major social problem.* Their early nineteenth-century founders expected public school systems to eradicate crime, poverty, and ignorance, and equally grandiose aims have reverberated through educational promotions ever since. Schools would ensure the commitment of immigrants to the new world, improve sexual morals, compensate for the influence of family poverty, and foster economic growth. The superiority of its schools, so it was argued, had gained the victory of the North over the South in the Civil War; German technical education had defeated France on the battlefields only a little less than a decade later; in 1957, Sputnik showed that Russian educational superiority threatened American national security; and, we are told, the mediocrity of American education more than any other factor threatens national security at this very moment.[13]

Democratic theory fostered the resilient popular commitment to public education as both the cornerstone of democracy and the key to the solution of virtually every major social problem. Between the early and mid–nineteenth century, a distinctive structure of democratic politics emerged in America. Four of its features are especially important: (1) early universal white male

suffrage; (2) the formation of a party system through which political activity was channeled; (3) the mobilization of urban political
activity by local machines; (4) widespread participation in politics
evident, particularly, in high rates of voter turnout. American
public education assumed its unique form partly because of the
coincidence of its birth with the origins of this special American
democracy. The form of democratic politics helped shape education's structure and forge its base of support, while American
ideas about democracy loaded public education with high expectations by stressing its role as the key agent for equalizing opportunity, providing an informed electorate, and unifying a diverse
people.[14]

The problem with these inflated expectations for public education has been threefold. First, they have deflected attention
away from the more attainable and legitimate, if less global, aims
of schools and colleges. Second, they have distracted energy from
the search for more realistic solutions to great problems. Third,
they have set up periodic disillusionment with educational institutions when it has become obvious that institutions could not
deliver on their promises.[15]

(5) *Like most social benefits, educational facilities have been expanded only
when innovation would serve the interests of the affluent more than the poor.*
Consider, for instance, the creation of the new key institution in
nineteenth-century school systems: the public high school. Although advocated in part as a way to improve the life chances of
the poor, high schools served affluent families best. After all, they
were the ones who could forgo the earnings of children for an
extra few years, and they are the ones who had been spending
their own money on private academies. High schools offered them
a wonderful way to educate their children at home and to have the
whole community share the expense. These differential benefits
have been a major source of middle-class attachment to public
education. A similar argument could be made about the expansion
of higher education in the late nineteenth and early twentieth
centuries. Precisely because it has delivered high benefits to the
middle class, public education (and I include public universities)
has retained a tenacious hold on popular favor and remained
resistant to structural change. (Analogous reasons explain both
the passage of Social Security legislation in 1935 and—in contrast
to forms of public assistance called welfare—its expansion and
continued ability to resist all but modest alterations.)[16]

(6) *The educational establishment has become an independent force that mediates the process of educational change.* Little more than a century ago, educators, largely isolated from each other, unprotected by civil-service regulations or tenure, lacked any effective professional associations or collective power. However, within a generation, the first public-school men had built both national professional associations and urban bureaucracies. As a result, they improved their career prospects and increased their power to foster or resist educational change. Although demographic growth, public indifference, unions, and skilled leadership all have played parts, exactly how and when educators transcended their historically vulnerable and weak position remains a story told primarily in fragments. Nonetheless, its result is a vast, interlocking bureaucracy that connects school administrators at the local level with city, state, union, and even national officials. Despite internal disagreements, the power of this educational establishment to shape and channel reform is awesome.[17]

(7) *Universities have tried, and failed, to dominate schools.* In the nineteenth century, university entrance requirements exerted a powerful influence on secondary-school curricula. Because entrance requirements were not standardized, students often had to choose very early the university or college they hoped to attend and to shape their studies accordingly. No clearer example of this asymmetrical relation between colleges and schools exists than the Committee of Ten, appointed in 1890 by the National Education Association, to make curricular recommendations for high schools. The committee's chairman was the president of Harvard, Charles William Eliot, and university men (there were no women) dominated its membership. By the First World War, university control of the NEA and related organizations had ended, as public-school men gained increased power and influence. As a result, the NEA's next major report, *The Reorganization of Secondary Education* (1918), usually called the "Cardinal Principles of Education," was written by a committee dominated by public-school men. In these same years, professors of education (first appointed in universities late in the nineteenth century, usually in philosophy departments) began a sustained drive for autonomy that resulted, first, in separate departments of education and, by the 1920s, in independent schools within universities. In the process, education professors, their power sustained by the demand for high-school teachers, trained administrators, and research (all generated by exploding

secondary-school enrollments) increasingly isolated themselves from their academic colleagues.[18]

After World War II, and especially after Sputnik, academics outside schools of education tried to reassert their influence on public schools through new curricula, consulting, and elite teacher-training programs for liberal-arts graduates, but the lasting results of their efforts have been meager for two reasons: first, the strength and impenetrability of professional bureaucracies and, second, the unexamined assumption that professors of physics, math, English, or history know best what should be taught in the public schools and how it should be presented. This assumption reflects the arrogance of the professoriat and the imperialism of the universities. The idea that universities can save public education by adopting schools and rejuvenating their faculties (a proposition stressed not long ago in a meeting of presidents and other high-ranking administrators from prestigious universities at Stanford) reflects a lack of humility in the face of past relations between universities and schools and an unwillingness to examine the characteristics and limits of the interaction between them. Indeed, the eagerness of universities to seize on the new educational panic to reassert their influence over public education is one of the more sleazy aspects of the whole episode.[19]

(8) *In the last twenty-five years, the legitimacy of the schools has eroded sharply.* Consider the implications of two observations about public education in late nineteenth- and early twentieth-century America. First is the discipline in urban schools. Observers, especially those from other countries, repeatedly commented on the order in city classrooms. Young, slightly trained women in urban schools often taught fifty or seventy-five children within the same classroom. By and large, they did not have discipline problems. Indeed, the worst discipline problems appear to have been in small country schools.[20] Second, in the late nineteenth and early twentieth centuries blacks had an extraordinarily high rate of school attendance. In Philadelphia, for instance, northern-born teenage blacks stayed longer at school than did the sons and daughters of any other ethnic group, and black children born in the South also had extraordinary rates of attendance. Indeed, everywhere historians have looked, blacks showed an extraordinary commitment to education.[21]

These two examples show the legitimacy of public education. No teacher can keep order when the legitimacy of her authority, and, indeed, that of the school itself are in question. Children do not forgo work to stay in school if they and their parents do not believe it has some purpose. The greater the sacrifice required (and for blacks in Philadelphia who were at the bottom of the occupational ladder it was very great), the stronger must be the belief in the institution's legitimacy and efficacy. By contrast, the turbulence of urban schools today, the need for armed policemen in the corridors, the lax attendance and high dropout rate among children of the urban poor—all show the eroding legitimacy of public education in the eyes of its clients. The question is, then, what sustained that legitimacy before and why has it eroded in recent years?

The answer, of course, lies partly in the general erosion of legitimacy among social institutions. The often-observed litigiousness of the post-Watergate era reflects public unwillingness to trust or take on faith any of the major social institutions: medicine, law, politics, welfare, or schools. The legitimacy of these institutions has declined because they have been shown to distribute their benefits unevenly, because their self-protective masks have been partly exposed, and because everyone knows they do not deliver what they promise. But there are specific factors as well with each one. With the schools, one of these has been the connection between education and jobs. I suspect that black faith in the schools began to erode around the time of the Great Depression, when it became unmistakably clear that advanced education was unable to break the barriers of racism and assure well-educated blacks access to professional and business careers. With whites, the situation has been less serious, but in the 1970s and early 1980s advanced degrees no longer guaranteed access to high-paying, professional work, and simple prolonged school attendance no longer guaranteed a comfortable berth in the upper middle class. Nor did schools seem capable of resisting the cultural transformation of adolescence. Despite the vast amount of money they consumed, their students turned increasingly to drugs, sex, and social protest; appeared to learn less; and could not even be sure of a good job if they graduated.[22]

(9) *Educational change is the result of conflict and contradiction, not planned policy.* The eroding legitimacy of schooling is one of the great contemporary sources fueling attempts at educational reform. Witness the recent spats of reports all expressing severe dissatisfaction with public education. Other sources are contradic-

tions between schooling and political values; race and gender conflicts; and the Cold War. The exploding contradiction between social structure and political ideals fueled the Civil Rights Movement and became the greatest source of educational change since the 1950s. The contrast between the Soviet Union's military and technological supremacy and America's alleged weakness touched off the last educational panic (as well as the recent one) and stimulated the reform movement that introduced the new math, the new physics, and other curricular innovations. An opposite impulse, the distrust of hierarchy, the revulsion with materialism, the longing for community, the skepticism toward technology, and the search for alternative lifestyles energized what have been called the romantic reforms of the 1960s and early 1970s: open classrooms, soft pedagogy, a relaxation of rigor, and an attack on authority. Indeed, all the major educational movements or changes in modern history (the creation of public school systems, the origins of high schools, the development of modern universities, to name three examples) resulted from conflict and contradiction, not planning. The moral is a certain humility about the ability of planning to initiate fundamental change and about the power of abstract rationality as a social or institutional force. Experts play an important but limited role as facilitators and servants of power (or its challengers). They rarely, if ever, initiate great changes by themselves. Nor can they effectively resist them.[23]

(10) *Educational policy always represents a choice among alternative possibilities.* The myth of inevitability is the greatest form of social control. Like the belief in the divine origins of the social structure that ordered medieval life, the idea that a modern society can organize its affairs in only one way serves to make anyone proposing fundamental change appear mad, malevolent, or, at the least, naive. The same can be said about the reification of the market: the separation of the economy from politics and the accompanying assertion that the marketplace is a mysterious, quasi-divine entity that works in predictable, unalterable ways. This reification of contemporary institutional arrangements and circumscription of alternative possibilities has been one great disservice rendered by modern social science. Social science has legitimated the view that the world we have is the only one possible. Existing forms of bureaucracy and stratification, the organization of work, the role of institutions—all may be unfortunate. They may leave us alien-

ated, depressed, angry, or unfulfilled. Unfortunately, they represent the only possible organization of modern life. Our only sensible course, therefore, is to recognize their inescapability and make our peace, helped along the way by therapists, (in Marcuse's term) "repressive desublimation," or, now, experts in management.[24]

History undermines the myth of inevitability. At every point, policies represented a choice among alternatives debated by sane, reasonable people. In the world of work, labor historians and historians of technology are showing how the reorganization of production reflected not the imperatives of production but management's drive to gather to itself control of the work process. In the history of education, I have argued that early in the nineteenth century, four different models of the organization of public schooling competed with each other; elsewhere I have tried to show how the history of social welfare also reflected a choice among alternative policies. With its mask of inevitability stripped away, history becomes much more interesting: a story of struggle, possibility, and hope.[25]

(11) *The history of educational reform traces an alteration between periods of soft and hard pedagogy and between emphases on environment and heredity.* In no period has most commentary praised education. As a consequence, reform, meaning a desire to change or improve the schools, always is present. What alters are its goals, assumptions, and style. These oscillate between two major poles. One is the shift between environment and heredity as explanations for learning problems. In optimistic periods of reform, such as the 1840s or the 1960s, environment predominates as the explanation for individual achievement and behavior (not only in schools but in crime, mental illness, and other areas of social policy as well). When reforms seem to have failed, the search for explanations usually turns eventually to heredity. It happened in the 1850s and 1870s, to take the earliest example. It started again at the end of the 1960s, to take the most recent, with the work of Arthur Jensen, Richard Herrenstein, and the sociobiologists. Hereditarian theories are invariably pessimistic, or, to their supporters, realistic. Their effect is to reinforce harsh, punitive policies and existing patterns of inequality.

The other pole in the reform oscillation is the shift between soft and hard styles of pedagogy, therapy, criminology, and so on. Clearly, these, too, are related to reform moods. Environmentalism and a soft pedagogy that stresses the interests of learners, values the role of experience in education, and deemphasizes authoritarian practices usually accompany each other. So do a stress on heredity and hard pedagogy. Thus, the current emphasis on discipline, homework, and rigid promotion policies is a predictable accompaniment to the disenchantment with the soft reforms and environmentalism of the 1960s and early 70s.[26]

Hereditarian theory also supported the invention of learning problems. Schools usually blame students for their failure to learn, but learning problems, as Daniel Calhoun argues in a brilliant analysis, are inventions. In the early nineteenth century, parents assumed their children could learn what schools taught, and they blamed any failures on teachers. Indeed, Horace Mann defined intelligence as a quality developed through education, not a fixed ceiling on potential. Only later in the nineteenth century did schoolmen begin to redefine learning failure as the fault of students and intelligence as an inherited, fixed quality. This displacement of responsibility for educational failure from teachers to students served nicely to excuse schools for their educational failures.[27]

(12) *For over a century, the dominant style of educational reform has been centralized and bureaucratic.* Throughout the modern history of education, reformers often have concentrated on what they believed to be excessively decentralized and unprofessional administration. As a consequence, they defined reform as tightened administrative procedures and professionally directed, systemwide innovation. The first generation of school promoters in the nineteenth century successfully advocated the creation of urban school systems, age-graded, hierarchical, centrally administered, tax-supported, and compulsory, taught by specially trained teachers. In the Progressive era, a great deal of reform energy concentrated on improving the professional administration of school systems and replacing large, elected ward-based school boards with smaller ones appointed, if possible, on an at-large basis. Although reformers often succeeded in changing the administrative framework of educational systems, they had much less influence on what happened within classrooms and on the results of schooling. Indeed, the history of educational reform shows the bankruptcy of top-down reform as a strategy of educational change.[28]

(13) *The concept of "public" has shifted its meaning throughout American history, and the boundaries between public and private have been fluid and problematic.* Most discussions draw a sharp line between "public"

and "private," as in public education. They assume that "public" includes both finance and management: the funding of schools through taxes and their management by centralized bureaucracies. In fact, the combination of finance and management emerged only in the nineteenth century. In the seventeenth and eighteenth centuries, "public" implied education carried on in a school rather than in a home. By the late eighteenth and early nineteenth century it began to mean schooling open to a broad cross-section of the community, even though administered by self-perpetuating boards of trustees. Indeed, states provided for secondary education by giving money to academies, which today we would call private schools, and they funded religious groups and voluntary associations that tried to supply nondenominational schools for the poor. Only later, for a combination of social and political reasons, did public education begin to mean schools both supported by taxes and controlled and managed by public authorities. "Public," therefore, is a historically contingent concept, and no one arrangement of educational facilities can claim exclusive title to its mantle. Still, educational reform remains trapped within a definition created to suit nineteenth-century circumstances, defending a concept whose time may have passed, unwilling to consider alternative meanings that could alter the control and results of schooling.[29]

By ignoring history, we have replicated the same unsuccessful reform strategies over and over again; reified a definition of public education forged to fit early and mid-nineteenth-century America; and ignored the contingent, protean meaning of public in America's past. We have refused to recognize that the dream of common schooling is dead, wounded first by differentiation between and within schools early in the twentieth century, killed by the social ecology of cities and suburbs after World War II.[30] In the process, we have ceded authority to bureaucracies, remote from children and parents, buffeted by politics and self-interest. We have allowed the re-creation of pauper school systems within large cities; now, we realize, the schools do not serve even our affluent youngsters very well. None of the reform energy lavished on schools throughout their history, none of the federal dollars poured into them in recent years, none of the professors of education who have trained their staffs and studied their operation, has been able to prevent this disaster. Is it not at least time to stop wandering within the same debates?

Notes

1. There were, of course, some exceptions. Three of them are Frank Tracy Carlton, *Economic Influences upon Educational Progress in the United States 1820-1850* (1908; reprint, New York: Teachers College Press, 1965); Merle Curti, *The Social Ideas of American Educators: With a Chapter on the Last Twenty-Five Years* (Totowa, N.J.: Littlefield, Adams, 1959); and Thomas Woody, *A History of Women's Education in the United States*, 2 vols. (1929; reprint, New York: Octagon Press, 1966). For an account of the early history of the field, see Lawrence A. Cremin, *The Wonderful World of Elwood Patterson Cubberly: An Essay on the Historiography of American Education* (New York: Teachers College Press, 1965). Cubberly, a professor of educational administration at Stanford and an important national figure, typified the problems with the field.

2. The works especially important in starting the rejuvenation of the history of education are Paul H. Buck, Clarence Faust, Richard Hofstadter, Arthur Schlesinger, Jr., and Richard Storr, *The Role of Education in American History* (New York: Fund for the Advancement of Education, 1957); Bernard Bailyn, *Education in the Forming of American Society: Needs and Opportunities for Study* (Chapel Hill: University of North Carolina Press, 1960); and Lawrence A. Cremin, *The Transformation of the School: Progressivism in American Education, 1876-1957* (New York: Random House, 1961).

3. For a historical legitimation of recent trends in American educational reform, see Diane Ravitch, *The Troubled Crusade: American Education 1945-1980* (New York: Basic Books, 1984). For a commentary on her book, see Michael B. Katz, *Reconstructing American Education* (Cambridge, Mass.: Harvard University Press, 1987), ch. 5.

4. The best study of the earlier relation between the Cold War and educational reform is Joel Spring, *The Sorting Machine: National Educational Policy since 1945* (New York: McKay, 1976).

5. National Commission on Excellence in Education, *A Nation at Risk: The Imperative of Educational Reform*, Report to the Nation and the Secretary of State, U. S. Department of Education, April 1983.

6. For an example of leading university educators climbing aboard the excellence bandwagon, see the report of a meeting of six major university presidents at Stanford in 1983: "A New Pledge to Help US Public Schools," *Boston Sunday Globe*, Aug. 28, 1983, p. A20.

7. The best account of the origins of the modern university is Laurence R. Veysey, *The Emergence of the American University* (Chicago: University of Chicago Press, 1965); the important source for revising ideas about the antebellum college and the late nineteenth-century university is Colin B. Burke, *American Collegiate Populations: A Test of the Traditional View* (New York: New York University Press, 1982).

8. Ivar Berg, *Education and Jobs: The Great Training Robbery* (New York: Praeger, 1971).

9. Christopher Jencks et al., *Inequality: A Reassessment of the Effect of Family and Schooling in America* (New York: Basic Books, 1972); Samuel Bowles and Herbert Gintis, *Schooling in Capitalist America: Educational Reform and the Contradictions of Economic Life* (New York: Basic Books, 1976), esp. pp. 102-48 and 201-23; Michael B. Katz,

The Irony of Early School Reform: Educational Innovation in Mid-Nineteenth Century Massachusetts (Cambridge, Mass.: Harvard University Press, 1968).

10. Peter O. Muller, *Contemporary Suburban America* (Englewood Cliffs, N.J.: Prentice-Hall, 1981); Kenneth T. Jackson, *Crabgrass Frontier: The Suburbanization of the United States* (New York: Oxford University Press, 1985); Ira Katznelson and Margaret Weir, *Schooling for All: Class, Race, and the Decline of the Democratic Ideal* (New York: Basic Books, 1985).

11. Richard Edwards, *Contested Terrain: The Transformation of the Workplace in the Twentieth Century* (New York: Basic Books, 1979).

12. Virtually every serious book or article on the history of education touches on the way the great group conflicts in American life have played themselves out in education. For one good example that stresses ethnicity and race, see Paul E. Peterson, *The Politics of School Reform 1870-1940* (Chicago: University of Chicago Press, 1985).

13. Virtually every historian of education has commented on America's faith in the power of formal education. See Henry J. Perkinson, *The Imperfect Panacea: American Faith in Education, 1865-1965* (New York: Random House, 1965), and Rush Welter, *Popular Education and Democratic Thought in America* (New York: Columbia University Press, 1962).

14. On the relations between democratic theory and politics and public education see Welter; Katznelson and Weir. On the structure of democratic politics, see also Richard L. McCormick, *From Realignment to Reform: Political Change in New York State, 1893-1910* (New York: Cornell University Press, 1979), pp. 11-24, and Ira Katznelson, *City Trenches: Urban Politics and the Patterning of Class in the United States* (New York: Pantheon, 1981), esp. ch. 3.

15. For an early example of disillusionment spawned by unrealistic expectations, see Katz, *Reconstructing American Education*, ch. 3.

16. On high schools, David F. Labaree, "The People's College: A Sociological Analysis of the Central High School of Philadelphia, 1838-1939" (Ph.D. diss., University of Pennsylvania, 1983); Joel Perlmann, "Curriculum and Tracking in the Transformation of the American High School: Providence, R.I., 1880-1930," *Journal of Social History* 19 (Fall 1985): 29-55, and "Who Stayed in School? Social Structure and Academic Achievement in the Determination of Enrollment Patterns, Providence, Rhode Island, 1880-1925," *Journal of American History* 72 (Dec. 1985): 588-614. On the expansion of higher education see Veysey and Burke. On Social Security, see James T. Patterson, *America's Struggle against Poverty, 1900-1980* (Cambridge, Mass.: Harvard University Press, 1981), ch. 4, and Michael B. Katz, *In the Shadow of the Poorhouse: A Social History of Welfare in America* (New York: Basic Books, 1986), ch. 8.

17. On origins of education as a profession, see David Tyack and Elisabeth Hansot, *Managers of Virtue: Public School Leadership in America, 1820-1980* (New York: Basic Books, 1982); Peterson; and Katz, *Reconstructing American Education*, ch. 3.

18. On the Committee of Ten see Theodore R. Sizer, *Secondary Schools at the Turn of the Century* (New Haven: Yale University Press, 1964); Edward A. Krug, *The Shaping of the American High School*, vol. 1, 1880-1920; vol. 2, 1920-41 (Madison: University of Wisconsin Press, 1969); Arthur G. Powell, *The Uncertain Profession: Harvard and the Search for Educational Authority* (Cambridge, Mass.: Harvard University Press, 1980); Michael B. Katz, "From Theory to Survey in Graduate Schools of Education," *Journal of Higher Education* 6 (June 1966): 325-34.

19. Spring; "A New Pledge."

20. David Tyack, *The One Best System: A History of American Urban Education* (Cambridge, Mass.: Harvard University Press, 1974), pp. 50–56; for a fictional example of the disorder in small country schools, see Edward Eggleston, *The Hoosier Schoolmaster* (1871; reprint, New York: Hill and Wang, 1957).

21. The Philadelphia observations are based on my unpublished research using manuscript census material. Some other observations on black enthusiasm for education are Louis R. Harlan, *Booker T. Washington: The Making of a Black Leader, 1856–1901* (New York: Oxford University Press, 1982), p. 33; Allen H. Bullock, *A History of Negro Education in the South from 1619 to the Present* (Cambridge, Mass.: Harvard University Press, 1967), pp. 25–28; Thomas Jesse Jones, *Negro Education*, Report of the Bureau of the Interior (Washington, D.C.: Government Printing Office, 1917), pp. 3, 280, 287; Howard N. Rabinowitz, *Race Relations in the Urban South, 1865–1890* (Urbana: University of Illinois Press, 1980), p. 157.

22. On thesis that there was a new culture see Philip Slater, *The Pursuit of Loneliness: American Culture at the Breaking Point* (Boston: Beacon Press, 1970).

23. On the limits of educational planning, I have been influenced by Henry Levin, "The Limits of Educational Planning," unpublished draft, April 1977, and Katznelson. Charles E. Lindblom and David K. Cohen, *Usable Knowledge: Social Science and Social Problem Solving* (New Haven: Yale University Press, 1979) also is important on the limits of social science. An excellent account of the educational reform movements of the 1960s is Allen Graubard, *Free the Children: Radical Reform and the Free School Movement* (New York: Pantheon, 1972).

24. One of the many sources for the discussion of the separation of the market from politics is Frances Fox Piven and Richard A. Cloward, *The New Class War: Reagan's Attack on the Welfare State and Its Consequences* (New York: Pantheon, 1982), pp. 42–44.

25. The major book reorienting the history of technology is David Noble, *America by Design: Science, Technology, and the Rise of Corporate Capitalism* (New York: Knopf, 1977). For my explication of the four models, see *Reconstructing American Education*, ch. 2; for my views on welfare, see *In the Shadow of the Poorhouse*.

26. Arthur R. Jensen, "How Much Can We Boost IQ and Scholastic Achievement?" *Harvard Educational Review* 39 (1969): 1–123; Katz, *Irony*, part 2. On the rise and problems of sociobiology, as well as the misuses of hereditarian theory, see Stephen Jay Gould, *The Mismeasure of Man* (New York: Norton, 1971). The major science founded on hereditarian theories in the early twentieth century was eugenics; see Daniel J. Kevles, *In the Name of Eugenics: Genetics and the Uses of Human Heredity* (New York: Knopf, 1985).

27. Daniel Calhoun, *The Intelligence of a People* (Princeton: Princeton University Press, 1973), pp. 70–132.

28. The best source for the history of school administration is Tyack and Hansot. For an excellent account of the struggle over centralization in early twentieth-century New York City, see David C. Hammack, *Power and Society: Greater New York at the Turn of the Century* (New York: Russell Sage Foundation, 1982), pp. 259–99. See also the discussions in Katznelson and Weir and in Peterson.

29. For an elaboration of this point, see Katz, *Reconstructing American Education*, ch. 4.

30. This is one important message of Katznelson and Weir.

꧁ ꧁ ꧁

Scholarship and Public Policy

JOHN BRADEMAS

Over the past few years, there has been a near tidal wave of reports urging reforms in American elementary and secondary schools, colleges, and universities. This debate about the quality and purposes of education provides an appropriate context for a discussion of scholarship and public policy. Let me explain these terms as I shall use them. By "public policy," I refer chiefly to the laws, regulations, and rhetoric of the federal government, while by "scholarship," I mean the activities of teaching, learning, and seeking new knowledge that are carried on in the nation's colleges and universities.

My perspective derives from three sources. The first is personal. For nearly half a century my Hoosier mother was a teacher in the public schools of Indiana and Michigan, and her parents were teachers, too. My father, a Greek immigrant, used to say, "John, I'll probably not leave much money to my children but I will leave you all a first-class education"—and he did. I was privileged to study at Harvard and Oxford, and among my two brothers, my sister, and me, there are nine earned degrees. Then, as a member of Congress for twenty-two years and, throughout that time, a member of the House Committee on Education and Labor, I took

---

Portions of this essay have appeared in different forms in speeches and lectures I have delivered on similar topics.

part in writing most of the legislation enacted between 1959 and 1981 in support of schools, colleges, universities, and other institutions of learning and culture in our country. Finally, since 1981, as president of New York University, I obviously continue to be preoccupied with education. So it is as former legislator and now leader of the nation's largest private university that I write of the changing federal role in education, the present condition of scholarship in the United States, and current national policies toward it.

The Federal Role in Education

The question of the connection between public policy and scholarship is, of course, not new. The government has been involved in education in one way or another for a century and a half, with federal initiatives adapting to the changing needs of a growing nation. The benchmarks of that evolution are well known:

> As early as 1787, Congress, through the Northwest Ordinance, reserved land for public schools.
>
> Nearly a century later, the Morrill Act made possible the establishment of land-grant colleges and universities.
>
> The G.I. Bill of World War II, the most sweeping federal program of aid to education ever enacted, afforded millions of returning veterans, including me, the means to go to college.
>
> The National Defense Education Act of 1958 provided federal funds for improving the teaching of mathematics, science and foreign languages.

Each era has produced its own stimulus and rationale for the use of federal tax dollars to help education. The movement toward land-grant colleges in the 1860s took place in the context of America's entrance into the industrial age and the necessity to prepare students in the sciences, mechanical arts, agriculture, and other subjects essential to that time. The G.I. Bill arose from a sense of national obligation to our returning soldiers.

In 1958 the justification for an expanded federal role in education came with the Soviet launching of Sputnik. With the passage of the National Defense Education Act, a new federal purpose in education was articulated: "The national interest requires . . . that the federal government give assistance to education for programs which are important to our national defense." I entered Congress the year following enactment of the NDEA, sought to be and was assigned to the Committee on Education and Labor, and remained on the committee through my service in Congress.

Four Commitments

Here briefly is what we in Washington, during my years in Congress, sought to accomplish.

First, we made—and when I say "we," I include presidents, senators, and representatives of both parties—a commitment that education would be accessible to those likely to be excluded.

Obviously, I cite here the Elementary and Secondary Education Act of 1965, which for the first time provided substantial federal funds to grade schools and high schools, with particular attention to the teaching of disadvantaged children. In addition, there were Head Start, the Job Corps, the Neighborhood Youth Corps, Upward Bound, and all the other components of the War on Poverty. We also created vocational education and manpower training programs as well as a measure on which I labored long, the Education for All Handicapped Children Act.

To secure talented but needy young men and women a chance for a college education, presidents of both parties—Eisenhower, Kennedy, Johnson, Nixon, Ford, and Carter—as well as Democrats and Republicans in Congress, put in place—from the National Defense Education Act through a series of higher-education laws—a fabric of grants, loans, and work-study jobs.

We made a second commitment during my time in Washington—to assist our institutions of culture. The milestones on this path included the National Endowments for the Arts and the Humanities as well as programs to help public libraries and museums. I was proud to have been a champion of all these measures on Capitol Hill.

There was a third commitment—to strengthen international studies at our colleges and universities. Here I cite the International Education Act of 1966 and other efforts to encourage teaching and learning about the peoples and cultures of the rest of the world.

A fourth commitment was to research. Support from the national government has been crucial in enhancing our understanding of ourselves and our universe through, among other entities, the National Science Foundation, the National Institutes of Health, and the National Institute of Education.

These then were the four commitments that guided and informed our actions as lawmakers for education when I was on Capitol Hill.

Scholarship and the Nation's Aspirations

In the years since I left Washington, D.C., for Washington Square, there has appeared a flurry of studies and reports about the adequacy and direction of scholarship in our country. Surely one reason for these analyses is the American people's growing recognition of the significance to their own individual lives and to society as a whole of what happens—or does *not* happen—in our classrooms, libraries, and laboratories. Nearly all these reports agree on the following conclusions:

> First, higher education is the key to individual social and economic advance. The nation's colleges and universities enable millions of young men and women to develop their skills, hone their talents, and better their lives.
>
> Second, the enterprise of higher education lies at the heart of a powerful and expanding economy. The research and scholarship conducted on American campuses were major springboards from which we launched our extraordinary economic growth following World War II, and our universities will be a critical determinant of our economic health in the remainder of this century and beyond.
>
> Third, colleges and universities are indispensable to our national security. To design sophisticated weapons systems or implement $300 billion annual defense budgets is simply not possible without highly trained scientists, technicians, and analysts. In like fashion, university-level education is central to our foreign policy. History and the social sciences and knowledge of cultures and languages other than our own are as essential to our diplomacy and the defense of our borders as are arms.

Beyond the instrumental ends served by institutions of higher learning—broadening individual opportunity, strengthening the economy, securing our international position, and enhancing the quality of our national life—there is another dimension to the contribution of our colleges and universities. Simply put, the world's wealthiest and most powerful free society has an obligation to foster the life of the mind as an important end in its own right. As the inheritors of Western civilization, we have a duty to preserve and add to that legacy for generations to come.

Challenges Facing Higher Education

Given the evident importance of scholarship to our most fundamental national aspirations, what are the forces now determining the landscape of American higher education? I shall briefly indicate the most significant factors.

The shrinking pool of high-school seniors over the next decade is a fact facing all academic institutions. By 1996 the number of Americans 18 to 22 years of age will have fallen by nearly 30 percent. At the same time, there is a shift toward older learners. One-third of today's college and university students are aged 25 or more.

Other demographic changes will also profoundly affect higher education. For example, racial and ethnic minorities comprise an increasing proportion of the young, and by 1990 will account for 30 percent of all 18- to 22-year-olds. But statistics show that blacks and Hispanics are less likely to graduate from high school and therefore less likely either to be prepared for or to go to college.

The composition of the next generation of college students will present one set of challenges to our institutions of learning. Another set revolves around what the students will be taught once on campus. In the last two decades, the liberal arts have been falling out of favor, with undergraduates not persuaded that the study of philosophy or history or literature can prepare them for careers in a competitive marketplace. Fortunately, more and more colleges and universities, like New York University, are now making the case that a liberal education is vital to professional as well as personal development—and leading figures outside the academy, especially from the world of business, are reinforcing this attitude.

Another challenge facing colleges and universities is to build and maintain faculties of high quality. In areas such as engineering and computer science, faculty vacancies are already a serious problem. The allure of industrial and corporate life for some of our ablest professors is often irresistible; better salaries and superior laboratories are the most obvious advantages. In other fields the problem is nearly reversed. The depressed employment market in the humanities and social sciences means that faculty turnover is limited; tenured faculty, in effect, block the progress of younger academics.

There is, not surprisingly, evidence that for the nation's most intellectually promising young men and women, academic careers are losing their attractiveness. In their recent book, *American Professors: A National Resource Imperiled*, Howard R. Bowen and Jack H. Schuster estimate that to meet future teaching and research needs, American colleges and universities must recruit nearly half a million persons into professorial ranks over the next twenty-five years. Yet the authors report that there has been a gravitational shift of students—among them the most gifted—*away* from careers in the academy.

There will also be, in the years ahead, several financial challenges confronting colleges and universities: the costs of faculty salaries, rebuilding facilities, and student aid. In the case of New York University, operating in high-cost New York City adds significantly to our expenses.

At the core of an institution of higher learning are its scholars and teachers. Generating the resources to continue properly to compensate faculty will be an ongoing imperative for every college and university. Retaining current faculty and attracting outstanding young scholars as junior faculty will require both fair salaries and access to modern equipment and facilities.

To perform the tasks of the twenty-first century, the academic enterprise must also rebuild itself physically. After decades of neglect and inadequate support, the infrastructure of our colleges and universities—the laboratories, libraries, classrooms, and equipment that support research and teaching—is in an alarming state of disrepair. The needs in this area are staggering—some estimates run as high as $10 billion for equipment and $20 billion for facilities.

And, finally, the costs to students of attending college, particularly a private one, have steadily risen. In the face of mounting tuition, colleges and universities must find ways to ensure that qualified students who lack the financial means are not for that reason turned away. At New York University, during my years as president, we have more than doubled the amount of university resources committed to student financial aid.

⌘

NOW I HAVE PRESENTED a snapshot of the problems and pressures— demographic, academic, financial—facing American colleges and universities. To master these various challenges will require a vigorous response from all levels of government, as well as from foundations, corporations, and individual donors.

Recent Policy Recommendations

What are some of the recommendations for action by the federal government to deal with these problems?

Virtually all of the recent studies are extremely critical of present national policy toward higher education and research. Four years ago, I served on the bipartisan National Commission on Student Financial Assistance, and I chaired its subcommittee on graduate education. Our commission's report, issued in December 1983, warned of "signs of trouble and erosion" in the nation's graduate capacities, including serious shortages in doctoral talent, obsolete laboratories and outdated library collections, and the potential loss of a generation of scholars in certain fields. The commission members unanimously agreed that the support of the federal government is indispensable to excellence in graduate education.

In a series of powerful speeches, Erich Bloch, director of the National Science Foundation, has identified serious deficiencies in the nation's research capabilities and has called for a greater commitment from the federal government. In the spring of 1986, a report entitled *A Renewed Partnership* was issued by a Panel on the Health of U.S. Colleges and Universities. This committee, co-chaired by David Packard, chairman of Hewlett-Packard and former secretary of defense, and Professor Allan Bromley of Yale University, was created by the White House Science Council at the request of Dr. George A. Keyworth, at the time science adviser to the president.

The conclusions of both Bloch and the Packard-Bromley panel are on all fours with each other and with those of the National Commission on Student Financial Assistance. In the past decade, says Bloch, there has been a troubling decline in doctorates in mathematics, the physical sciences, and engineering, with the Soviet Union and Japan turning out proportionately more engineers than the United States. Beyond his concern about the poor condition of university laboratories and equipment, Bloch is also disturbed by the nation's research priorities. The military portion of the federal research and development budget has ballooned during the Reagan years from about half to nearly three-fourths.

The report on the status of academic science prepared by the White House Science Council group—the Packard-Bromley panel—also deplores the deterioration of facilities, obsolescence of equipment, and shortages of science and engineering faculty. "Our universities today," warn these experts, "simply cannot respond to society's expectations for them or discharge their national responsibilities in research and education without substantially increased support." Both Bloch and the White House panel argue strongly for a *doubling* of federal support of basic research conducted at universities.

And what are some of the "expectations" and "responsibilities" to which our universities must attend? Two areas are of growing concern: our competitive strength in an increasingly globalized economy and our national security in an increasingly dangerous world.

The decline of American productivity and so of American competitiveness in the world economy is stirring concern in a variety of quarters, from the Oval Office to Main Street. An October 1986 article in *Fortune* magazine noted that "the largest single factor [that] contributed to the doubling of output per manhour over the past forty years . . . has been the forward march of U.S. science and technology."

Everywhere today there are signs of warning. The American share of the world high-tech market dropped in 1986 in seven of ten sectors. The National Academy of Sciences said recently that Japanese and other foreign countries now supply "critical components" for American missiles, electronic warfare devices, and other advanced weapon systems. And an essay in a Fall 1986 issue of *Science* declared, "The collapse of U.S. productivity growth is the most severe and persistent of recent economic problems."

So salient is the apprehension about the decline in American productivity that more and more voices are urging renewed attention to education, research, and development as essential ingredients to restoring America's economic position in the world. Among those making this case are the President's Commission on Industrial Competitiveness; the bipartisan Congressional Caucus on Competitiveness; the Council on Competitiveness, formed by John K. Young, president of Hewlett-Packard; and the National Governors Association.

All these voices call for more, not *less*, action by the federal government.

NOW WHERE DOES my analysis lead?

First, I have described the historic commitments made to learning and culture by the government of the United States. Second, I have asserted that investment in our colleges and universities is essential to our future as a free people—to individual opportunity, our economic strength, our national security, our quality of life. Third, I have indicated both major changes in the topography of higher education and principal challenges to the system. Fourth, I have cited several recent recommendations for public policy toward scholarship and the virtual consensus they represent.

Because as a member of Congress I dealt for over two decades with education legislation, because Ronald Reagan would turn back the clock on schools, colleges, and universities, and because I believe current policies pose an unprecedented danger to what I have called "scholarship," I should now like to examine their effect.

Whether they emanate from the president, Congress, or regulatory agencies, these policies are implemented in three ways, through budgets, taxes, and regulations.

The Reagan Record

Unfortunately, although more Americans are recommending a greater investment in teaching and learning, the administration of Ronald Reagan in its budgetary, tax, and regulatory policies is more hostile to education than any administration in the nation's history. Indeed, it is today obvious that the commitments presidents and Congresses made during my own years in Washington are being eroded.

Mr. Reagan has repeatedly attempted to weaken the role of the federal government in support of education. His budgets have called for deep slashes in aid to schools, colleges, and universities. His secretary of education, the highest-ranking official in our government dealing with education, has made public statements contemptuous of American colleges and universities and the students who attend them. And the president has supported changes in our tax laws that will work great damage to schools as well as colleges and universities, both public and private.

The Reagan record on education over the last six years provides substantial evidence for the validity of these charges. Ronald Reagan has never made a secret of his desire to reduce—indeed eliminate—the role of the federal government in education. Eleven years ago, in a speech in Minnesota, Mr. Reagan advocated the abolition of the Office of Education in what was then the Department of Health, Education, and Welfare. Former Governor Reagan said at that time, without qualification, that the federal government "should not be involved in education."

As president, Mr. Reagan has fostered a concise legislative program for education: do away with the Department of Education; encourage prayer in public schools; offer vouchers to persuade students to attend private schools; and change federal regulations, including those aimed at enforcing civil rights, improving opportunities for the handicapped and disadvantaged, and protecting the free exchange of information and ideas.

It is ironic that the National Commission on Excellence in Education, whose members were all appointed by President Reagan's secretary of education, should have produced a report that did not even mention—let alone recommend—a single one of Mr. Reagan's proposals.

The Reagan administration has also pressed massive cuts in most education budgets, including Chapter 1 ESEA programs; help in teaching handicapped children; and grants and loans to college and university students.

Despite all its rhetoric about the importance of education to our national life, the Reagan administration is pursuing a course of action that is undermining the schools, colleges, and universities of the United States. These are strong words but justified.

Budgets

As a university president, I have been particularly distressed by the Reagan higher-education budgets. I choose three examples from the fiscal 1988 budget to make my point: university-based science research and development; international studies; and student financial aid.

The Reagan proposals for academic research and development present a mixed picture. The President seems to be giving with one hand and taking away with the other. The administration seeks a large boost in money in fiscal year '88 for basic research through the National Science Foundation, a result of the strong leadership of Erich Bloch. Nevertheless, once again, the administration is urging cuts in funds for the National Institutes of Health, which account for forty percent of federal support of university science.

Although the amounts involved are modest, Mr. Reagan is also continuing his campaign, waged year after year, to kill support for another area where, in the new international economy, we need all the information and wisdom we can get—international studies. The president remains hostile to such investment despite the judgment of such persons as former Defense Secretary Weinberger and former Secretary of State Kissinger that knowledge of foreign languages, cultures, and political and social systems is vital to the nation's security—as the Iran-contra fiasco surely demonstrates.

But the worst casualty of the Reagan '88 budget is financial assistance to college students. In every budget this administration has proposed since 1981, Mr. Reagan has called for deep cuts in aid to talented but needy students. In fiscal 1988 the administration would chop student aid by a full forty-five percent below the amount Congress voted for fiscal year '87, from $8.2 billion to $4.5 billion! If enacted, the White House '88 budget would force all but the very, very poorest students to turn to loan programs that would make going to college much more expensive and would substantially increase student indebtedness.

Moreover, the much-vaunted and supposedly new Income-Contingent Loan program, introduced with such fanfare by Secretary of Education William J. Bennett, would no longer subsidize interest on student loans and would link repayment schedules to a student's earnings after college. Some experts estimate that student borrowers would have far larger bills to pay and would stay in debt for decades.

This program is really not new. In 1986, Congress rejected the administration's bid for $90 million for the same scheme, said the proposal required further study, and voted $5 million for a pilot program. Suddenly, without knowing if the experiment even works, the administration wants to escalate it to $600 million.

One of the most scathing critiques of this Income-Contingent Loan idea comes from Boston University President John R. Silber, who advanced a similar proposal ten years ago. President Silber warns that the administration's plan will mean "very much higher" interest rates than those he had envisioned, and that the maximum annual repayment is "a crippling 15 percent of income," nearly *twice* the percentage he had recommended!

Despite Mr. Reagan's allegations, the impact of these and the other student-aid cuts he urges would fall heavily on students from low- and middle-income families. As of the autumn of 1983, nearly half the undergraduate students receiving some form of federal assistance were from families of incomes below $15,000 and eighty percent from families with incomes of less than $30,000.

Nor is there truth to the administration's continued allegations that the aid programs are too generous and that students and their families should pay a larger portion of college costs. At New York University, eighty percent of our overwhelmingly low- and middle-income-family students work part-time, and nearly two-thirds of them depend on some form of financial aid. Across the country, between 1979–80 and 1983–84, students receiving aid and their families increased their share of the cost of going to an independent college or university by seventy-two percent; these families were paying an average of $5,700 a year.

Moreover, more and more students at both private and public colleges and universities are having to borrow to meet their college costs. According to a report released in December 1986 by the Joint Economic Committee of Congress, a decade ago, in 1975–76, loans constituted less than a fifth of total financial aid (from college, federal, and state sources), but by 1985–86, more than *half* such assistance was in the form of loans. In 1985–86, the average student borrower graduated from a private college with nearly

$9,000 in loans to repay, and from a public college, with a $6,685 debt.

"The rising cumulative debt of college students that is documented in this paper is disturbing," Congressman David R. Obey of Wisconsin and Senator Paul S. Sarbanes of Maryland, former chairman and current chairman, respectively, of the committee, said in issuing the report. "We do not know whether we are overburdening a generation, whether these loans can be repaid, whether undergraduate debt burdens are discouraging young people from attending graduate schools or whether young people are being pressured away from important but lower-paying careers because of the salary demands which such debt may impose." The Obey-Sarbanes report is all the more reason to view with much skepticism an Income-Contingent Loan plan that would mean still greater debt for American college students.

Indeed, one possible result of the Income-Contingent Loan program is that the present generation of borrowers would be paying off their college debts in the future at the same time that they would be struggling to help pay for the college education of their children. Another danger, according to Harold Howe, the former United States commissioner of education, is that we could see "a substantial decrease" in the proportion of women, low-income, and minority students attending college.

Tax Reform

Although the tax-reform bill President Reagan signed into law on October 22, 1986, represents major improvements in making the tax code fairer, the measure also contains provisions that threaten serious harm to the nation's colleges and universities. First, the legislation will tax scholarships and fellowships to the extent that students do not use the stipends for tuition and equipment, a particular hardship for graduate students paying for room and board. Second, deductions for interest on student loans will be phased out, another cost increase for students. Third, the new legislation mandates a $150 million ceiling per institution on access to tax-exempt financing by *private but not public* colleges and universities. And finally, the law will reduce giving to higher education by eliminating the charitable deduction for nonitemizers and by imposing a minimum tax on gifts of appreciated property.

So at a time when, both in the interests of our competitiveness in the world economy and our national security, voices on every hand urge greater investment in education, we are in effect imposing new tax burdens on the colleges and universities of the United States and on the students who attend them.

As I write in 1987, Secretary Bennett is out on the stump attacking colleges and universities for raising tuition. Yet the policies he and his administration are pursuing—cuts in student aid, increased costs of student borrowing, higher costs for renovating research facilities, as well as tax changes that will reduce private contributions to higher education—all these factors are directly responsible for generating more pressure for the steeper tuitions Mr. Bennett tells us he deplores.

The cumulative effect of these several provisions of the Tax Reform Act is a serious loss for American higher education generally and a particular blow to independent colleges and universities, a bizarre result for an administration that rhetorically praises the private sector of American life.

Regulations

As if the impact of these budget and tax measures were not damaging enough, colleges and universities have also had to be concerned about another set of potentially harmful federal policies—regulations. In February 1986, for example, the Office of Management and Budget, without any prior consultation with the university community, announced that overhead charges on federal research grants would be limited to twenty-six percent of the direct cost of the research with a still lower cap of twenty percent to be applied in 1988. As David Packard, cochairman of the White House Science Council panel, said, "The [Office of Management and Budget] did precisely what we recommended they not do," adding that "the OMB lacks any understanding of what the problem is all about."

Fortunately, leaders of the research community were able to work out with OMB representatives a mutually acceptable formula for paying overhead charges. But universities must still anticipate further attempts to make them pay a greater portion of indirect costs of research.

Free Flow of Information and Ideas

There is one other matter that must concern all those dedicated to the free flow and exchange of information and ideas. Through regulatory and other administrative actions, the Reagan White House is attempting to restrict access to such flow and exchange in ways that have ominous implications for an open society. For example, the administration has

> sought to narrow the scope of the Freedom of Information Act, which guarantees public access to most government documents;
>
> barred entry of foreign speakers into the United States for fear of what they might say;
>
> urged lifetime censorship on over 150,000 employees of the federal government, denying them the right to publish without government approval;
>
> attempted to block the exchange of unclassified information at scientific meetings;
>
> issued guidelines that would reduce the collection and dissemination of information developed by federal agencies on which both government and the private sector rely; and
>
> expanded the reach of prepublication review of research financed by the government.

Importance of Independent Higher Education

Here I must draw attention to another depressing consequence of current national policies toward higher education. Taken together, they pose a particular threat to independent colleges and universities.

The United States, it must be recalled, is the only country in the world with a major system of private higher learning, one not under government control. Private institutions, heavily dependent for income on tuition, are especially endangered by, for example, cuts in student aid. Twenty years ago, some fifty percent of American college and university students were enrolled at independent institutions; today, less than a quarter attend private institutions. In my view, if we take seriously our words about the value of *pluralism* in higher education, we must look to the conditions of our private as well as our public colleges and universities.

I note that five years ago, in May, 1981, I was present at the University of Notre Dame in my home congressional district when President Reagan declared, "If ever the great independent colleges and universities . . . give way to and are replaced by tax-supported institutions, the struggle to preserve academic freedom will have been lost."

The Reagan Mismatch

The president was right but his policies have failed to match his rhetoric:

> A president who promises to make America competitive presses budget and tax measures that favor our competitors.
>
> A president who praises the place of private values in public policies pursues a course especially damaging to the private colleges and universities of the land.
>
> A president who paints a future of "Star Wars" defense shields and a giant atom-smasher urges a budget that is blind to the link between such visions and the educated men and women needed to make them come true.

For from where are these highly trained people to come if not from the nation's colleges and universities? President Reagan has not seemed to understand the close connection between the achievement of goals he himself espouses and a strong system of higher education.

Bipartisan Tradition

Here let me reiterate a fundamental fact about federal support for learning and research over the last generation. It has always been bipartisan. Today's battle over appropriate policies toward higher education is not between Democrats and Republicans. Rather the struggle is between, on the one hand, the bipartisan tradition of legislators, presidents, and other public officials of both parties who have worked together to strengthen our colleges and universities, and, on the other, a narrow, ideological view that would undermine them. Evidence for this assertion came in the spring of 1985 from the secretary of education in President Reagan's first term, Terrel Bell. In an article in the *Phi Delta Kappan*, Bell, a Utah Republican, wrote of his battles while in office with "the lunatic fringes of ideological political thought" and "zealots" pressing "radical and off-the-wall ideas."

More recently, Bell chaired the National Commission on the Role and Future of State Colleges and Universities, whose report was issued in November 1986. The study strongly deplores the Reagan attacks on student aid and concludes, "Public officials who propose budget reductions in education at a time when the republic is handicapped by the burden of an undereducated populace are unthinkingly abetting an act of national suicide. . . ."

In fact, some of the most stinging criticisms of Mr. Reagan's higher education policies have come from members of Congress of his own party. I noted some Republican responses when the fiscal '88 higher-education budget was presented to Congress. Said Senators John C. Danforth of Missouri, "absolutely wrong"; Pete V. Domenici of New Mexico, "inconceivable"; and Robert T. Stafford of Vermont, "I am very, very deeply disappointed."

Clearly Republicans as well as Democrats on Capitol Hill understand, even if the President does not, that when Mr. Reagan savages education, he is directly threatening both the prosperity and the security of the United States.

Conclusion

In this essay, I have written of the commitments made to education by past governments, have indicated some of the major challenges facing higher education today, and have noted several significant recommendations for mastering them.

I have contrasted these proposals with budgetary, tax, and regulatory policies now being pursued in Washington and have also commented on the opposition in Congress on the part of both Republicans and Democrats to the Reagan administration's continued attacks on colleges and universities.

Even as I look with apprehension and dismay at the impact on American colleges and universities of the policies of the present administration, I take some comfort from the composition of the Hundredth Congress. For, if this great republic is to survive, we must invest more than we have been doing in educated men and women.

I conclude my analysis with the eloquent words of warning of Alfred North Whitehead: "In the conditions of modern life, the rule is absolute. The race which does not value trained intelligence is doomed."

I do not believe the American race is doomed, so long as the American people and the men and women they choose to lead them acknowledge the value of such intelligence and insist on the resources to support it.

Philanthropy as Moral Discourse

ROBERT L. PAYTON

If thought makes free, so does the moral sentiment. The mixtures of spiritual chemistry refuse
to be analyzed. Yet we can see that with the
perception of truth is joined the desire that it
shall prevail. That affection is essential to will.
Moreover, when a strong will appears, it usually
results from a certain unity of organization, as if
the whole energy of the body and mind flowed in
one direction. . . . Whoever has had experience of
the moral sentiment cannot choose but believe in
its unlimited power. . . .

But insight is not will, nor is affection will. Perception is cold, and goodness dies in wishes; as
Voltaire said, 'tis the misfortune of worthy people that they are cowards; "un des plus grands
malheurs des honnêtes gens c'est qu'ils sont des
lâches." There must be a fusion of these two to
generate the energy of will. . . .

The one serious and formidable thing in nature is
a will. Society is servile from want of will, and
therefore the world wants saviours and religions.
One way is right to go: the hero sees it, and
moves on that aim, and has the world under him
for root and support. He is to others as the world.
His appropriation is honor; his dissent, infamy.

> The glance of his eye has the force of sunbeams.
> A personal influence towers up in memory only
> worthy, and we gladly forget numbers, money,
> climate, gravitation, and the rest of Fate.[1]

Emerson understood that benevolence is not enough. For kindly feeling to become beneficent, for good will to become action, requires a coalescence of insight and affection—of recognition of a problem and a concern for those affected—fused "to generate the energy of will." Emerson argues that ordinary people are immobilized by cowardice: they are brought to action by persons of will and purpose. Those of strong will are the catalyst of the spiritual chemistry that makes up the moral sentiment. Without leaders, without direction and focused purpose, most of us would remain stuck in our doubt and confusion in the face of the great moral demands of life.

The organization of efforts to make things better, or to make them less bad, is philanthropy. It begins with perception: someone has to *see* suffering and to recognize it for what it is. That requires imagination—not simply the sensitivity of the observing novelist or anthropologist, but imagination linked to moral sentiment, moral sentiment linked to action. To these is added organization. The Good Samaritan, coming to the aid of a stranger in need at some risk to himself, is acting as an individual. It is the transformation of moral sentiment and imagination into collective action that has shaped the core of the philanthropic tradition.

The thesis of this essay is that the moral agenda of society is put forward within the philanthropic tradition. Philanthropy's contribution to moral discourse is as critic of the other institutions of society—even, on occasion, as critic of itself.

Robert H. Walker, in *Reform in America*, describes a cycle of reform. The first phase is a time of discovery, of recognition that something is wrong, marked by competing definitions of what the problem is. A second phase is completed by competing proposals for change. The first cycle takes place as voluntary initiatives of private citizens; the second is marked by movement of those new insights into public policy. To cite one of Walker's paradigm cases: slavery becomes an indigestible knot in the stomach, and abolition brings temporary relief; the negative achievement of abolition eventually inspires hope that there is a fuller pattern of citizenship not yet achieved; legislation begins to redefine the qualifications of citizenship. Voluntary initiatives lead eventually to reform of the law.[2]

The moral sentiment is not, of course, confined to the philanthropic sector. Politicians and government officials sometimes interpret their roles and responsibilities in order to enhance the social consequences of their actions—as happened so often during the eighteenth and nineteenth centuries, when merchants aligned themselves with religious leaders to create communities, to build schools and hospitals, churches and markets.

Notions of enlightened and humane government are based on empirical evidence as well as on theory; notions of socially responsible business corporations are supported by fact as well as by ideology. But the case has been well made by James Douglas in *Why Charity?* that the operations of the marketplace are theoretically indifferent to public goods and that the acts of government must be categorical rather than responsive to individual needs. These inherent constraints on the first two sectors create opportunities for the third—indeed, require the third.[3] The rhetorical role of philanthropy is to point out the deficiencies of social institutions—whether those deficiencies occur by design or by default. What is different about the philanthropic tradition of the West, then, most extensively manifest in the United States, is that the genius of organization has amplified the sporadic actions of individuals into a loose system, a tradition of moral sentiment in action, a moral sector parallel to that of the political and economic. Law protects these private initiatives for the public good; tax policy encourages them.

Within the third sector are two kinds of activity: initiatives that respond to recognition that things have gone wrong and people are suffering, and initiatives that propose opportunities to enhance the quality of life. The definition of philanthropy that emerged in the late nineteenth and early twentieth centuries links the two: it defines the purposes of philanthropy as those of identifying the causes of human suffering and social misery and developing strategies to eliminate them. Philanthropy as moral discourse has since deferred somewhat to the demands of social science. Moral claims are validated or rejected by survey research, on the one hand, or reduced to echoes of ideology by analysis, on the other. Skepticism has been brought to bear systematically on the claims and methods of beneficence.

The case against philanthropy is not necessarily misanthropic, but it often exhibits harshness. Emerson himself, in "Self-Reliance," complained

> . . . do not tell me, as a good man did today, of my obligation to put all poor men in good situations. Are they *my* poor? I tell thee, thou foolish philanthropist, that I begrudge the dollar, the dime, the cent, I give to such men as do not belong to me and to whom I do not belong . . . your miscellaneous popular charities; the education at college of fools; the building of meeting-houses to the vain end to which many now stand; alms to sots; and the thousandfold Relief Societies;—though I confess with shame that I sometimes succumb and give the dollar, it is a wicked dollar which by and by I shall have the manhood to withhold.[4]

There is a widely held point of view that true social betterment on a large scale cannot come about by voluntary action. "Charity must be coerced," as economist Barbara Bergmann once put it. Voluntary action must be superseded by the obligations of citizenship. Benevolence requires beneficence to have meaning; privileges dependent on voluntary action must be followed by rights, by enforceable claims. Voluntary action is too often undermined by free riders; free riders will contribute their share only when compelled to do so. This point of view also contends that in a democracy the resources for social good should be gathered by the state through taxation and allocated through established processes by representatives and agents of the commonweal.

Recent political developments in the United States, however, have given weight to contrary arguments. It is complained that dependence on public solutions to social problems—as reflected in the programs of the New Deal and the Great Society—leads to state interventions that imperil freedom and drain a diminished treasury. Western European welfare states have begun to back away from social commitments taken for granted in the recent past. The competition of the new international marketplace has encouraged philosophies of public welfare that identify enlightened charity with job creation. As Maimonides declared 750 years ago, the highest form of charity is to help a person become self-supporting. It is still a beguiling notion: public welfare drains the treasury; job creation fills it up. Welfare increases taxes; job creation increases profits. George Gilder has even argued that it is altruism that inspires the marketplace: those who take economic risks do so not out of self-interest only, but out of an understanding that their actions will benefit others as well.

In the wake of the welfare state's decline, there are also increasing signs that Western Europe and Japan are encouraging a larger and more active private philanthropic practice to make up for some of the reductions in public spending for social goods. These nations now borrow eagerly from the American experience. The Japanese are busily establishing foundations and organizing corporate philanthropy; British and French universities are turning to business corporations and even to alumni for financial support.

Although attracted by the possibility of offsetting public expenditures by private giving, these countries have not yet discovered that the moral agenda of government is given form in the voluntary and nonprofit third sector. Emerson's four elements of insight, affection, will, and leadership, empowered by organization, assert the claims, even though Emerson himself opposed them:

> If an angry bigot assumes the bountiful cause of Abolition, and comes to me with his last news from Barbadoes, why should I not say to him, "Go love thy infant; love thy wood-chopper: be good-natured and modest; have that grace; and never varnish your hard, uncharitable ambition with this incredible tenderness for black folk a thousand miles off."[5]

It is out of the competing rhetoric that the moral vision of some people becomes the moral standard of the nation as a whole. Nor does the process end there: it is the function of philanthropy as moral discourse to point out the gaps between the ideal and the actual—whether it be in terms of civil rights, the claims of the poor and defenseless, or the protection of the natural environment.

The high aspiration of philanthropy is inseparable from low technique. Egoism is on the same scale as altruism and cannot be wholly removed from it. The sublime in the philanthropic tradition is often deflated by the mundane. Giving money is inseparably linked to raising money. Raising money often requires appeals to emotion rather than clean, objective, logical demonstration. As scholars and artists find to their dismay, merit is not always self-evident to prospective patrons. There is a widespread inability to remain inspired to do good while using guile and pressure to make doing good possible.

The evidence for my thesis is to be found in particular cases, and they lie conveniently at hand. It is helpful to imagine what it would mean to have to deal with these cases *without* a third sector, leaving them exclusively to the agencies of government and marketplace. What would America be, in theory, without its philanthropic tradition?

I. *International Human Rights*

The popular singer Paul Simon performed at a benefit concert in Zimbabwe recently with a group of South African musicians. Simon has also recorded a new album, *Graceland*, described by him in *U.S. News & World Report* as rooted in "black music on the other side of the Atlantic." Simon says, "I knew 'Graceland' had political implications and just hoped that the music would be interpreted as a positive statement insofar as the black peoples of South Africa were concerned."[6]

Beyond the commercial recording and concert, the so-called benefit—at which those in attendance share in entertainment contributed by performers—or other social gatherings where the excess of income over expense is donated to charity, is designed to raise funds for the cause and at the same time to attract broader public attention.

These two concerts were part of an international philanthropic endeavor, a kind of secular missionary activity. Popular culture exploits its appeal to recruit new followers to the cause of human rights. There is also an appeal to an ill-defined sense of solidarity, a joining of hands across borders and across racial and ethnic lines to give participants a sense of strength and momentum. Beneficent interventions of this kind—to help the poor of the world, to bring down the racist government of South Africa— are often applauded by those who find other forms of cultural imperialism unacceptable.

The antiapartheid movement in the United States has been sustained almost entirely by philanthropic effort. It is unusual in not being primarily dependent on ethnic ties, as is the effort to relieve the oppression of Jews in the Soviet Union or to support rebellion in Northern Ireland, to cite two more typical examples. The American opposition to apartheid gathers its support in this country from those who are most strongly committed to the advancement of civil rights.

Certain styles of moral discourse seem to be effective and appealing to some groups. Common patterns of behavior and perceived analogies appear over time among diverse and previously unrelated causes. These sometimes lead to the formation of coalitions along ideological lines. The emergence of social movements out of this process is only dimly understood and is too little studied by philanthropic practitioners.

Those engaged in philanthropic practice give little evidence of being concerned about philanthropic theory. The function of philanthropy as moral discourse remains hidden. For example, one moral issue that is seldom publicly faced by supporters of rebellion in Northern Ireland or resistance to apartheid in South Africa is that of offering money and moral support without sharing directly in the mortal risks entailed.

A major failure of much philanthropic activity intended as *moral* action is that it thus often appears to be empty symbolism, obscuring rather than sharpening the moral issues. The search for rhetorical impact requires suppression of detail and complexity. In the heat of the struggle there is little time or sympathy for structured moral discourse, especially among those whose philanthropic role may mask political ambitions or the search for financial gain.

Moral discourse in philanthropy should be—but seldom is—candid about its own persuasive devices. The ethics of rhetoric is given less attention than are the moral objectives to be won by rhetorical means. Ends are thus commonly and uncritically used to justify means. Action overwhelms reflection. (And Emerson asks, "If malice and vanity wear the coat of philanthropy, shall that pass?")

Because philanthropic intervention in behalf of others has its greatest consequences for those helped rather than for those helping, the ethic of responsibility is also weak. Those whose philanthropy is based on moral absolutes find themselves mired in inconsistency in a world where good and evil are so haphazardly distributed and so difficult to disentangle.

A small child from the Philippines is brought to Washington for surgery to correct severe congenital deformities of the hands and feet. The surgery is performed by professional medical staff members who have volunteered their services, in a religiously affiliated hospital that donated its facilities. This act of mercy is the work of the Washington chapter of an organization called Operation Smile, "founded in 1982 to improve medical treatment of children of other countries."[7]

Religion accounts for almost half of the private giving in America, and churches and other religiously inspired organizations enlist the efforts of tens of millions of volunteers. Religious organization is behind large numbers of day-care centers and homes for the elderly and infirm, and religious denominations founded many, if not most, hospitals and colleges. Religious values based directly on biblical injunctions continue to color philanthropic activity.

It is a common American practice, originating in Christian universalism and made possible by the nation's relative affluence, to make its medical resources available to citizens of other countries, as in the case of Operation Smile. This practice calls us to rise above the commonplace that "charity begins at home," at least while absorbing substantial costs in the treatment of a child from a foreign country, although large numbers of American children lack medical care for which their need is presumably as great as that of the child from the Philippines.

Operation Smile and other organizations argue for a universal beneficence, sustained most generously by Americans until such time as other, less advantaged nations acquire medical resources of equal quality. Yet, "Thy love afar is spite at home," Emerson argued. Many would still agree.

II. Domestic Poverty

A. M. Rosenthal, who wrote a book about the Kitty Genovese case in 1964 (in which a woman was attacked and murdered while thirty-eight people watched from different vantage points without taking action to help), now sees himself as "the 39th witness."

"Almost every day of my life," he writes in a *New York Times* column, "I see a body sprawled on the sidewalk. . . . Some show signs of life; others are totally still. I assume they are all alive but I never stop to find out or even bend over to see if I could possibly be of some help."[8]

The familiarity in large cities in the United States of the "people wrapped in cardboard," those "bag ladies shuffling in the night streets to keep warm," is acute and distressing. Rosenthal's failure to do anything about their plight leads him to classify himself among those moral cowards who failed to come to the help of Kitty Genovese. He is angry—at himself and "at the cops and the hospital people for not taking them somewhere they can be taken care of."

Social history suggests that few of us are able to accept all people in distress as equally deserving of our assistance. (Recall Emerson's derisory reference to "alms for sots.") Some people seem to be in greater need than others, to be more deserving of help.

Howard University was recently the scene of a "mock tribunal" to "dispel the myths of the homeless." According to a report in the *Washington Post*, homeless men and women told about their experiences in shelters and how they came to be homeless in the first place.

> The room fell silent as David Hamilton Jones, 47, came forward on crutches. Jones said he once worked as an electrical engineer for companies that contracted with the federal government. For him, health problems that kept him from working caused financial problems, and he found it difficult to find a place to live. He told the audience he wants to work. "I'm not looking for a handout."[9]

In modern societies, needs have come to be defined increasingly as rights. The moral rhetoric seeks to persuade us that rights are not only political but economic and even cultural. A central moral issue of philanthropy, then, is the way in which we choose, establish, and affirm such rights. One approach is for philanthropic voices to bring pressure to bear on the public authorities. Bishop John R. McGann, of the Roman Catholic Diocese of Rockville Centre in New York, argues in a *New York Times* essay that "affordable housing is a basic human right."[10] The bishop urges an end to the curtailment of federal funds for the housing of the elderly and the handicapped, "in light of the grave moral responsibility of government to be deeply involved in such a critical need of its citizenry."

The antipoverty activist Mitch Snyder recently concluded a hunger strike that successfully preserved a public building as a shelter for the homeless in Washington. The hunger strike is by now a familiar device to win public sympathy for a cause and also to bring public pressure to bear on officials. Personal witness of this kind, in its many familiar variations in recent times, is an essential ingredient of American philanthropic discourse.

Charles Hyder, self-identified by his sign "Fasting Physicist," had lost 160 pounds (of an original 310 at the starting point six months earlier) when he received a message from Mikhail Gorbachev: "Your spiritual strength is needed to continue the struggle for preventing a nuclear catastrophe. For that reason, we urge you to stop your hunger strike."[11]

In the rhetoric of philanthropy, basic needs come before less urgent ones. Corporal alms often come before spiritual alms, as Thomas Aquinas said many centuries ago. The elderly and the handicapped and small children presumably have a more pressing claim on philanthropic resources than does the unemployed electrical engineer. Still, the engineer's need may be more easily met and dealt with, while those other claims seem endless.

There is no national assessment of the philanthropic effort as a whole, no "National Philanthropic Policy" established by Congress. We have only a gross calculation of how much money is contributed and to which areas of concern it is directed. We have, of late, estimates of the numbers of volunteers and rough breakdowns of what they do. National philanthropic priorities change depending on media coverage, economic conditions, and prevailing ideological winds. How then do we choose among the myriad of opportunities to do good?

One quandary of philanthropy is the priority given to needs near at hand when there is suffering elsewhere. One answer is to balance them: the sponsors of the United States portion of the Live Aid concert later organized Hands across America. The former fundraising effort was aimed at the plight of starving people in Africa, the latter at the plight of those in poverty in this country.

As Guido Calabresi and Philip Bobbitt have pointed out, some public choices have tragic side effects.[12] Calabresi analyzed, for example, the method of allocation of kidney dialysis machines. The number of machines available was determined to be significantly smaller than the life-dependent demands on them. A first-order solution is to limit categorically those who are eligible to have access to the machines (by age group, for example). A second-order solution is to provide more machines; implicit in this solution is a further reallocation that directs more medical resources to those suffering from kidney disease and less to those suffering from other diseases.

Those who cannot face the consequences of first-order choices turn to second-order choices, but discourse about the moral implications of second-order choices tends to be ignored by those whose entry into the matter is an agonizing first-order emergency. As Calabresi points out, some first-order solutions are morally intolerable, even though equally tragic second-order consequences may follow if we avoid them.

Philanthropy as moral discourse is cacaphonic. Those who believe that philanthropy represents a sector (as politics and economics are sectors) often indulge the babel of claims as if it were guided by a Smithian invisible hand. The philanthropic marketplace is a triumph of free enterprise, scarcely restrained by the gentle guidance of the IRS. Anyone captured by a moral cause can organize and seek to enlist others to serve the same cause.

The evangelical preacher and faith healer Oral Roberts, an early exponent of the electronic church, captured national attention by announcing that he would be dead within a year if he was not successful in raising $8 million to relieve financial pressures on the medical center he founded in Oklahoma. According to the evangelical Protestant monthly *Christianity Today*:

> "I desperately need you to come into *agreement* with me concerning my life being extended beyond March," states a fund-raising letter signed by Roberts. "God said, 'I want you to use the ORU medical school to put My medical presence on earth. I want you to get this going in one year or I will call you home!'" Roberts said he received this message last March. . . .
>
> Calvin College communications professor Quentin Schultze, a student of Christian fund raising, criticized Roberts's latest

appeal, saying it reflects poorly on Christian organizations. But he added: "You've got to see it in the context of a man who has a tremendous amount of pressure on him. He's at the top of an organization that has to bring in millions of dollars each year to keep things going. . . ."

Critics say Roberts's approach to raising funds, even if sincere, constitutes a kind of moral blackmail. . . .[13]

Philanthropy as moral discourse is most often couched in terms that reflect immediate personal experience. Sammy Davis, Jr., the entertainer and motion-picture actor, almost died of liver disease. According to an interview in *Newsday*, Davis now believes that because he has survived his illness he has a responsibility to help others similarly afflicted. Davis expresses the common experience of a calling to philanthropic action: "Maybe that's one reason I have survived. . . . I think I was put here to do more than sing 'Bojangles' and 'Candyman.'"[14]

A man named David Tilman was the subject of a recent newspaper profile in the *Daily Progress* of Charlottesville. The reporter expressed admiration for Tilman's capacity for voluntary service to the Boy Scouts and as a member of the volunteer fire department and rescue squad while at the same time holding down a full-time job with the telephone company. "I just figure the Boy Scout work is more important . . . so I go with that. That's one reason I quit the National Guard (after 22 years of service), was because of the Boy Scouts."[15]

The newspaper profile was one of a series on "Piedmont People," a familiar journalistic device to lend support to philanthropic work as a community service. Our democratic populism wants us to believe that ordinary people participate in the moral discourse of philanthropy as much as powerful organizations or famous personalities.

THE STRONG WILL and sense of purpose that Emerson wrote about is transformed by moral aspiration. As Emerson saw so clearly, the moral sentiment can be foolish as well as practical, fraudulent as well as self-sacrificing. We must judge them all. Our answer to the claims of the helpless and the moral arguments of those who come to their aid is a measure of our civility, our humanity, and our good sense.

Notes

The examples I have chosen reflect my recent parochial reading habits as a former resident of New York now resident in Virginia, but the kinds of evidence offered here will be found in the newspapers of every American community.

1. Ralph Waldo Emerson, "Fate" in *The Conduct of Life*, in *Emerson: Essays and Letters*, ed. Joel Porte (New York: Library of America, 1983), pp. 956–57.

2. Robert H. Walker, *Reform in America: The Continuing Frontier* (Lexington: University Press of Kentucky, 1985), introd. and part 2.

3. James Douglas, *Why Charity? The Case for a Third Sector* (Sage Publications, 1983).

4. Emerson, "Self-Reliance," in *Essays and Letters*, pp. 262–63.

5. Emerson, "Self-Reliance," p. 263.

6. "A Songwriter's South African Odyssey" (conversation with Alvin P. Sarnoff), *U.S. News & World Report*, March 2, 1987, p. 74.

7. "Operation Smile: Medical Help over Miles," *Washington Post*, Feb. 23, 1987, section 4, p. 1.

8. A. M. Rosenthal, "The 39th Witness," *New York Times* (Long Island ed.), Feb. 12, 1987, section 1, p. 31.

9. "Dispelling the Myths of the Homeless," *Washington Post*, Feb. 15, 1987, p. B3.

10. "Affordable Housing Is a Basic Human Right," *New York Times* (Long Island ed.), Jan. 25, 1987, section 1, p. 25.

11. "Personalities," *Washington Post*, Feb. 28, 1987. Mr. Hyder's hunger strike was still under way as this was written.

12. Guido Calabresi and Philip Bobbitt, *Tragic Choices* (New York: Norton, 1978).

13. "Did Oral Roberts Go Too Far?" *Christianity Today*, Feb. 20, 1987, vol. 31, pp. 43–45.

14. "People," *Newsday*, June 18, 1985.

15. Lawrence Hardy, "Search for David Tilman Could Lead Number of Places," *Daily Progress*, Feb. 22, 1987.

IV

ӘＬ ӘＬ ӘＬ

FOREIGN POLICY

The True Sentiments
of America

DENIS DONOGHUE

And we Americans are the peculiar, chosen people—the Israel of our time; we bear the ark of the
liberties of the world.

MELVILLE, *White-Jacket*

I.

There is no question of describing "the American mind," any
more than "the Irish spirit," "the English character," or "the
French temper." These phrases would remove from time and
process the ensemble of notions they propose to establish. They
are rhetorical essentialisms, positing in each case a spirit floating
free from any ostensible manifestation. They imply that there is
something, a quality independent of change and time and process,
that can't be exemplified by any evidence that may be produced.
Only the phrase is adequate, with such adequacy as language has:
beyond the phrase, there is an incorrigible absence.

It is not clear why we maintain the desire that these phrases
mark, unless it is that, having lost the indigenous gods of people
and place, we want to call back divinity by spiritualizing various
collective entities. It is a vain endeavor. If we want to restore to

our interests a further qualitative character, we can find it only as an adjectival relation to our historical nouns.

But even if we put aside the project of an essence, we are not thereby restricted to the enumeration of phenomena. It is reasonable to speak of a type, and of the discourse that governs it as a typology, because a type is distinguished from an essence by arising from historical considerations. A type is a pattern or a structure, disclosed first by history and then by the permanent significance of that history. When Henry James referred to "the complex fate of being an American," he did not propose an essentialism; he marked a type of historical experience, and called it American. Any observation that takes account of the same source and reflects upon it has the same validity. It would be reasonable to say, for instance, that one of the distinguishing signs of American culture is the degree to which Americans question its character, or whatever they deem its character to be, and force it to declare itself, submitting its quality to the judgment of moral or aesthetic principles. Such a remark is merely a cultural notation, issuing for what it is worth from certain historical and social observations, and it may be tested by appeal to the conditions at hand.

But sometimes the conditions are such as to provoke in those who otherwise merely cope with them a sense of taking part not only in an enterprise of great pith and moment but in an affair of destiny. I have been reading through some of the documents in American political history, which come to a first fulfilment in the Declaration of Independence (1776) and develop beyond that through the Federalist and anti-Federalist papers to the Constitution (1787) and the Bill of Rights (1791). What seems striking in the early documents is not that the Founders saw themselves in a dramatic light—the birth of a nation could hardly be seen in anything less—but that the inaugural sense has persisted and is still maintained in strikingly personal terms. Certain men came together to do certain things. Even now, the founding documents are interrogated not for their objective meaning but for the intention the Founders apparently if not comprehensively entrusted to those words. Written constitutions are not always perused in this spirit. Irish citizens don't consult the Constitution of 1937 to see what those who wrote it intended. The questions are rather: what does such-and-such a provision in the Constitution mean, and is the matter at hand—something the government proposes to do—

compatible with it or not? But the American Constitution is regularly construed as a treasury of collective intentions: what it means is what certain men may be judged to have had in mind. It is assumed that the framers of the Constitution, for instance, were the providential custodians of a distinctively personal entity, the sentiment of America. Many citizens regard as impious any attempt to dissociate the Constitution from the deducible intent of the Founders.

My concern is not with the founding motives in their bearing upon the conditions that provoked them, but with those motives insofar as they gathered up other historical sentiments in America and, after their dramatic expression in the War of Independence, established their privilege at large. I am not claiming that these motives at some point transformed themselves into an essence that we identify as American, or that in some other respect they aspired to the ineffable character of mystery. But they may have come together, or have been brought together, to form a distinctive typology, adjectival to the conditions that produced it. Some of these motives can be seen at a glance in one man.

II.

In February 1765, two years after the satisfactions of the Peace of Paris, John Adams wrote in his diary:

> I always consider the settlement of America with reverence and wonder, as the opening of a grand scene and design in Providence for the illumination of the ignorant, and the emancipation of the slavish part of mankind all over the earth.[1]

We may let that stand without comment for the moment. But we should place beside it *A Dissertation on the Canon and Feudal Law*, which Adams published in August 1765, and *The True Sentiments of America*, which he published in 1768. These documents argue that the true sentiments of America are those that the New England settlements fostered upon the principles of love and freedom, and that the false sentiments are those that found their tyrannical form in feudalism and the Canon Law of Rome. From the Reformation to the first settlement of America—"God in his benign providence raised up the champions who began and conducted the Reformation"—Adams saw the gradual spreading of knowledge in Europe, and the weakening of tyranny.

Beside these episodes, we may set another, the correspondence between Adams in Quincy and Jefferson in Monticello; both old men, retired from political life, mulling over gone times but finding local strength enough to discuss, in addition, the question of "natural and artificial aristocracies," Napoleon, the character of grief, the new University of Virginia, and Flourend's experiments on the functions of the nervous system in vertebrate animals. The noblest letter is Jefferson's of October 12, 1823, in which he refused to allow any third party to compromise the understanding between him and Adams, but Adams's letters are nearly as fine as Jefferson's, as grand in their generosity.

These episodes bring together three motives which seem to me to have a certain privilege in American history, literature, and politics. First, the diary of February 1765 enhances the common American assumption that America has been marked out as having a redemptive mission not only in its own territory but throughout the world. In *Redeemer Nation: The Idea of America's Millennial Role*, Ernest Lee Tuveson has studied this assumption from the seventeenth century to the twentieth. The conviction that America is the new Israel is as clear in Increase Mather and Jonathan Edwards as it is in John Adams. Indeed, in 1765 Adams merely resumed an old motif, America's exceptional destiny. The sentiment adhering to it brought together the notion of a religious *renovatio* in New England, the westward march of civilization, the Roman conviction of *imperium*, the botanical analogy by which a plant transplanted from its original setting becomes stronger in new ground—"flourishes in America with an augmented lustre," as Ezra Stiles put it, twenty years later than Adams, in *The United States Elevated to Honor and Glory* (1785).

The sentiment still persists. Woodrow Wilson's version of it— "America had the infinite privilege of fulfilling her destiny and saving the world"—is echoed in Ronald Reagan's State of the Union messages. America is to play the crucial redemptive role in history and establish democratic government throughout the world: it is taken for granted that democracy has the indisputable validity of natural law.

Sometimes the millennial ambition has seemed wild, but mainly to foreigners. The English clergyman Andrew Burnaby, who visited the colonies in 1759–60, reported with dismay that "an idea strange as it is visionary has entered into the minds of the generality of mankind, that empire is travelling westward; and every one is looking forward with eager and impatient expectation to that desired moment, when America is to give law to the rest of the world."[2] From time to time, American administrations have restrained their millennial ambitions for pragmatic reasons: there have been several versions of the Monroe Doctrine, based on a consideration of what at a particular moment might or might not be possible: no intervention was attempted in Afghanistan; the response to the Russian appropriation of Eastern Europe was merely verbal. But a direct relation between fulfilling America's destiny and saving the world is regularly invoked, even when the experience of American intervention in Korea, Vietnam, Cuba, Nicaragua, and other countries has been wretched or, as in Chile, disgraceful. The ambition to give law to the rest of the world is always at least considered, as if it amounted to America's destiny and were not at all accurately described as a mere exercise of power. American wars are regularly presented as crusades. There is always a readily recognizable enemy, Communism, in our own day and obsessively in the past fifty years, as if there were only one form of evil in the world. Above all, there is the sentiment of a fresh start for the world in the hands of Americans. Adams implies that the New England settlements were separated from the corrupt Old World so that they might start again in innocence. Canon Law and feudal law were only the most blatant forms of the Old World's corruptions. A new era had begun.

This motive partly accounts for the determination of American writers to transcend the local marks of corruption—dispossessed Indians, enslaved blacks—by appeal to a comprehensive diction of unity. The desire is as evident in Jonathan Edwards's "Thoughts on the Revival" and Emerson's lectures ("The American Scholar," for instance) as in Whitman's *Leaves of Grass*. The sense of local disunity must have been acute if it needed such hyperbole to appease it. "Manifest destiny" could only be acclaimed if by a rhetoric of *etiam peccata* the otherwise disfiguring signs of inequality could be dispelled by a vision encompassing good and evil. The future is the only tense in which such a vision might be located.

The second motive was defined by Adams's sense of the Reformation as a divinely awarded opportunity. God had produced great men to defeat anti-Christ, to curb the power of Rome, and to break the vicious conspiracy between Rome and feudal

Europe, which, until the Reformation, had kept multitudes in bondage. It is difficult to estimate the degree to which this suspicion of Romishness persists, or indeed to say what would count as evidence. Does it count that, in American literature, when a corruption distinctly European has to be given a particular locale, it becomes a choice between Paris and Rome? Or that, in *William Wetmore Story and His Friends*, Henry James remarks that London, Paris, and New York are cities in which the spirit of the place has long since "lost any advantage it may ever have practised over the spirit of the person," but that the Rome of words that he felt impelled to conjure was "a rare state of the imagination, dosed and drugged, . . . by the effectual Borgia cup, for the taste of which the simplest as well as the subtlest had a palate"?[3] Perhaps it doesn't count, especially now that it has become difficult to think of the Roman Catholic Church as a pervasive and therefore sinister power. In *Character and Opinion in the United States*, Santayana referred to the assimilating capacity of American life and offered as an instance of it the conviction that a Roman Catholic lives in America without any feeling of friction: he is entirely at peace, and "cheerfully American." It is wonderful, Santayana remarked of the Roman Catholic, "how silently, amicably, and happily he lives in a community whose spirit is profoundly hostile to that of his religion."[4] If any change has occurred in the conditions of the Roman Catholic in America in the past sixty or seventy years, it is that they have become even more congenial. But the Borgia cup is still to be tasted, on the rare occasions on which the Church is identified with murderous cardinals and lecherous popes. Hatred of Rome, as in Adams's *Dissertation*, is by now an exotic passion, but a much diminished version of it may still be found.

The third motive, as we find it in the correspondence between Adams and Jefferson, may be called Enlightenment rationalism. Ezra Pound offered the letters as proof that in the years between 1760 and 1830 there was indeed a civilization in America. "Nothing surpasses the evidence that CIVILISATION WAS in America, than the series of letters exchanged between Jefferson and John Adams, during the decade of reconciliation after their disagreements."[5] Pound recurred to the letters, with the same admiration, in the *Guide to Kulchur, Jefferson and/or Mussolini*, and Canto 31; in each, he ascribed the "sanity and civilisation" of Jefferson and Adams to the Encyclopaedists and the rich culture held in common by Bayle and Voltaire. After the death of Van Buren in 1862,

Pound argues, the conditions were never again favorable to the mutual bearing of public and private merit.

But this is to run ahead of my theme. What the correspondence between Jefferson and Adams mainly shows is that in their day there was a context of discourse in which it was possible to discuss such questions as public order, taxation, the relative dangers of populace and aristocracy, the privilege of property, the matter of money and the banks. The arguments between Federalists and their opponents disclose the same condition. At any moment it is hard to say what Jefferson or Adams believed, so far as their religious convictions went, or to what extent they put under supernatural disposition the values they revered. Locke and Montesquieu account for whatever passed between Jefferson and Adams as political philosophy: the lessons of history were to be taken seriously and for their exemplary value, but no appeal to historical instances could be decisive. Adams favored more government and more clearly established continuity than Jefferson did: he maintained residual affection for monarchy, if not for a particular king. But they both assumed that by taking thought a man could reach the right decision, and that he might then persuade other men to act upon it.

The correspondence also shows, however, much misgiving, on each side, about government as such. Adams's insistence upon checks and balances throws some doubt upon his confidence in the institution of a central government: it was a necessity at best, and they should make the most of it. I mention this only to suggest that the transition from the post-Puritan world of Jonathan Edwards to the Enlightenment rationalism of Adams and Jefferson and thence to the individualism of Emerson was not abrupt. Emerson didn't fret about institutions, having left the Christian one, the only one that mattered. His common attitude was that if you found yourself a member of an irksome institution you should either leave it or put up with it: it was not a crucial matter. Adams and Jefferson were good enough federalists to work for unity, but they were good enough Americans to prefer informal coherences if any could be had. One of the intentions of the Founders was to curb the tyranny of the majority, to set a limit upon ostensibly democratic demands, and to guarantee the privilege of white skin and property.

But my theme is not the conflicts involving property, money, and power that led to the Civil War, or the matter of states' rights and federal rights, which made the war inevitable, or even the sacrosanctity of the Union, which the South had to be forced to acknowledge. I am positing, even in the signatories to the Declaration of Independence and the framers of the Constitution, sufficient misgiving about the theory and principle of a federal government to make Emersonian individualism, when it was proffered, an appeasing resource. Again, no violent change was entailed. Just as Adams gathered up the motives he received from the New England settlers, so he indicated that a slight change of tone would be enough to make further development easy. Where the Puritans spoke as if with tongues of fire about a divine blessing to be manifested in New England, Adams spoke of domestic felicity, which, if satisfactorily established, would be seen as blessed by God. Pound had an interest in presenting Enlightenment rationalism as the decisive cultural style of an America worth comparing with the finest instances of Italian Renaissance power. But in fact the transition from Edwards to Adams was a gentle process, and the further transition to Emerson was hardly more turbulent. A nudge of self-confidence was enough to reach Emerson's "Self-Reliance."

But it may be useful to interpose between Adams and Emerson a passage from de Tocqueville, to show how malleable the terms of American discourse were.

III.

"I am persuaded," de Tocqueville wrote in the second volume of *Democracy in America*, "that in the end democracy diverts the imagination from all that is external to man and fixes it on man alone." Among a democratic people "poetry will not be fed with legends or the memorials of old traditions":

> But Man remains, and the poet needs no more. The destinies of mankind, man himself taken aloof from his country and his age and standing in the presence of Nature and of God, with his passions, his doubts, his rare prosperities and inconceiveable wretchedness, will become the chief, if not the sole theme of poetry, among these nations.[6]

It may appear that God, nature, and man form a triad sufficiently inclusive to sustain a major poetry. But if God were to lose his

thunder, disappear or absent himself, wait in silence till summoned—if, supposing further, we were living in the middle of the
nineteenth century and we had our heads full of progress and
perfectibility and man's command over nature, then our triad
would not hold, the tension of three terms would slide into the
omnivorousness of one of them. Enlightenment rationalism found
it easy to invoke nature instead of God. A further nudge, the
secularization of spirituality, would complete the rhetorical process. "God without thunder" can't become anything but man,
especially if the human imagination is endowed with capacities
declared to be divine. Wallace Stevens's formula is anticipated, in
effect: "We say God and the imagination are one. . . ." Even if the
identification depends upon our saying it and upon no other pro-
ducible evidence, we have reduced God to ourselves. What then of
nature? It can only mean the conditions that surround us, and if
we are still in America and in the nineteenth century, we increasingly see the conditions as divided into two kinds: those we have
made in our own image, as cities and towns, so that nature is
already transformed into culture, and those residual intimations
of a nature we have neither created nor yet transformed, the
landscape that appeases our guilt and remains for a few more
years virgin land.

Are we touching upon the familiar complaint of American
writers from Cooper to Henry James, that the country is socially
too thin, too empty of social structures to allow for a complex
relation between the individual and society? Not quite. Besides,
we have James's other word for it, that despite this emptiness
Hawthorne made himself a major writer just by being American
enough. We have Howells's insistence, in reply to James, that
what remains to a country bereft of Epsom and Derby is—everything. This is not the question. The question in the nineteenth
century, and in our own time, is: Do Americans feel that their
institutions, such as they are, genuinely mediate whatever they
take reality to be? Or that the common sense of reality is humil-
iated by those institutions?

It is my impression—and what can I have but an impression?—that the civic sense in America has always been half-
hearted. As a visitor, I have long been surprised at the readiness of
Americans to believe the worst of their doctors, teachers, lawyers,
judges, industrialists, politicians—as if they assumed that particular men and women are corruptible in advance by the professions

they enter. In other countries a profession seems to be thought innocent and serviceable until it is proved guilty. I am compelled to associate the American suspicion of professions and institutions with the conviction, familiar to readers of American literature, that value is not here and now but in "a world elsewhere."

Admittedly, there are changes of mood. In "Reality in America"—one of the essays collected in *The Liberal Imagination*—Lionel Trilling complained, partly on the evidence of the wrong-headed reception of Dreiser and James, that in America reality is always deemed to be "material reality, hard, resistant, unformed, impenetrable, and unpleasant," and that the only mind felt to be trustworthy is the one that "most resembles this reality by most nearly reproducing the sensations it affords."[7] An account of the general sense of reality in America at present would not, I think, endorse Trilling's essay. Dreiser and the naturalistic writers akin to him are no longer admired or indeed much read. James has won. Indeed, I continue to find it odd that readers of American literature, agreeing upon little else, now concur in a general sense of the literature: that it is the "site" of an attempt to create in language and style an environment of freedom that has never been available otherwise in American society. "Reality" may still be hard, unpleasant, and so forth, but in that character it is no longer deemed to be morally or aesthetically compelling. The effort to create a new style answerable to the desire for freedom is meant to release, as Richard Poirier says in *A World Elsewhere*, "hitherto unexpressed dimensions of the self into space where it would encounter none of the antagonistic social systems which stifle it in the more enclosed and cultivated spaces of England and of English books, the spaces from which Lawrence escaped to the American West."[8] The new space is to be created first in language and style and, later, in personal and social life. We imagine freedom, before enjoying it.

The reasons for which Lawrence went west are more complicated than Poirier's reference implies. F. W. Bateson once described Romanticism as the shortest way out of Manchester: there is nothing uniquely American in that desire. What is odd is the fact that the sentiment Poirier describes was felt even by unencumbered American writers in the nineteenth century, to whom the social system in which they found themselves could hardly have been deemed oppressive or stifling. The Concord of Emerson and Thoreau was as much a "West" as Lawrence ever found in

Taos: no wonder Henry James thought that in Concord one's introspective powers had to serve as a social resource, and that Emerson's life there could be represented as one of reading, walking in the woods, and the daily addition of sentence to sentence.

I can only infer that the reason why American writers have presented social systems mostly as a nuisance is that they regard their true lives as lived, on principle, apart from them; "beyond culture," in Trilling's phrase. The fact that in Thoreau's Concord there was a relatively mild system in force didn't deter him from feeling disgusted that there was any. Otherwise I can't explain why so many Americans hold themselves ready to live "beyond culture" if given half a chance. Trilling was not the only social critic to feel dismayed by evidence that many Americans, and not merely the young, insist on standing apart from the common culture and enjoying "an autonomy of perception and judgment." His reservations in regard to modern literature arose from his sense that it fostered the belief that a primary function of art and thought is "to liberate the individual from the tyranny of his culture."[9] He was shocked that by, say, 1965 so many Americans seemed determined to define their lives according to private values and to declare the independence of an adversary society congenial to this desire.

There is no question of blaming Emerson, Thoreau, and Melville for the invention of an adversary culture. There is—or should be—all the difference in the mundane world between imagining a state of being and living it out. But the reduction of God to the human imagination is not an innocuous act—still less so if the imagination is then outlandishly enhanced to give the impression that what has taken place is not a reduction.

IV.

It is for this reason that Frost and Stevens are, among the indigenous as distinct from the cosmopolitan American poets, the most characteristically American—and most clearly so in their diverse relations to Emerson. Emerson in one of his many guises is readily compatible with the version of self-reliance that, as readers of Frost, we call social Darwinism. Stevens's relation to Emerson— the Emerson of "The Snow-Storm"—is such that many of his poems, as Hugh Kenner was the first to say, present an immensely resourceful mind staring bewildered upon an opaque and unpeopled universe. What else is there, except words? You would never divine from Stevens's poems that they were written in a city and that beyond the city there were more than two hundred million Americans going about their business. In those poems, even the sublime

> comes down
> To the spirit itself,
>
> The spirit and space,
> The empty spirit
> In vacant space.[10]

Or it comes down to the imagination in any of its moods.

Perhaps the poem to read, in this context, is Stevens's "The Blue Buildings in the Summer Air," because it starts by recalling Cotton Mather, his books, what he believed, what he preached, his sense of heaven and earth. The other truth Mather's voice tried to overwhelm is represented by a mouse in the wall of his church, interminable and at last successful in its destructive capacity. Stevens's poem, as if it were placed exactly halfway between the early "Sunday Morning" and the late "To an Old Philosopher in Rome," almost adverts to both in the fourth of its five stanzas:

> Look down now, Cotton Mather, from the blank.
> Was heaven where you thought? It must be there.
> It must be where you think it is, in the light
> On bed-clothes, in an apple on a plate.
> It is the honey-comb of the seeing man.
> It is the leaf the bird brings back to the boat.

If that is all it is, was it worth what Cotton Mather spent to declare it? He could as well have lived on cakes and ale. But what Mather meant to himself and to God is not what he means to Stevens, who sees him now through Emerson, Whitman, Santayana, Nietzsche, and Pater. If there is a blank, it is in Stevens's eye, to recite a figure from Emerson that Stevens would not have wanted to find brought against him.

Is there a political consequence to this, as well as a metaphysics prior to it? The readiness of Americans to think the worst of their institutions, the common insistence on living beyond culture, the reduction of God to the human imagination and that to a desperate inventiveness—are these several unrelated motives or one motive in several forms?

What are the consequences of getting into the habit—because it is a habit—of thinking that what is commonly deemed to be reality is not real, and that the only true reality is the "world" each of us constructs in private? It is entirely possible to construct such a world, and to endow it with large-scale intimations of freedom. Stevens is the poet of such a possibility: his poems transpose the appurtenances of the common, deceived world—of heroes and masters and slaves—into spiritual equivalents. His "Examination of the Hero in a Time of War" offers an alternative to thinking about Audie Murphy and General Patton and Churchill and the saturation bombing of Dresden, an internal sense of heroic values for which only the subjective imagination and an amenable language are required. It then becomes possible to conjure an ironic relation to ordinary goings-on, letting them be what they happen to be.

But there is a price to be paid: you must allow the goings-on to pass, in practice, into the hands of those who want to administer them. The people who insist upon creating an adversary culture bear some responsibility for the emergence of such a man as Alden Pyle in *The Quiet American*, whom we might choose to set aside as a mere vehicle of Greene's hostility to America if we had not the irresistible image of Colonel North to deal with. Pyle's destructive innocence—"'They were only war casualities,' he said. 'It was a pity, but you can't always hit your target. Anyway they died in the right cause.'"—is contiguous to the other forces that produce a Colonel North and let him blunder about the world with missionary zest, serving his country and fulfilling its manifest destiny with the fanaticism of a good conscience. In such a context, America's axiomatic mission seems appalling, and the conviction of manifest destiny an outrage. Surely there is sufficient evidence that there are millions of people in the world who don't want to become middle-class American Democrats or Republicans?

V.

And yet if we look at these matters from a slightly different angle, we have to qualify our sense of them. If you were to read American literature, knowing nothing further about American habits and sentiments, you would conclude that the culture it arises from is radically divided, that "the power of blackness" is incorrigible. But if you looked at the general culture, so far as that is visible, you would think it to a remarkable degree homogeneous. You would report that the Puritan fathers established a form of life in the middling way, free of social exorbitance either of the aristocratic or of the popular kind. You would also report that the middling way is still the accepted paradigm of American life. Indeed, your sense of the paradigm would be so strong that you would read the literature again and decide that its blackness was notional, a metaphysical footnote to social values universally accepted, a dissenting scruple within consent. I don't dispute the American provenance of the sentiments represented by such phrases as "beyond culture" and "a world elsewhere." They accurately describe the literature. But the adversary culture they denote now seems, looked at aslant, a nuance of the dominant culture rather than a repudiation of it. It is odd that everything we think of as "Emersonian" is compatible with expansionist metaphors, the figures of capacity and possession, in the society Emerson addressed. His essays may be read not as providing a better alternative to capitalism but as showing how the figures and sentiments of capitalism may be internalized. Property is real estate, but it may also be a sentiment, a mode of one's subjectivity, and remain compatible with real estate. This is as true of Frost and Stevens as it is of Emerson and Whitman. Think of their metaphors—of outer and inner weather, land and landscape, of building a house to live in and escape from and come back to: what we are mostly aware of is the continuity between such figures and their internal or subjective enlargements.

What we keep coming back to, as to a motive of explanatory force, is the sentiment of America. It has often been treated with irony—"America the Beautiful," "The American Dream"—and often as the value that goes beyond irony and makes the sardonic sense of life feel ashamed of itself.

VI.

To represent the idea of America, the irony to which it is vulnerable, and the sentiment that in turn receives the irony and survives

it, I can't think of a writer more winning than F. Scott Fitzgerald—unless perhaps the Hart Crane of "Voyages II," "The
seal's wide spindrift gaze toward paradise"—nor can I quote, as
every student of American culture has quoted, a passage more
eloquently just to that idea than the ending of *The Great Gatsby*.
Nick has come down to the beach to take a last look at the houses
and to think of Gatsby's dream:

> Most of the big shore places were closed now and there were
> hardly any lights except the shadowy, moving glow of a ferry-
> boat across the Sound. And as the moon rose higher the ines-
> sential houses began to melt away until gradually I became
> aware of the old island here that flowered once for Dutch
> sailors' eyes—a fresh, green breast of the new world. Its van-
> ished trees, the trees that had made way for Gatsby's house,
> had once pandered in whispers to the last and greatest of all
> human dreams; for a transitory enchanted moment man must
> have held his breath in the presence of this continent, com-
> pelled into an aesthetic contemplation he neither understood
> nor desired, face to face for the last time in history with some-
> thing commensurate to his capacity for wonder.[11]

The sense of wonder needs to be provoked by an object, but
to keep itself going or to hold itself steady thereafter, the object is
not needed; all the better if it recedes. In that mood the mind
fancies that it is in harmony with the principle of things—and not
merely with things, but with the principle, of which the things are
mere particles. In this, wonder differs from analysis, it lifts its
eyes beyond the object to the life that no object can do more than
annotate. Nick, looking at the landscape, removes its constituents—the inessential houses—so that he may imagine it afresh.
He turns the island into an imagined thing, displacing the thing
that might otherwise be merely reported or transcribed. Imagining it in the light of a larger perspective—"as the moon rose
higher"—he peoples it with Dutch sailors, their eyes filled with
wonder continuous with his own. The trees whisper to the sailors,
of girls, the landscape flowing, flowering, receptive. But lest the
vision remain too Gauguinesque, "pandered" keeps us mindful of
the other part of the dream, the serpent in this garden: it can only
be historical time. For the moment, the scene is given over to
beginnings, long before the Puritans arrived with their consciences girded for battle. It is a "style of distance," the detail held

at poise—"man must have held his breath"—the art of the picture rather than that of the picturesque. But the beginning is not exempted from history. Before the paragraph is finished, Nick's mind changes its perspective again. The enchanted moment, "face to face," yields "for the last time in history." He means, I assume, that man's dream must be transposed from history to myth, if the sentiment of presence and the capacity for wonder are to be renewed. Myth, like the idea of America, is a form within history, but because it is an idea it is not entirely subject to temporal process, it may be recovered at any time whenever the desire for it is renewed.

Meanwhile it is a real question whether the idea of America is more safely entrusted to the future, Gatsby's "orgiastic future that year by year recedes before us," as Nick puts it, or to a past at once historical and inaugural. *The Great Gatsby* ends upon that issue: the future recedes before us, "so we beat on, boats against the current, borne back ceaselessly into the past"; the heroism consists in the desire and not in any fulfilment that succeeds desire. Fitzgerald, too, looks back to Emerson, particularly to the "original relation to the universe" that Emerson proposed—an emblem to which no missionary or millennial destiny necessarily corresponds.

But Fitzgerald's paragraph has, I think, something more to say to us. It may help us to bring together, or to hold usefully apart, two motives in American culture that I have not been able to reconcile. Let me try again.

The passage I've quoted from *The Great Gatsby* projects a landscape and a sense of wonder which it provoked; or, alternatively, a sense of wonder and a landscape that gratified it. There is no need to choose between these emphases. Fitzgerald's sense of the past accords with the modern conception of history as "a recapitulation of a probable past in a merely mental present."[12] It is the merely mental character of the posited present, in language, that gives him the boon of constituting a secondary world of freedom. The freedom is relative to social and otherwise terrestrial constraint, but it is no poorer for that consideration. On each side of the scene, another set of values may be supposed, if only upon the absence of them. On one side, a sensory image, what the Dutch sailors merely saw before seeing the wonder of it. On the other, there is the meaning of the image, after the wonder of it, the meaning as a permanent possession of any American mind capable of apprehending it. It is not fanciful to posit a gap, as if spatial and temporal, between the image and its meaning. Erich Auerbach has shown, in his *Mimesis*, that the Old Testament was often placed in an exegetic context that "removed the thing told very far from its sensory base, in that the reader or listener was forced to turn his attention away from the sensory occurrence and toward its meaning."[13] Not only would the meaning be found later than the sensory image, and in other places, but it would be involved in quite different needs and discourses. It would be possible to manage the image according to one discourse, and project its meaning upon another plane and according to a different structure of discourse.

If this is feasible, then American culture could proceed with two apparently separate discourses. One of them would involve a commitment to the sensory image, the local conditions, seen without wonder. We may call this motive Franklinism, but it would be just as reasonable to call it Pragmatism, and think of William James, John Dewey, and their successors. Its discourse would happily deploy the words of action, work, betterment, commerce, communications. The projection of meanings at a distance from the sensory image would suggest not only American Transcendentalism but every effort to find a "place" for meanings chiefly sustained by the desire of them and the linguistic concession that makes them at least notionally accessible. The first motive would point to daily transactions and their diverse apprehension in realism and naturalism; the second to the tradition from Emerson to Stevens according to which, whatever else is sacrificed, it is never the imagination or its projected meaning. The gap between image and meaning would also offer the dangerous possibility of bringing them together in the same necessarily equivocal scene, as in Hawthorne's pages of twilight. The reason why *The Scarlet Letter* and *The House of the Seven Gables* seem, in one mood, the work of the devil is that they are understandable only as obscure commentaries on naively progressive texts of commerce and communication. It is because Hawthorne brings together images and meanings that his culture tactically holds apart that he seems infernal. More commonly, American culture holds apart the motives we describe by such phrases as "within culture" and "beyond culture," "the ordinary world" and "a world elsewhere." By holding them apart, it can then engage in tolerable relations between different motives. What is sinister in Hawthorne is that his fictions incriminate history and myth, events and meanings, images and their phosphorescent afterlife among needs they never had to recognize.

VII.

So where are we? Hawthorne is the dark side of Fitzgerald's moon, prophet of a sternly un-Dutch interior. More than any other American writer, he impels us to question the millennial destiny, or at least to glance at the ways in which it has been questioned.

It must be a cursory glance, but nearly everything that may be said by way of rebuke to the destiny claimed has been implied by F. R. Leavis, especially in his allusion to "the vision of our imminent tomorrow in today's America: the energy, the triumphant technology, the productivity, the high standard of living and the life-impoverishment."[14] Leavis didn't subject his sense of America to any sustained experience of visiting it: he assumed that it was well enough described as the extreme form of what he denounced as technologico-Benthamite culture. He thought it appalling that England should become, as it showed every intention of becoming, "just a province of the American world." He conceived, too, what I can only regard as a wild fancy, that if England were to defeat the processes of "Americanization," America itself would turn back from its dreadful course: "hope of salvation for America depends upon our success in the creative battle here, where we can still open it, and wage it, and resolve to win (or not to lose)." It is hard to know, reading such sentences, where to begin to comment on them; perhaps with a "yes, but . . . ," the "but" just as assertive as the "yes."

Another way of dealing with the millennial motive is to claim that it is, in any case, premature; we don't even know what form the remaining years of the century will take. It is quite possible that developments in Japan, China, and Russia will modify the American agenda to the point at which the visionary afflatus will appear absurd. In the meantime I find congenial a passage in *The Consequences of Pragmatism* in which Richard Rorty praises Santayana for avoiding the conviction "that America is what history has been leading up to, and thus that it is up to American philosophy to express the American genius, to describe a virtue as uniquely ours as our redwoods and our rattlesnakes." American philosophy, according to Rorty, has not taught "that the combination of American institutions and the scientific method would produce the Good Life for Man." Besides:

> There is no reason to think that the promise of American democracy will find its final fulfilment in America, any more than Roman law reached its fulfilment in the Roman Empire or literary culture its fulfilment in Alexandria. . . . Even if, through some unbelievable stroke of fortune, America survives with its freedoms intact and becomes a rallying point for the nations, the high culture of an unfragmented world need not center around anything specifically American. It may not, indeed, *center* around anything more than anything else: neither poetry, nor social institutions, nor depth psychology, nor novels, nor philosophy, nor physical science. It may be a culture which is transcendentalist through and through, whose center is everywhere and circumference nowhere.[15]

The irony that Rorty affixes to the "Good Life for Man" is fully justified: something has been achieved if a more modest aim is sought, according to un-Promethean auspices. The right note is sounded, I think, by the title of Kenneth Burke's novel, which opts for one step at a time: specifically, *Towards a Better Life.*

Notes

1. Quoted in Ernest Lee Tuveson, *Redeemer Nation: The Idea of America's Millenial Role* (Chicago: University of Chicago Press, 1968), p. 25.

2. Andrew Burnaby, "Travels in the Middle Settlements in North America in the Years 1759 and 1760," quoted in Tuveson, p. 101.

3. Henry James, *William Wetmore Story and His Friends* (London: Thames and Hudson, 1903), p. 209.

4. George Santayana, *Selected Critical Writings*, ed. Norman Henfrey (Cambridge: Cambridge University Press, 1968), 1:50.

5. Ezra Pound, *Selected Prose 1909–1965*, ed. William Cookson (London: Faber and Faber, 1973), p. 117.

6. Alexis de Tocqueville, *Democracy in America* (New York: Modern Library, 1945), p. 371.

7. Lionel Trilling, *The Liberal Imagination* (New York: Harcourt Brace Jovanovich, 1978), p. 12.

8. Richard Poirier, *A World Elsewhere* (New York: Oxford University Press, 1966), p. 40.

9. Lionel Trilling, *Beyond Culture* (New York: Harcourt Brace Jovanovich, 1965), preface.

10. Wallace Stevens, *Collected Poems* (London: Faber and Faber, 1955), p. 217.

11. F. Scott Fitzgerald, *The Great Gatsby* (London: Bodley Head, 1958), pp. 268-69.

12. Jonathan Bishop, *The Covenant: A Reading* (Springfield, Ill.: Templegate, 1982), p. 32.

13. Erich Auerbach, *Mimesis: The Representation of Reality in Western Literature*, trans. Willard R. Trask (Princeton: Princeton University Press, 1953), p. 48.

14. F. R. Leavis, *Nor Shall My Sword: Discourses on Pluralism, Compassion and Social Hope* (London: Chatto & Windus, 1972), pp. 60, 133.

15. Richard Rorty, *The Consequences of Pragmatism* (Minneapolis: University of Minnesota Press, 1982), pp. 69-70.

꙾꙾꙾

Dreams of Perfectibility: American Exceptionalism and the Search for a Moral Foreign Policy

JAMES CHACE

Not so long before Ronald Reagan's fall from political grace, the president boldly defined the kind of foreign policy Americans have traditionally wanted to believe in. "The ultimate goal of American foreign policy," he said, "is not just the prevention of war but the extension of freedom—to see that every nation, every person someday enjoys the blessings of liberty."[1] It was a characteristically American desire uttered by a man who had made it his mission to restore American pride and power. Within a few months, however, the moral foundations of his foreign policy were shown to be hollow. To treat with an authoritarian regime, seemingly committed to terrorism as an arm of its foreign policy, in order to assist what the president called "freedom fighters"—as was the case when the Reagan administration sold arms to the Iranians and with the proceeds financed the rebels fighting the Sandinistas in Nicaragua—falsifies any reasonable connection between the requirements of national security and the desire to spread the blessings of democracy.

Americans are, after all, most comfortable with a foreign policy imbued with moral purpose. Even when the pursuit of justice has led to unintended consequences, even when our ideals have concealed from ourselves as well as from others motivations of a darker and more complex nature, we have preferred a policy that at least rhetorically is based on moral purpose rather than self-interest. For almost a half-century now, the American mission has been to protect the world against the threat of communism or, in its modest moments, against the threat of Soviet expansionism.

In perhaps the most recent incarnation of this mission, President Reagan, in his State of the Union message of February 1985, said that the United States must support freedom fighters from Nicaragua to Afghanistan. To meet the threat to America's global interests, the Reagan administration even devised a doctrine that was supposed to do more than contain the Soviet Union—"the focus of evil in the modern world"[2]—it sought to roll back the Soviet threat, in both its ideological and geopolitical expressions.

The innovation of the Reagan Doctrine, according to one of its most articulate supporters, was its intent to reverse the trend toward "Soviet acquisitions (albeit only at the periphery, where there is no threat of general war)." But this was only part of a larger vision of America's role in the world: "The elements are simple: Anticommunist revolution as a tactic. Containment as the strategy. And freedom as the rationale."[3]

The notion of America as a crusading force for freedom—a recurrent motif in American foreign policy—had been noticeably absent when the Vietnam War was drawing to a close. The Nixon Doctrine promised only that America would use surrogates (such as Iran) to police regions deemed vital to American interests (such as the Persian Gulf). Otherwise, President Nixon and his foreign-policy adviser Henry Kissinger preferred to avoid moral issues in favor of a policy of *Realpolitik* that lay largely outside the American tradition. At least partly in response to the amorality of power politics, President Carter was elected as a man who wanted to give foreign policy a moral thrust. America, he said, had a "historical birthright" to promote political freedom worldwide, and in particular to encourage the growth of democracy in the Third World.

The Reagan Doctrine, however, with its emphasis on anti-communism and intervention, harked back to an earlier phase of the Cold War, when the postwar realists, while rejecting spheres of influence, were prepared to weld Wilsonian idealism to American power. For President Truman and Dean Acheson, perhaps the most gifted secretary of state since John Quincy Adams, realism implied the measured use of power to implement American idealism. The containment of the Soviet Union, originally designed for Europe, was such a policy: the Truman Doctrine in 1947 promised military and economic aid only to Greece and Turkey. But it contained dangerously ambiguous phrasing that called up the specter of an overweening moral crusade—that the United States should "support free peoples who are resisting subjugations by armed minorities or by outside pressures."

To secure congressional support for the emergency aid, Truman felt compelled to invoke the rhetoric of the spreading danger of communism worldwide instead of emphasizing the more limited aim of American intervention in the eastern Mediterranean as necessary to the regional balance of power after British withdrawal. It was Acheson, after all, who, when briefing congressional leaders prior to Truman's speech, used the troubles in Greece to evoke the global danger to the United States of the Soviet expansionism. "These congressmen had no conception of what challenged them," Acheson explains in his memoirs, "it was my task to bring it home." He then went on to paint a stark picture of what might happen, first in the eastern Mediterranean, and then worldwide, saying that America's failure to act

> might open three continents to Soviet penetration. Like apples in a barrel infected by one rotten one, the corruption in Greece would infect Iran and all to the east. It would carry infection to Africa through Asia Minor and Egypt, and to Europe through Italy and France, already threatened by the strongest domestic Communist parties in Western Europe. The Soviet Union was playing one of the greatest gambles in history at minimal cost.[4]

Acheson was in fact wary of any overextension of American power; it was not until the North Koreans crossed the thirty-eighth parallel that he fully embraced the need for the United States to make a global response to what Truman and he perceived as Soviet expansionism.[5]

The universalist concept of American purpose and power was spelled out more fully ten years after the Truman Doctrine in the Eisenhower Doctrine. Ostensibly designed to deal with instability in the Middle East after the failure of the Anglo-French expedition to restore Western control of the Suez Canal, the new doctrine enlarged the American commitment to contain not only communist power but to maintain the status quo in any nation even indirectly threatened by communism. Not only would economic aid be granted; so would American forces, "to secure and protect the territorial integrity and political independence of such nations requesting such aid against overt aggression from any country controlled by Communism." Throughout the Eisenhower years an almost Manichean view of the world as a struggle between the forces of good and evil, between freedom and totalitarianism—or what was called the Free World and international Communism—prevailed. It was universalism run rampant. The existence of evil had rarely been so clearly identified, along with the existence of an American morality whiter than white.[6]

Throughout the Cold War, then, the mission of the United States had been that of both crusader and exemplar.[7] As a crusader America had tried to roll back communism—militarily in Korea when Truman and Acheson allowed General Douglas MacArthur to cross the thirty-eighth parallel and strike north into North Korea in an effort to unify the country; rhetorically under Eisenhower and Dulles, when the Soviet-bloc nations of Eastern Europe were led to believe that the United States would intervene to aid them in escaping Soviet control; both rhetorically and militarily under Reagan, as the United States sought to arm anticommunist guerrillas in Asia, Africa, and Latin America. (In Vietnam, our most tragic war, rollback was never even contemplated; instead, a classic policy of containment was tried, but in a region of only marginal strategic importance and in support of an ally whose domestic base was fatally weak.)

Historically, America has generally fulfilled her mission as a crusader for freedom by acting alone. But whether as simply the champion of freedom in a benighted and sinful world, or as an activist seeking to make the world safe for democracy, America has viewed herself as exceptional, ordained to play a singular role in world affairs—and never more so than today.

IT WAS ALEXANDER HAMILTON who warned us to reject "idle theories which have amused us with promises of an exception from the imperfection, weaknesses and evils incident to society in every shape." He asked in *The Federalist*: "Is it not time to awaken from the deceitful dream of a golden age and to adopt as a practical maxim for the direction of our political conduct that we, as well as the other inhabitants of the globe, are yet remote from the happy empire of perfect wisdom and perfect virtue?"[8] But Hamilton was not heeded. Instead, America was deemed an extraordinary nation—"an asylum for mankind," as Thomas Paine wrote in *Common Sense*.

In the view of Arthur Schlesinger, Jr., the Founding Fathers stressed the fragility of the new nation—"the idea of America as an experiment, undertaken in defiance of history, fraught with risk, problematic in outcome."[9] It was an understanding that did not endure. After the War of 1812, a new nationalism swept the land. If it was not the view of the Founding Fathers that moral values should play the controlling role in determining American foreign policy, in Schlesinger's view, in the century after 1815 Americans "stopped thinking about power as the essence of international politics. The moralization of foreign policy became a national penchant, nor did the subsequent return of the republic to the world power game much enfeeble that cherished habit."[10]

America's was to be a unique destiny. In the year 1796, according to Henry Adams's history of the Jefferson administration, the House of Representatives debated whether to insert in the Reply to President Washington the assertion that the United States was "the freest and most enlightened [nation] in the world."[11] As Adams describes Jefferson's idea of the American mission, the third American president

> aspired beyond the ambition of nationality, and embraced in his view the whole future of man. That the United States should become a nation like France, England, or Russia, should conquer the world like Rome, or develop a typical race like the Chinese, was no part of his scheme. He wished to begin a new era.

Hoping for a time when the world's ruling interests should cease to be local and should become universal. . . . he set himself to the task of governing, with this golden age in view.[12]

No one celebrated Jefferson's vision of a new era more tellingly than Ralph Waldo Emerson. He called himself "a seeker with no Past at his back."[13] In his essay "The Young American," Emerson strikes at the heart of the matter: "After all the deduction is made for our frivolities and insanities, there still remains [in America] an organic simplicity and liberty . . . not known to any other region."[14]

The critique of American perfectibility was not long in coming; it came not in political discourse but in the writings of the classic American novelists, most notably Nathaniel Hawthorne and Herman Melville. In the rising nationalist fervor that swept Americans forward in an expansionist drive that would yield them a continent, political rhetoric—even when harshly critical of expansionism, as it sometimes was during the Mexican War—did not question the American aspiration to liberty for all peoples. The means, not the ends, were the issue. But the artist had no such mission, and it was the artist who perceived the darker side of the American dream. In "The Birthmark," Hawthorne describes the single blemish that seems to disturb the beauty of the wife of the scientist Aylmer. The mark itself is in the shape of a small red hand against her pale skin, a symbol of his wife's liability "to sin, sorrow, decay, and death." These very characteristics are, of course, the signs of mortality. But Aylmer cannot accept them. In trying to enforce man's control over nature, he gives his wife a potion he has invented to remove the flaw. The experiment appears to succeed, for the birthmark fades away. Her beauty is perfect. But she is dead.

Unlike Hawthorne, Melville first appears as the quintessential American man of action, the man who exists outside history. "We are the pioneers of the world," he proclaims in *White-Jacket*, "the advance guard set on through the wilderness of untried things, to break a path in the New World that is ours." He is attracted by the happiness of an Eden, glimpsed for the first time in the South Sea islands he visited as a sailor. But later his tales darken. In "Benito Cereno," an American sea captain, Amasa Delano, comes upon a drifting Spanish slave ship and, innocently, boards it to help. What he does not realize is that the captain,

Benito Cereno, has been made captive by the slaves, who have revolted and seized the ship. When Delano himself is threatened by the slaves, he asks in wonderment: "But who would want to kill Amasa Delano?" Unwittingly, he has been drawn into the evils of the Old World. Experience, in the guise of the Spanish sea captain, is akin to corruption; the revolt of the slaves is compared to a rush from darkness into light. Yet, paradoxically, that revolt threatens the American's life.[15]

By middle age Emerson himself doubted the redeeming value of the American newness. In "Experience," published in 1844, he comes to resemble Hawthorne: "It is very unhappy, but too late to be helped, the discovery we have made, that we exist. That discovery is called the Fall of Man."[16]

∽∾

THE WARNING AGAINST the search for perfection in an imperfect world never became part of the rhetoric of American foreign policy. It was, after all, a policy that was singularly successful. It ensured American security from the Atlantic to the Pacific and seemed bent on removing all threats to the vulnerable new Republic. A literature in any way tending to subvert the extraordinary freedom of action we had in pursuing America's exceptional destiny was necessarily disregarded—except when read as tales of adventure and gothic mystery. It was, of course, a freedom made possible by America's geographical apartness from the great powers. The new nation, as Jefferson described her, was "separated by nature and a wide ocean from the exterminating havoc of one quarter of the globe."[17] But these blessings did not lead to an isolationist America. On the contrary, the advice of Washington and Jefferson to avoid entangling alliances allowed the new nation to act unilaterally in pursuing an activist role in the Western Hemisphere, even when this risked war with England and Spain. And in the period of American expansion overseas, the ideology of American righteousness was able to be spread far more easily throughout the globe as long as America was unencumbered by powerful allies who might actually question American exceptionalism.

Moreover, the American democratizing mission, whether in the guise of America as crusader or as exemplar (echoing John Quincy Adams's words urging the nation to be "the well-wisher to the freedom and independence of all"), was a role other nations might both envy and wish to destroy.[18] In preserving American exceptionalism, then, the chief executive was duty bound to ensure American security from foreign threats. Jefferson was well aware of the vulnerability of the new nation. For that reason he was prepared in 1802 to "marry ourselves to the British fleet and nation," on the day "that France takes possession of New Orleans."[19]

"The essence of genius of Jefferson's statesmanship," Henry Adams wrote at the end of the nineteenth century, "lay in peace."[20] By securing—peacefully—Louisiana from France, Jefferson helped provide for the security of the United States. He did it without war, though he was willing to risk war. "Peace is our passion," Jefferson said, "and wrongs might drive us from it. We prefer trying *every* other just principle, right and safety, before we would recur to war."[21]

John Quincy Adams, like Jefferson, was a man who believed that America stood as an exemplar of freedom. Like Jefferson, he was also a leading expansionist. He may have been skeptical of whether other nations, particularly those of Latin America, were capable of enjoying the blessings of liberty as they were enjoyed in the United States—but he was certain that America had a unique destiny to fulfill.

The expansion of the United States across the continent, first through the efforts of Jefferson and John Quincy Adams, and later at the expense of Mexico, was firmly linked to the notion of the American destiny as a moral absolute. But that same special quality of the American nation and society—the result of enlightened government, an extraordinary geographical position, and a wealth of natural resources—also appeared to make the United States an obvious target for the world's aggressive or subversive forces. The Monroe Doctrine may have been made possible by the British fleet, and it may have been designed ostensibly to protect American shores against French, Russian, and Spanish power, but the fact remains that American governments were deeply troubled by British power. Even though England was a liberal, parliamentary state, her imperial ambitions seemed to threaten not only American territorial integrity but also the American democratizing mission itself.

By World War I, the United States had extended the boundaries of her interests to the far Pacific. The acquisition of the Philippines not only prevented the islands from falling into the hands of a foreign power but also achieved a missionary goal. So cruel, however, was the American occupation of the islands, with perhaps as many as 200,000 Filipino lives lost, that our behavior there seemed, if anything, to contradict America's sacred duty. The philosopher William James, saddened and angry, wrote a passionate condemnation of what America had done.

> There are worse things than financial troubles in a Nation's career. To puke up its ancient soul, and the only things that gave it eminence among other nations, in five minutes without a wink of squeamishness is worse; and that is what the Republicans would commit us to in the Philippines. Our conduct there has been one protracted lie towards ourselves.[22]

Public opinion had its intended effect on our subsequent interventions in the Western Hemisphere. Never again was our behavior so iniquitous as it had been in the Philippines.

A new kind of nationalism seemed to be needed after the excesses of the Spanish-American War, a nationalism that would turn Americans away from the seductions of empire, so reminiscent of the vices of the Old World, and toward the task of renovating the Republic of democratic dreams. The new spirit of patriotism was best summed up in 1909 by Herbert Croly, later editor of the *New Republic*, in *The Promise of American Life*. Croly, who also believed in a policy of economic independence for the common man, thought that there was "every reason why the American democracy should become in sentiment and conviction frankly, unscrupulously and loyally nationalist." Walter Lippmann, in *Drift and Mastery*, published on the eve of the First World War, spoke of an American patriotism that would come to mean "love of country and not hatred of other countries."[23]

Even Woodrow Wilson's invasion of Mexico in 1914 was done not in the name of empire, but rather to impose a government sympathetic to the United States, preferably a democratic government. Wilson was also wary of interference by European powers in Mexico's affairs and was prepared to act unilaterally to protect American interests that might be so threatened. When he learned that a German freighter laden with armaments was prepared to land in the Mexican port of Vera Cruz, he sent American marines to occupy the city—without congressional authority. It was the ironic paradox of Wilson's foreign policy that only by interfering in the affairs of other nations could the United States wage its campaign for self-determination for all peoples.

Wilson's zeal to spread the blessings of democracy provided America with a truly global role. When Americans entered the First World War, they did so not only to protect their physical security from the menace of the German empire but also, in Wilson's words, "as the disinterested champions of right." And when Wilson sat down with his allies at Versailles after the victory, he was convinced that America's new global responsibilities had come "by no plan of our conceiving, but by the hand of God who led us in this way." In his desire not to redress the balance of the Old World but to remake it, he bore with him the principle of self-determination and the covenant of the League of Nations. The American flag, as he put it, was "the flag not only of America but of humanity."[24]

Unable to compromise with his domestic opponents over the issue of American participation in the League of Nations, Wilson remained convinced of the unique mission of the United States. In his last speech, made in 1919 when he was urging ratification of the League by the Senate, he spoke of the American soldiers who had died crusading for a new world of democratic nations:

> I wish sane men in public life who are now opposing the settlement for which these men died . . . could feel the moral obligation that rests upon us not to go back on those boys, but to see the thing through, to see it through to the end and make good their redemption of the world. For nothing less depends on this decision, nothing less than the liberation and salvation of the world.[25]

The Senate, of course, refused to ratify the League.

Paradoxically, Wilson and his isolationist antagonists shared the desire to avoid the iniquitous old system of the balance of power as devised by the Europeans and as practiced by Clemenceau's France. And America's encounter with Europe on the battlefront and at the conference table only strengthened the conviction of America's exceptional destiny. The interwar period was not, strictly speaking, one of American isolationism—except for participating in the security systems of Europe. We used troops in Guatemala, Honduras, Nicaragua, the Dominican Republic, and Haiti. But as European penetration was no longer a threat to the region, the United States moved to withdraw its troops and settled instead for a policy of using local forces to maintain order—and American hegemony. At the same time, clothed in moral righteousness, Americans were only too ready to sign international agreements as long as they were couched, like the Kellogg-Briand peace pact, in idealistic terms.

It was not until the election of Franklin Delano Roosevelt that the country found a president who combined the idealistic aspirations of the Founding Fathers to create a republic of virtue and their realistic appraisal of the need to seek temporary alliances to ensure our security. Like Hamilton, Roosevelt counseled against the dangers of exceptionalism: "Perfectionism, no less than isolationism or imperialism or power politics, may obstruct the paths to international peace."[26] Like Hamilton's, his warnings were largely disregarded after the Second World War was won.

THROUGHOUT THE YEARS of the Cold War, the notion of America as a crusader, as a force for freedom, seems to have become engraved on the national consciousness. But spreading freedom, if it is to be America's peculiar destiny, is likely to be a lonely task. America's allies have not shared her missionary zeal to roll back communism. They see America's obsession with spreading democracy in the Western Hemisphere, particularly in the Caribbean and in Central America, as a traditional great-power concern to preserve a sphere of influence. They prefer a policy of detente with the Soviet Union in Europe. Except toward their former colonies in Africa, they remain generally disinterested in the ideological struggles of the Third World. It is likely, then, that the United States will continue to pursue a largely unilateral course as it strives to fulfill its singular missionary role.

In extending the perimeter of its security interests far beyond the reaches of this hemisphere, however, the United States will find that any crusade for freedom will sorely test its moral, to say nothing of its physical, resources. For example, the need to treat with dictators in order to further American interests has always been difficult to reconcile with America's democratizing mission. It seems undeniable that in the long term American interests are far more likely to be advanced by supporting democracies than by supporting dictatorships. Nonetheless, the national interest has often required that America aid regimes that are distasteful, or even ultimately dangerous—most notably during the Second World War, when we were allied to the Soviet Union.

To suggest that the United States temper its missionary zeal is not to say that America should abandon itself to a foreign policy devoid of moral concern. This was the policy Henry Kissinger and Richard Nixon followed to a great extent—a Bismarckian foreign policy that relied on manipulating the balance of power. It aimed to deal with our adversaries without imposing moral structures, without self-righteousness, and without moral demands. But despite the short-term successes of Nixon and Kissinger, the question inevitably arose: Could the United States build a domestic base for its foreign policy unless such a policy contained a fair measure of moralistic zeal? The answer, supplied by both Jimmy Carter and Ronald Reagan, was no.

The deepening crisis in American foreign policy, then, stems from our inability to balance the pursuit of the national interest, wherever that may lead, with the democratizing mission. No American foreign policy can succeed without such a balance. But we must beware of mounting quixotic crusades to make the world safe for democracy and, in so doing, finding ourselves isolated in a hostile world. We come back once again to Hamilton, who urged a policy for nations that was not "absolutely selfish," but rather "a policy regulated by their own interest, as far as justice and good faith permit."[27] Justice and good faith are not drawn from dreams of perfectibility. They are instead the practical goals of a realistic American mission.

Notes

1. *New York Times*, Oct. 7, 1986, p. A12.

2. Speech in Orlando, Fla., March 8, 1983.

3. See Charles Krauthammer, "The Poverty of Realism," *New Republic*, Feb. 17, 1986, p. 16.

4. Dean Acheson, *Present at the Creation* (New York: Norton, 1969), p. 219.

5. See Harry S. Truman, *Years of Trial and Hope*, vol. 2 of *Memoirs* (Garden City, N.Y.: Doubleday, 1956), p. 403.

6. See James Chace, "American Jingoism," *Harper's*, May 1976, pp. 37–44.

7. See Robert W. Tucker, "Exemplar or Crusader? Reflections on America's Role," *National Interest*, no. 5 (Fall 1986), pp. 64–75.

8. *Federalist*, no. 6.

9. Arthur Schlesinger, Jr., "The Theory of America: Experiment or Destiny?" in *The Cycles of American History* (Boston: Houghton Mifflin, 1986), p. 12.

10. Schlesinger, "National Interest and Moral Absolutes," in *The Cycles of American History*, p. 70.

11. Henry Adams, *History of the United States of America during the Administrations of Thomas Jefferson* (New York: Library of America, 1986), p. 108.

12. Adams, p. 101.

13. See Irving Howe, *The American Newness* (Cambridge, Mass.: Harvard University Press, 1986), p. 22.

14. Ralph Waldo Emerson, "The Young American," in *Essays and Sketches* (New York: Library of America, 1983), p. 228.

15. See James Chace, "How Moral Can We Get?" *New York Times Magazine*, May 27, 1977, pp. 38, 40.

16. Emerson, "Experience," in *Essays and Sketches*, p. 487.

17. Jefferson citation in S. E. Morison and H. S. Commager, *The Growth of the American Republic* (New York: Oxford University Press, 1940), 1:320.

18. See Tucker, p. 64; see also Philip Geyelin, "The Adams Doctrine and the Dream of Disengagement," in *Estrangement*, ed. Sanford Ungar (New York: Oxford University Press, 1985), p. 219.

19. Jefferson to Robert Livingston, April 18, 1802; quoted in Adams, p. 277.

20. Adams, p. 299.

21. Jefferson to Sir John Sinclair, June 30, 1803; quoted in Adams, p. 300.

22. William James to Henry Lee Higginson, Sept. 18, 1900; cited in Bliss Perry, *Life and Letters of Henry Lee Higginson* (Boston: Atlantic Monthly Press, 1921), 2:429.

23. See Chace, "American Jingoism," pp. 37–44.

24. *Ibid.*

25. *Ibid.*

26. Franklin D. Roosevelt, State of the Union Address, Jan. 6, 1945, in *The Public Papers and Addresses of Franklin D. Roosevelt, 1944–45 Volume: Victory and the Threshold of Peace* (New York: Harper & Brothers, 1950), p. 498.

27. Alexander Hamilton, Pacificus, no. 4, July 10, 1793.

CRITICAL: (decorative ornament)

Presidents and Nuclear Weapons and Truth: Some Examples, from Roosevelt to Nixon

McGEORGE BUNDY

Nearly fifty years into the nuclear age, people everywhere are still struggling to come to terms with the multiple revolution wrought by the Bomb. Although there is danger of misunderstanding in any approach to the history of those years from the perspective of a single nation, however strong, and a single office, however high, there is also much to be learned from what American presidents have and have not done and said.

Nine presidents have now addressed themselves to the Bomb. None has made a perfect record, but none has wholly failed. Except at Hiroshima and Nagasaki, the weapons have not been used by any country against another, and the exception has more to do with the war it ended than with the Bomb itself. Given the vivid sense of danger created by what happened to those two cities and earlier at Alamogordo, what is most remarkable about the record now before us is that further nuclear warfare has been avoided. Presidents have had their role in that result. There are also less gratifying lessons in the record. Presidents have had a hard time telling the truth about the Bomb, and their failures have had costs.

The first and most reticent of the nuclear presidents was Franklin Roosevelt. The subject came to him as a deep secret, and he kept it that way; indeed, that was one of his three basic decisions. He had accepted the notion of secrecy that came with Albert Einstein's famous letter of 1939, and he strongly reaffirmed the principle on October 9, 1941, when he made his own real decision to press forward. On that day he heard from Vannevar Bush that the ablest scientific judges in Britain and America were now convinced that a workable atomic bomb could be made, quite possibly in time to decide the war. This was information entirely different in its import from the general warning of possibilities that had come from Einstein and led only to slow and wary committee work.

Roosevelt decided at once (1) to go ahead, (2) to do it in the deepest secrecy, and (3) to keep all policy questions under his own control. Bush would press ahead as fast as possible with further analysis, and he understood that if the results were affirmative, he could expect full and immediate approval of the fastest possible program of development and production. Meanwhile, every decision of policy above the level of research and development, indeed every authorization to work on such policy questions, would be reserved to the president himself. To keep it secret, to get it quickly, and to keep all questions of policy firmly in his own hands—all three were fateful decisions. All remained unchanged while Roosevelt lived, and each was a better choice in 1941 than in 1945.

The decisive reason for secrecy in 1941 was as good as it was simple. The most important imperative connected with the possibility of a bomb was that Adolf Hitler must not be the first to have it. That imperative was as obvious to Roosevelt as to the anti-Nazi physicists who persuaded Einstein to write in the first place. It was just as important not to stimulate German nuclear ambition as it was to press forward the American effort. Given the extraordinary energy and prowess in warfare then attributed to Hitler as the master of *Blitzkrieg*, it was entirely natural that men should fear a German bomb. Nuclear fission itself had been discovered in 1938 in a German laboratory. It would have been extraordinarily foolish to make a public challenge to Hitler. Thus at the outset the secrecy of the enormous adventure was entirely justified.

When it was first made, Roosevelt's decision to reserve all questions of policy for himself was equally reasonable. In large part, it was no more than a consequence of the decision to go forward in secret. The undertaking could be kept secret only if it was protected from American public notice, and that required an enterprise shielded from all the ordinary processes of our open democratic society. But military secrets were acceptable in October 1941, and still more so after Pearl Harbor. The project was soon entrusted to the War Department, and the number of those "in the know" was kept as small as possible. If that restriction left broader questions in the hands of just one man, Franklin Roosevelt in October 1941 was more than ready to accept that result. He was totally preoccupied in that season by the enormous task of engaging American strength against aggressors on the march—a task greatly complicated by inescapable public debate. To be able to keep the policy problem of the Bomb in his own pocket must have been a comfort.

In their October meeting Bush proposed a policy committee. Roosevelt accepted the proposal, and the committee was named, but its structure and history showed the President's real preference. Everyone on the six-man committee was already inescapably a part of the secret. Roosevelt and Vice-President Henry Wallace had already been informed, Wallace because Bush had sought him out as the only scientifically literate member of the Cabinet. Henry Stimson and George Marshall, as secretary of war and Army chief of staff, would be involved in any case when the War Department undertook the work, and Vannevar Bush and James Conant were the scientific administrators already responsible both for research and for the basic recommendation to go forward. There were no strangers on the committee, and no one who would fail to understand who was retaining the power to decide.

But what is still more interesting about this committee is that it never met. Bush kept its members informed, but he fully understood that his real boss was the president, and when he needed a decision he got his "OK, FDR" from one man. Roosevelt watched the program develop, worried about it intermittently, talked about it as much alone with Churchill as with any American, and pushed the policy decisions ahead of him just as much as he could. Only the question of relations with London was forced to decision, and the exception did not show the president at his best. What he wanted was what would keep his partner Churchill and his own subordinates content; he did not himself try to understand just what the nuclear relation between London and Washington should be—only that it should be friendly. The final memorandum of agreement that he initialed with Churchill, late in 1944, pledged full postwar cooperation, but he never dared to share it with any of his American advisers.

Wrapped in secrecy and protected by the enormous privilege and power of the president as wartime commander-in-chief, the question of what he would do with the bomb when he got it went unexamined, even while military planning for its use against Japan went forward. In the last six months before Roosevelt's death, Bush and Conant tried repeatedly to bring to life the process of planning for policy after the Bomb became a reality, but their effort broke against the interacting fatigue of Roosevelt and Stimson. When FDR died, the government of the United States had barely scratched the surface of two great questions on which decisions would be forced by the first successful test—the question of wartime use and the question of international cooperation in controlling the new force. There were imperfections in Harry Truman's process of considering these great questions, but one of the largest difficulties he had to face was not of his own making: not only the new president but those around him had to begin from a standing start.

We come back here to secrecy. Weariness at the top and the pressure of other responsibilities were also strong forces, but without the protective power of the secrecy which had become so strong and thick, it would have been impossible to keep the policy questions off the agenda of the American government. The mystique of the secret had gained in power every year, even while the original reason for it was growing weaker. As the American program multiplied in its magnitude and momentum, so it became ever less likely that Hitler was ahead, and by the autumn of 1944 there was decisive evidence of the feeble and fractionated character of the German effort. There was now no overriding danger in a public announcement of the purpose of the Manhattan Project. What made that unthinkable was simply that men had learned to treat the whole enterprise as unmentionable except among those "in the know." The secret was buried too deep to be exposed to thought.

We cannot know how Roosevelt would have handled a process of deliberation that he never allowed, and we have only fragmentary and inconclusive reports of his own opinions. He certainly encouraged Niels Bohr, in their one meeting, to believe that he understood the importance of an approach to the Russians, and he once told Felix Frankfurter that the whole subject "worried him to death," but his talks with Churchill, Stimson, and Bush were all inconclusive. We do know that he fully understood the magnitude of the matter. He made the point himself publicly once in a nationwide radio broadcast on election eve, November 6, 1944:

> [W]e must consider the devastation wrought on the people of England, for example, by the new long-range bombs. Another war would be bound to bring even more devilish and powerful instruments of destruction to wipe out civilian populations. No coastal defense, however strong, could prevent these silent missiles of death, fired perhaps from planes or ships at sea, from crashing deep within the United States itself.

Roosevelt's audience did not know what he was talking about when he spoke of "even more devilish" weapons, but we do. Moreover, the documentary records at Hyde Park make it clear that the language of this passage was his own. We cannot know how a Roosevelt who set himself free from secrecy would have addressed this topic with his countrymen and the world, but it is impossible to avoid a feeling of regret that he never came close to this great task.

HARRY TRUMAN'S LARGEST DECISIONS were made quickly and have since been debated at great length. He never doubted that it was necessary to use the weapon against Japan, and the targets he chose were those recommended by others. He later approved a bold plan for international control, but he also chose not to pursue any real Soviet-American negotiation, and Stalin made the same choice. Truman also moved without hesitation toward the hydrogen bomb in 1949–50, and it appears that no one ever told him of the existence of a chance to hold back that fateful choice by seeking an agreement with Moscow that such devices would never be tested. The point was made at the time in a remarkable paper written by Enrico Fermi and I. I. Rabi, but no one made it to the president. Yet Truman understood from the start that the Bomb was no ordinary weapon, and he firmly sustained Roosevelt's position that decisions about these weapons must be presidential.

Truman's underlying mistake was to believe in the Bomb as an American secret. He never knew of the crucial early contributions of scientists in Britain, and he never understood that the American head start in manufacture conferred no long-term advantage. Truman was himself still instinctively downgrading Russian capabilities when he left office. From 1945 onward he encouraged belief in a great American secret. When the Russians got the Bomb and spies were discovered around Los Alamos, too many Americans too easily believed that the Russians had the Bomb only because they had stolen the secret. Only the president could have prevented that destructive misunderstanding, and because in some degree he shared it, Harry Truman never tried.

WITH DWIGHT EISENHOWER MATTERS BECAME more complex. On the one hand, in October 1953, Eisenhower personally approved a top-secret paper called "Basic National Security Policy" in which it was stated that: "In the event of hostilities, the United States will consider nuclear weapons to be as available for use as other munitions." On the other hand, Eisenhower's personal supervision of all the international crises of his two terms was both intense and cautious, with the result that no such crisis led to the use of nuclear weapons. There were men around Ike who strongly believed in establishing by action the principle that the basic policy paper asserted, but again and again Eisenhower held back from the Bomb—over Korea in 1953, over Vietnam in 1954, over Quemoy and Matsu in 1955 and 1958, over Berlin in 1958-60. What he approved in verbal policy he never approved in practice, and when he left office he had greatly reinforced American understanding that the Bomb was not just another weapon.

Eisenhower also understood and repeatedly tried to explain that in the nuclear arms competition enough was enough. He recognized from the beginning that the one fundamental requirement for American strategic nuclear forces was that they should never be open to destruction by surprise attack. They must always be able to survive and strike back with such power that the surprise attack would never come. This was no small requirement, but neither was it a matter of matching or outmatching every Soviet deployment. Eisenhower regularly resisted those who wanted the United States to have this or that weapons system merely because the Russians might be building it. Once it was said to be bombers, and later ballistic missiles. He had no use for what he called the "numbers game"; he held firmly to the standard that "we need what we need," and in fact his programs for developing new systems were timely and sufficient. Indeed, in gross megatonnage the warheads built in his time were excessive, as he himself, if too slowly, came to understand.

Yet what is remarkable about this prudent and generally successful handling of the American strategic deterrent is that in the heated public discussion of an asserted "missile gap" in Eisenhower's last years, the president allowed himself to be forced into a defensive position in which his efforts to explain and defend his program were generally outmatched by the cries of alarm from men who argued that the Soviet Union was moving decisively into a position of strategic superiority. Eisenhower's failure here was not in what he said but in what he did not say, and it had a double cause. First, he was inhibited by excessive respect for "secrets" about American forces that were not secret from Moscow. The most important such secret was that he was learning about Russian capabilities from U-2 flights, and while Krushchev knew of those flights (and complained about them privately), there were good reasons not to boast about their value before the "secret" was broken by the Soviet shoot-down of May 1, 1960. But Eisenhower was also secretive about other evidence that had no such sensitivity, evidence such as numbers of American weapons and their strength, arrangements ensuring the capacity to survive and reply, and the like.

Ike was also held back by a self-confidence that was both justified and irrelevant to his obligation of democratic leadership. He had a deep-seated belief that his lifelong record as soldier and statesman was itself a sufficient demonstration that he could be trusted. Who had a better capacity for judgment on such questions? Who had as much experience and as much information? Ike believed that there were real secrets here and that no outsider knew as much as he. Most of all, whose *job* was it? Eisenhower never fully accepted the notion that he must somehow demonstrate to the American public the quality of his performance on this most obviously presidential duty.

cₚₗ

JOHN F. KENNEDY, with the energetic and talented help of Robert McNamara, worked hard on the nuclear problem, and I believe he understood it as well as any president of the nuclear age. He understood before he came to office that the Bomb was not at all like other weapons, and he recognized throughout his time that the president who got into a nuclear war would not be happily remembered. His handling of two major crises—over the freedom of West Berlin and Soviet missiles in Cuba—was careful and successful, and eventually Khrushchev accepted from Kennedy the proposal for an Atmospheric Test Ban Treaty that Eisenhower had first put forward in 1959. Kennedy and McNamara understood as clearly as Ike that what was vital was adequate second-strike strength, and from among the many new systems they found under development in 1961 they made excellent choices, strongly reinforcing three systems designed in the 1950s that remain familiar twenty-five years later: land-based missiles, submarine-based missiles, and intercontinental bombers.

Yet there were two important failures in what Kennedy and McNamara said about what they were doing. The first was a continuing insistence that they had reinforced the strategic *superiority* of the United States, and that this achievement was important. Kennedy was probably more at fault here than McNamara. He had taken part in Democratic assertions of a dangerous missile gap, and he was convinced that it was a political imperative to be able to claim first place.

Consider a passage from the very last of his presidential papers—a speech that he would have delivered on the afternoon of November 22, 1963.

> In Fort Worth, I pledged in 1960 to build a national defense which was second to none—a position I said, which is not "first, but," not "first, if," not "first, when," but first—period. That pledge has been fulfilled.

The text goes on to cite the increase in Polaris submarines, the increase in Minuteman missiles, the doubling of the numbers of strategic bombers and missiles on alert, and so on and on, to the conclusion that:

> We can truly say today, with pride in our voices and peace in our hearts, that the defensive forces of the United States are, without a doubt, the most powerful and resourceful forces anywhere in the world.

As a political speech for a Texas audience in 1963 the statement was prudent, and its quantitative claims were not wrong. But what it left out is what Kennedy himself fully understood—that at levels of survivable destructive power long since reached on both sides, there was *no such thing* as nuclear superiority. It is not a matter of pride for those of us who worked in the Kennedy administration that full public recognition of this deep reality had to wait for Richard Nixon. On this point indeed Eisenhower had done better than Kennedy.

There was a second and deeper difficulty in both Kennedy's time and Lyndon Johnson's: the hard question of deciding and explaining just what forces were necessary, and why. Eisenhower had worried in his last years about the thousands of big bombs and the massive plans of attack that his commanders favored, but he had not himself addressed the problem of strategic doctrine except at the elementary but fundamental level of guarding against surprise attack. With Kennedy's encouragement McNamara went further, and by going too far he became the first American leader to reach full understanding of what can and cannot be achieved in a world where both sides insist on having large survivable second-strike forces. McNamara's discovery, and the incompleteness of his public explanation, set in train a debate that still continues. On one side are those who believe in an enduring stalemate between two forces, neither of which can be used against the other without a common catastrophe. This position is strongly contested by people who believe that it is entirely possible for one side to become significantly better than the other in war-fighting capabilities, that such an advantage can be translated into effective blackmail or even strategic victory. Many in this second group came to believe that by the end of the 1970s the Soviet Union was achieving just such a superiority.

McNamara began by accepting the impressive argument of civilian analysts that it was wrong to think of strategic warfare as nothing more than the exchange of annihilating attacks on cities. If nuclear war ever came, the proper first targets would be those most dangerous to one's own forces and people. In the spring of 1962, first to the NATO Council in a secret speech in Athens, and then publicly at commencement in Ann Arbor, McNamara announced that "the principal military objective" in any nuclear war "should be the destruction of the enemy's military forces, not of his civilian population." In shorthand, nuclear strategy should be "counterforce," not "countercities." Additional forces sufficient to destroy the whole society of the enemy could be held in reserve to give any opponent "the strongest imaginable incentive to refrain from striking our own cities." The surface attraction of this new doctrine is apparent, and indeed there is durable truth in it. It is much better to hit military than nonmilitary targets, and it is wise always to have sufficient survivable forces in reserve.

But what McNamara soon discovered was that his new doctrine was generating a military demand for additional weapons and carriers at a level far beyond what he had anticipated. What would be needed to destroy the enemy's forces with any acceptable degree of completeness was very much more than what was needed to be able to make an unacceptably devastating reply to any surprise attack. Even very large additional forces would always leave surviving enemy weapons that could fire back, and even a small number of those would be too many. McNamara also recognized that such an enlarged American build-up would surely drive the Soviet Government to its own further build-up in reply. For the Soviet Union as for the United States the one plainly unacceptable situation would be the one in which an adversary might think himself able to make a first strike so successful that no unacceptably destructive reply need be feared. If the United States should attempt to achieve forces so strong that they could destroy the Soviet deterrent, the Soviets would feel the heaviest compulsion to frustrate that effort. Each side *must* keep its ability to make a devastating reply.

Thus both sides were caught in this situation: whatever might allow Americans to limit Soviet damage to the United States was exactly what might threaten Soviet confidence in Soviet capacity for second-strike destruction. In a secret memorandum to President Johnson at the end of 1964, McNamara put the point forcefully: "Our damage limiting problem is their assured destruction problem, and our assured destruction problem is their damage limiting problem." His own conclusion was clear: the capability for assured destruction was vital to both sides, and however desirable it might be in principle to limit damage from the adversary, there was no chance of achieving a capacity for counterforce attack that could reliably prevent a catastrophic reply. The survival of an assured destruction capability must be the primary criterion for American strategic deployment. Damage limiting was desirable but attainable only in a limited measure; it was therefore secondary.

What McNamara concluded was not at all that cities were better targets, after all, than military installations—he never thought that. Nor did he assert that it was in some way better to destroy than to defend. It was simply that each superpower would always insist on keeping its own capacity for a devastating reply, and it would be very much easier for each side to keep that capacity than for the adversary to take it away. What McNamara was reporting to Johnson was the result of extended and powerful analysis of the realities of the 1960s. Shared vulnerability to assured destruction was a condition, not a doctrine.

That condition has been accepted as the way things really are in every subsequent administration. Belief in this reality was central to the American decision of 1972 to enter the SALT I Treaty, which severely limited strategic defense systems. Even in 1987, in an administration many of whose members had denounced what they mistakenly called the *doctrine* of mutual assured destruction (MAD) for years before they came to power, the reality of the existing situation is admitted. Yet throughout this period it cannot be said that any leader ever fully explained this reality to Americans—not McNamara himself, not the two presidents he served, and not any successor. The condition continued, but the argument about it grew sharp.

As time passed, the shape of complaint shifted. When McNamara moved away from the criterion of having an effective counterforce capability to the criterion of having a survivable capacity for assured destruction, those opposed were mainly military men who believed correctly that the shift would limit their claims for the new weapons that could insure continued American "superiority." But in the 1970s, when believers in strategic defense and in war-fighting capabilities united in a renewed opposition to MAD, what moved them most strongly was a genuine but entirely unjustified fear of an emerging Soviet "superiority."

Lulled by MAD "doctrine," they believed, and falsely supposing that SALT I had made both sides safe, the United States was entering a decade in which it would become decisively number two. Every president from Eisenhower onward had understood that in the age of survivable overkill neither superpower could be effectively ahead in nuclear strength, but not one of them had ever made the case with sufficient strength to overcome the counterattack of the late 1970s that was launched by ardent believers in an imminent Soviet threat, many of them active in a group called the Committee on the Present Danger.

There are many elements in this failure, and a full explanation, even if I knew how to give it, would go far beyond the bounds of this essay. Let me instead remark on the particular contribution made by presidents, and especially by former presidents, to one important element in this continuing misunderstanding, namely the widespread belief that the existence of nuclear armament translates readily into effective atomic diplomacy. One reason for the persistence of this notion among believers in present danger is their susceptibility to what former presidents have claimed. Three in particular, by their later accounts, were successful practitioners of nuclear diplomacy—Truman, Eisenhower, and Nixon.

Truman's principal contribution to the mythology of atomic diplomacy relates to the Soviet withdrawal from northern Iran in 1946. Let me begin with some passages from an account of this case that I wrote some years ago:

> In April 1952 President Harry Truman told an astonished press conference that not long after the end of World War II he had given Joseph Stalin "an ultimatum"—to get his troops out of Iran—and "they got out." [Before the day was over the White House issued a statement saying that the President had not used the word "ultimatum" in its usual diplomatic sense, but what this clarification represents is almost surely damage control by Dean Acheson, not a change of heart by Harry Truman.]
>
> Truman was referring to events in March 1946, when the Soviet Union kept troops in northern Iran after the expiration of an agreed date for British and Russian withdrawal that had been honored by the British. The Soviet stance stirred a vigorous international reaction, and after three weeks of increasing tension there came a Soviet announcement of a decision to withdraw which was executed over the following weeks. Tru-

man never doubted that his messages had been decisive. Out of office, in 1957, he described his action still more vividly: "The Soviet Union persisted in its occupation until I personally saw to it that Stalin was informed that I had given orders to our military chiefs to prepare for the movement of our ground, sea and air forces. Stalin then did what I knew he would do. He moved his troops out." . . .

The only trouble with this picture is that no such message ever went to Stalin and no such orders to American officers. . . . Stalin's was a low-stake venture in an area of persistent Soviet hope. He pulled back when he found the Iranian government firm but not belligerent, his Iranian supporters weak, and the rest of the watching world critical. One of the critics was Harry Truman, and we need not doubt the strength of his feelings. But the messages he actually sent (all now published) were careful and genuinely diplomatic. The United States Government "cannot remain indifferent," and "expresses the earnest hope" of immediate Soviet withdrawal, all "in the spirit of friendly association." There is no deadline and no threat. What we have here is no more than an understandable bit of retrospective braggadocio. . . .

Truman's retrospective version of events was not harmless. Among stouthearted and uncomplicated anticommunists it became a part of the folklore showing that Harry Truman knew how to stop aggression by toughness, when in fact what he and his colleagues knew, in this case, was something much more important: that their task was to help keep up Iranian courage, but precisely *not* to confront Stalin directly. American diplomacy was adroit but not menacing. . . . Truman's messages . . . had expressly avoided the kind of threat he later came to believe he made. So his faulty memory led others to learn the wrong lesson.

Indeed, Truman's tale became still more dramatic as he grew older. In 1980, commenting to *Time* magazine on what *Time's* headline called the Good Old Days, Senator Henry Jackson remembered hearing from Truman that during the Iranian crisis he had summoned Andrei Gromyko to the White House and told him that Soviet troops should evacuate Iran within forty-eight hours—or the United States would use the new bomb that it alone possessed. "We're going to drop it on you," Jackson quoted Truman as saying. "They moved in twenty-four hours." The historical record reveals no connection whatever between this story and reality. All that is real is that Jackson believed it.

DWIGHT EISENHOWER'S PRINCIPAL contribution to the folklore of atomic diplomacy relates to the ending of the war in Korea in 1953. Eisenhower argued in his memoirs that nuclear threats were decisive in this instance, and there is not much doubt that he did in fact intend that a sense of nuclear danger should reach the Chinese government. Unfortunately for the legend, however, the decisive change in Chinese policy toward an armistice agreement came months before the warnings that Eisenhower cites in his own account. The relevant event that in fact precedes the Chinese shift—in which they gave up their long-standing demand that all Chinese prisoners in United Nations hands should be returned by force to Chinese control—is the death of Stalin in early 1953, not later messages from the new American president. There is no reason to doubt that Eisenhower was respected in Peking or that his determination was feared, but it is also clear that Eisenhower remembered matters in a way that does not find support in the record.

I do not intend to suggest by this comment that Eisenhower never practiced atomic diplomacy. What he sounded ready to do if necessary in the defense of Quemoy and Matsu, for example, is of great importance. It may well have prevented the loss of those islands, and it may also have been a powerful stimulus to both the Chinese Bomb and the Sino-Soviet split. But what concerns us here is that what Eisenhower taught about the power of atomic diplomacy was a lesson overstated by the teacher and overlearned by some of his American students.

THE MOST IMPORTANT of these students was Richard Nixon, and what he had to face in his first year as president was that whatever Eisenhower had or had not done with atomic threats in Korea in 1953, Richard Nixon could make no credible nuclear threat over Vietnam in 1969. Against all his initial beliefs and expectations, Nixon was forced to recognize, in the summer of 1969, that a nuclear threat over the continuing war in Vietnam could never be carried out, and that this reality was as clear to the enemy as it was to him. He had come to office believing that he could end the war by following Ike's example. He explained to trusted assistants like H. R. Haldeman that "the threat was the key" and that the Vietnamese must be brought to understand that the new president "has his hand on the nuclear button." Yet as he himself acknowledged years later, he could not use nuclear weapons because of both domestic and foreign opinion. He did deliver what he describes in his memoirs as an "ultimatum" in the summer of 1969, but he also describes that "ultimatum" as a "bluff" that was called by the men in Hanoi.

Yet this initial disappointment did not in fact prevent Nixon from developing his own happy memories of successful atomic diplomacy in other cases. Talking with Roger Rosenblatt of *Time* in the summer of 1985, he remembered three such episodes, and all three are empty boxes. Nixon asserts that the American nuclear alert called near the end of the Yom Kippur war of 1973 was effective in persuading the Soviet government to hold back, but quite aside from the question whether this alert was in fact his own decision—he was absent from the meeting, engulfed in the consequences of his Saturday night massacre over Watergate—Nixon's account neglects the other successful steps taken in the same night, steps to hold back the Israelis and to enlist Sadat himself against the notion of a joint Soviet-American intervention.

The other two cases are feebler still: Nixon asserts that the Americans successfully warned Moscow that they would not tolerate a Soviet attack on China in 1969, but the more careful memoirs of Henry Kissinger make it plain that no such message was sent. Finally, Nixon believes that in the war between India and Pakistan of 1971 he was ready for the nuclear option if necessary. But here he glides by the fact that the crisis he perceived was unreal—there was no Indian plan to destroy all of Pakistan, and there was certainly no American national readiness to use nuclear weapons on that issue. The Nixon administration, taken as a whole, is an almost continuous demonstration of the irrelevance of atomic diplomacy in the age of overkill; we would understand that reality better if Nixon himself did not prefer to paint imagined pictures of the statesman as nuclear chess player.

These vainglorious memories of nonexistent atomic diplomacy are important less for the wrong lessons they may teach to the Henry Jacksons of the world than for the historical realities they tend to obscure. The bomb in reality is a declining political force on the international scene, as indeed Nixon told Rosenblatt. Atomic threats are now unreal in all international disputes that are not truly matters of national life or death to a nuclear power, and if we go by their behavior and not their reminiscences we can see that recent American presidents have understood that reality, as indeed they have both understood and spoken the underlying truth on which it rests. That truth is that nuclear war is plainly a losing game for all concerned.

Back in 1957 Dwight Eisenhower spoke that underlying truth with his own special combination of energy and weariness: "I have told you this time and time again—I repeat it almost in my sleep: there will be no such thing as a victorious side in any global war of the future." Ronald Reagan has made the same thought one step stronger and sharper: "A nuclear war cannot be won and must never be fought." These propositions are not self-evident at all— not to all strategic analysts and not to all strategic plan-makers. They do not always govern the decisions of presidents themselves when they are considering what weapons to recommend and what arms-control proposals to resist. Yet they constitute a starting point from which the president who sets himself to the task can lead Americans to a new level of national understanding and in that process make a signal contribution to the lessening of the nuclear danger with which we are all required to live.

This is an essay in history, not in future prescription, so I do not attempt a platform for a new president. It is enough to say that there is no safe refuge in secrecy, none in the use of the Bomb, and none in refusing to explain. There is no remaining strength in atomic diplomacy and no prospect of usable strategic superiority—not for our Soviet rivals and not for us. On life-and-death matters we must respect each other's interests. The imperative of peaceful coexistence is as clear as the imperative against nuclear adventure. The president who clearly explains this basic reality will by that very act reduce the nuclear danger that is part of that reality and so take a high place among the presidents of the nuclear age, for all of whom, past, present, and future, the first of their responsibilities, always shared with the leaders of the Soviet Union, is that there shall be no nuclear war.

EPILOGUE

A Citizen Reads
the Constitution

E. L. DOCTOROW

Not including the amendments, it is approximately five thousand words long—about the length of a short story. It is an enigmatically dry, unemotional piece of work, tolling off in its monotone the structures and functions of government, the conditions and obligations of office, the limitations of powers, the means for redressing crimes and conducting commerce. It makes itself the supreme law of the land. It concludes with instructions on how it can amend itself, and undertakes to pay all the debts incurred by the states under its indigent parent, the Articles of Confederation.

It is no more scintillating as reading than I remember it to have been in Mrs. Brundage's seventh-grade civics class at Joseph H. Wade Junior High School. It is five thousand words but reads like fifty thousand. It lacks high rhetoric and shows not a trace of wit, as might be expected of the product of a committee of lawyers. It uses none of the tropes of literature to create empathetic states in the mind of the reader. It does not mean to persuade. It abhors metaphor as nature abhors a vacuum.

"A Citizen Reads the Constitution" was originally a talk given under the auspices of the Pennsylvania Humanities Council in September 1986. It appeared in slightly different form in *The Nation* on February 21, 1987.

One's first reaction upon reading it is to rush for relief to an earlier American document:

> We hold these truths to be self-evident, that all men are created equal, that they are endowed by their Creator with certain unalienable Rights, that among these are Life, Liberty and the pursuit of Happiness. That to secure these rights, Governments are instituted among Men, deriving their just powers from the consent of the governed. That whenever any Form of Government becomes destructive of these ends, it is the Right of the People to alter or to abolish it, and to institute new Government.

That is the substantive diction of a single human mind— Thomas Jefferson's, as it happens—even as it speaks for all. It is engaged in the art of literary revolution, rewriting history, overthrowing divine claims to rule and genealogical hierarchies of human privilege as cruel frauds, defining human rights as universal and distributing the source and power of government to the people governed. It is the radical voice of national liberation, combative prose lifting its musketry of self-evident truths and firing away.

Surely I am not the only reader to wish that the Constitution could have been written out of something of the same spirit? Of course, I know instinctively that it could not, that statute writing in the hands of lawyers has its own demands, and those are presumably precision and clarity, which call for sentences bolted at all four corners with *whereins* and *whereunders* and *thereofs* and *thereins* and *notwithstanding the foregoings*.

Still and all, an understanding of the Constitution must come of an assessment of its character as a composition, and it would serve us to explore further why it is the way it is. Here is something of the circumstances under which it was written.

The Background

The Constitutional Convention was called in the first place because in the postwar world of North America influential men in the government, in the Continental Congress, were not confident that the loosely structured Articles of Confederation, as written, could make permanent the gains of the Revolution. Without the hated British to unite them the states would revert to bickering and mutual exploitation. They had as many problems with one another as the classes of people in each state had among themselves, and men like George Washington and James Madison foresaw a kind of anarchy ensuing that would lead to yet another despotism, either native or from foreign invasion by the Spanish or again by the English. Many competing interests were going unmediated. The agrarian Southern states, with their tropical rice and cotton plantations, saw danger to themselves in export taxes applied to all their goods by the North Atlantic port states. The small states, like Delaware, felt threatened by their bigger neighbors, such as Pennsylvania. There was immense debt as a result of the Revolution, which debtors wanted to pay off with state-issued paper money—and which creditors, security holders, bankers, merchants, men of wealth, wanted returned in hard currency. There were diverse ethnic and religious communities, black slaves, white indentured servants. And there were Indians in the woods. The states not contiguous had little in common with one another. To a New Yorker, South Carolina was not the South; it was another kingdom entirely, with people of completely different backgrounds and with bizarre manners in speech and deportment—foreigners, in short. Georgia and South Carolina depended on slave labor to run their plantations. Slavery was abhorrent to many Northerners in 1787, and an economy of slaves was morally detestable.

It is important to remember that colonial society had existed for 150 years before the idea of independence caught on. That's a long time, certainly long enough for an indigenous class of great wealth to arise and a great schism to emerge between the rich and the poor. A very few people owned most of the land and were keenly resented. Three percent of the population controlled fifty percent of the wealth. People were not stupid; there was general knowledge of the plunder, legal chicanery, favoritism, privilege of name, and corruption of government officials that had created such inequity. In fact, it is possible that organization of public sentiment against King George is exactly what saved the colonies from tearing themselves apart with insurrections of the poor against the rich; that events like the Boston Tea Party and calls to arms by Jefferson and Tom Paine created the common enemy, the British, to unify all the classes in America and save, by diversion of anger and rage to the redcoats, the fortunes and hides of the American upper class. This was the class, as it happened, of most of the fifty-five men who convened in Philadelphia. Washington was perhaps the largest landowner in the country. Benjamin Franklin possessed a considerable fortune, and Madison owned several slave plantations.

There was an additional factor to make them sensitive. The convention had been called to consider amendments to the Articles of Confederation. The Continental Congress was even now sitting in New York City and doing government business, and not all that ineffectually. It was, for example, passing legislation outlawing slavery in the western territories. But rather than amending the Articles, the convention in Philadelphia was persuaded to throw them aside entirely and design something new—a federal entity that would incorporate the states. The agenda for this course of action was proposed by Governor Edmund Randolph of Virginia, who presented a number of resolutions for debate, and so it has come to be called the Virginia plan. But the sentiment for something new, a new federal government over and above state sovereignties, had the strong support of influential delegates from several venues. And so the convention got down to business that was actually subversive. It violated its own mandate and began to move in the direction the Federalists pushed it. It was because of this and because no one participating wanted, in the vigorous debates that were to ensue over the next months, to be confronted with a record of his remarks or positions, that the conventioneers agreed to make their deliberations secret for the entire time they sat, permitting no official journal of the proceedings and swearing themselves to a press blackout, as it were. That was to upset Jefferson greatly, who was off in France as a minister; the idea of such secrecy repelled him. Only Madison, fortunately for us, kept a notebook, which did not come to light until 1843 but which provides us the fullest account of those secret deliberations and the character of the minds that conducted them.

The Convention

What a remarkable group of minds they were. The first thing they did was constitute themselves as a Committee of the Whole, which gave them the power of improvisation and debate, flexibility of action, so that when the collected resolutions were decided on they could present them to themselves in plenary session.

Methodically, treating one thorny question after another, they made their stately way through the agenda. If something could not be resolved it was tabled and the next issue was confronted. Nothing stopped their painstaking progress through the maze of ideas and resolutions from which they slowly constructed a new world for themselves: who would make the laws, who would execute them, who would review their judicial propriety; should the small states balk at proportional representation, then the Senate would be created to give equal representation to every state. Some matters were easy to agree on—the writ of habeas corpus, the precise nature of treason. A reader of any of the dramatic reconstructions of their work (there is a small library of such books) has the thrill of watching living, fallible men composing the United States of America and producing its ruling concept of federalism, a system of national and local governments, each with defined powers and separate legal jurisdictions.

Through it all Washington sat up at the front of the room, and he never said a word. The less he said the more his prestige grew. They had settled on one chief executive, to be called a president, and everyone knew who it would be. He had only to sit there to give the delegates courage to persevere. Franklin, too, lent the considerable weight of his presence, only occasionally saying a few soft words or passing up a note to be read by the speaker. Franklin was an old man at the time, over eighty. At one point, when the proceedings were bogging down in dissension, he offered the recommendation that everyone stop and pray. The lawyers were so stunned by this idea that tempers cooled, probably just as he had intended, and the meeting went on.

And as the weeks wore on there slowly emerged among the delegates—or must have—a rising sense of their identity not only as Carolinians or Virginians or New Yorkers but as American nationals. A continental vision of nationhood lit their minds, and a collaborative excitement had to have come over them as day after day, month after month, they fantasized together their nation on paper. One cannot read any account of their deliberations without understanding how they improvised their social inventions from their own debated differences, so that a sort of group intellect arose that was smarter than any one man. It was wise with a knowledge of the way men act with power and from what motives and to what likely ends. This objectification of separate personalities and interests came of a unanimous familiarity with parliamentary method and was finally self-propelling. These men invented a country of language, and that language celebrated—whether in resolutions of moral triumph or moral failure—the idea of law. The idea of a dispassionate law ruling men, even those men who were to make and effect the law.

Enough resolutions having been put forth, a Committee of Detail was formed to get them into an orderly shape, and that was accomplished with the scheme of articles, and sections under the articles, grouping the resolutions about legislative, judicial, and executive branches, the rights and obligations of the states, the supremacy of the Constitution as law, and so on.

When the Committee of Detail had structured the composition and it was duly examined and considered and amended, a Committee of Style was formed—my favorite committee. It comprised William Samuel Johnson of Connecticut, Alexander Hamilton of New York, Madison of Virginia, Rufus King of Massachusetts, and Gouverneur Morris of Pennsylvania. Apparently Morris did the actual writing. And it is this document, produced by the Committee of Style and approved by the convention, that was called the Constitution of the United States. And for the first time in the various drafts there appeared in the Preamble the phrase "We the people of the United States," thus quietly absorbing both the seminal idea of the Declaration of Independence and the continental vision of federalism.

The Voice of the Constitution

So I come back to this question of text. It is true but not sufficient to say that the Constitution reads as it does because it was written by a committee of lawyers. Something more is going on here. Every written composition has a voice, a persona, a character of presentation, whether by design of the author or not. The voice of the Constitution is a quiet voice. It does not rally us; it does not call on self-evident truths; it does not arm itself with philosophy or political principle; it does not argue, explain, condemn, excuse or justify. It is postrevolutionary. Not claiming righteousness, it is, however, suffused with rectitude. It is this way because it seeks standing in the world, the elevation of the unlawful acts of men—

unlawful first because the British government has been overthrown, and second because the confederation of the states has been subverted—to the lawful standing of nationhood. All the *hereins* and *whereases* and *thereofs* are not only legalisms; they also happen to be the diction of the British Empire, the language of the deposed. Nothing has changed that much, the Constitution says, lying; we are nothing that you won't recognize.

But there is something more. The key verb of the text is *shall,* as in "All legislative powers herein granted shall be vested in a Congress of the United States which shall consist of a Senate and a House of Representatives," or "New States may be admitted by the Congress into this Union; but no new State shall be formed or erected within the jurisdiction of any other State." The Constitution does not explicitly concern itself with the grievances that brought it about. It is syntactically futuristic: it prescribes what is to come. It prophesies. Even today, living two hundred years into the prophecy, we read it and find it still ahead of us, still extending itself in time. The Constitution gives law and assumes for itself the power endlessly to give law. It ordains. In its articles and sections, one after another, it offers a ladder to heaven. It is cold, distant, remote as a voice from on high, self-authenticating.

Through most of history kings and their servitor churches did the ordaining, and always in the name of God. But here the people do it: "We the People . . . do ordain and establish this Constitution for the United States." And the word for God appears nowhere in the text. Heaven forbid! In fact, its very last stricture is that "no religious test shall ever be required as a qualification to any office or public trust under the United States."

The voice of the Constitution is the inescapably solemn self-consciousness of the people giving the law unto themselves. But since in the Judeo-Christian world of Western civilization all given law imitates God—God being the ultimate lawgiver—in affecting the transhuman voice of law, that dry monotone that disdains persuasion, the Constitution not only takes on the respectable sound of British statute, it more radically assumes the character of scripture.

The ordaining voice of the Constitution is scriptural, but in resolutely keeping the authority for its dominion in the public consent, it presents itself as the sacred text of secular humanism.

I wish Mrs. Brundage had told me that back in Wade Junior

High School. I wish Jerry Falwell's and Jimmy Swaggart's and Pat Robertson's teachers had taught them that back in their junior high schools.

The Sacred Text

Now, it is characteristic of any sacred text that it has beyond its literal instruction tremendous symbolic meaning for the people who live by it. Think of the Torah, the Koran, the Gospels. The sacred text dispenses not just social order but spiritual identity. And as the states each in its turn ratified the Constitution, usually not without vehement debate and wrangling, the public turned out in the streets of major cities for processions, festivities, with a fresh new sense of themselves and their future.

Every major city had its ship of state rolling through the streets, pulled by teams of horses—a carpentered ship on wheels rolling around the corners and down the avenues in full sail, and perhaps with a crew of boys in sailor uniforms. It was called, inevitably, the Constitution or Federalism or Union. Companies of militia would precede it, the music of fifes and drums surround it, and children run after it, laughing at the surreal delight.

Of all the ratification processions, Philadelphia's was the grandest. There was not only a ship of state, the Union, but a float in the shape of a great eagle, drawn by six horses bearing a representation of the Constitution framed and fixed on a staff, crowned with the cap of Liberty, the words THE PEOPLE in gold letters on the staff. Even more elaborate was a slow-rolling majestic float called the New Roof, the Constitution being seen, in this case, as a structure under which society took secure shelter. The New Roof of the Constitution stood on a carriage drawn by ten white horses. Ornamented with stars, the dome was supported by thirteen pillars, each representing a state; at the top of the dome was a handsome cupola surmounted by a figure of Plenty, bearing her cornucopia. I may smile at the quaint charm of that, but I'm reminded that to this very day we speak of the framers of the Constitution, not the writers, which is more exact and realistic and less mythologically adequate.

Behind the New Roof came 450 architects, house carpenters, saw makers and file cutters, just to let people know there was now a roof-building industry available for everyone.

A thirty-foot-long float displayed a carding machine, a spinning machine of eighty spindles, a lace loom, and a textile printer. There were military units in this procession, companies of light infantry and cavalry, and there were clergymen of every denomination. There were city officials and schools in their entire enrollments, but more prominent were the members of various trades, each dressed in its working clothes and carrying some display or pulling some float in advertisement of itself—sail makers and ship chandlers, cordwainers, coach builders, sign painters, clock- and watchmakers, fringe and ribbon weavers, bricklayers, tailors, spinning-wheel makers, carvers and guilders, coopers, blacksmiths, potters, wheelwrights, tinplate workers, hatters, skinners, breeches makers, gunsmiths, saddlers, stone-cutters, bakers, brewers, barber-surgeons, butchers, tanners, curriers, and, I am pleased to say, printers, booksellers, and stationers.

So heavily weighted was the great Philadelphia procession with those tradesmen and artisans, it could just as easily have been a labor day parade. The newly self-determined America was showing its strength and pride as a republic of hard work, in contrast to the European domains of privilege and title and their attendant poverty system. The Constitution was America de-Europeanizing itself. A kind of fission was taking place, and now here was a working-class republic, carried on the backs first of its citizen-soldiers dressed in rough brown and sober black, and then on the shoulders of its artisans and skilled workers. That anyway was the symbolic idea, the mythology that almost immediately attached itself to the ratified Constitution. From the very beginning it took on a symbolic character that its writers, worried always that they might never get it ratified, could not have foreseen. We speak of the "miracle at Philadelphia." That same impulse was working then: the celebration of the sacred text, miracles being beyond mere human understanding, a cause for wonder and gratitude—in a word, supernatural.

The Subtext

Yet it is true also of sacred texts that when they create a spiritual community, they at the same time create a larger community of the excluded. The Philistines are excluded or the pagans or the unwashed.

Even as the Constitution was establishing its sacred self in the general mind, it was still the work, the composition, of writers; and the writers were largely patrician, not working class. They tended to be well educated, wealthy, and not without self-interest. The historian Carl Degler says in *Out of Our Past*: "No new social class came to power through the doors of the American Revolution. The men who engineered the revolt were largely members of the colonial ruling class." That holds for the Philadelphia fifty-five. They themselves were aware of the benefits, if not to themselves then to their class, of the provision guaranteeing the debts incurred under the Confederation: the security holders, the creditors of America, stood to make a lot of money; at the same time, the debtors—the freeholders, the small farmers—stood to lose everything. It was a practical document in their minds. They did not think of themselves as Founding Fathers or framers or anything more august than a group of men who held natural stewardship of the public welfare by virtue of their experience and background. They were concerned to establish a free and independent nation, but also a national economic order that would allow them to conduct business peaceably, profitably, and in the stable circumstances deriving from a strong central government.

The ideals of political democracy do not always accord with the successful conduct of business. Thus, as the government was conceived in 1787 only the House of Representatives would be elected by popular vote. Senators were to be elected by state legislatures, and the president by an electoral college, meaning men like themselves who would command the votes of their localities. There was the sense in these strictures of a need for checks and balances against popular majorities. Furthermore, to come up with a piece of paper that diverse regional business interests could agree on meant cutting deals. One such deal was between the northeastern states and the southern. Importation of slaves would be allowed for twenty more years; in return only a simple majority in Congress would be required to pass navigational commerce acts that the sea-going Atlantic states much wanted. That odious deal appears, in part, in article 4 of the original Constitution. The exactness and precision of statute language in this case is used not to clarify but to euphemize a practice recognizably abhorrent to the writers:

No person held to service or labour in one State under the laws thereof, escaping into another, shall, in consequence of any law or regulation therein, be discharged from such service or labour, but shall be delivered up on claim of the party to whom such service or labour may be due.

There is no mention of the word *slave*, yet a slave in one state became a slave in all. The Virginia delegate, George Mason, to my mind the great inadvertent hero of the convention, warned his colleagues: "As nations cannot be rewarded or punished in the next world they must in this. By an inevitable chain of causes and effects, Providence punishes national sins by national calamities." If you affect the scriptural voice, he could have been telling them, you had better aspire to enlightenment, or the power of prophecy of your speech will work against you. And so it came to pass. That odious article worked through a historic chain of cause and effect like a powder fuse, until the country blew apart seventy-five years later in civil war. Not until 1865, with the passage of the Thirteenth Amendment, was slavery outlawed in the United States. And the monumental cost in lives, black and white, of that war, and the cost to the black people, the tragedy of their life in the antebellum South, and to American blacks everywhere since then (the state poll taxes that kept black people from voting in the South were not outlawed until the Twenty-Fourth Amendment was ratified, in 1964), shows how potent, how malignly powerful, the futuristic, transhuman Constitution has been where it has been poorly written. What was sacred is profane; there is a kind of blasphemous inversion of the thing.

In this formulation it is the power of the Constitution to amend itself, or, in writers' terms, to accept revision, that shows the delegates at their best. They knew what they had was imperfect, a beginning; Franklin and Washington said as much. Nevertheless, Mason refused to put his name to the constitutional document even after Franklin urged a unanimous presentation to the states—why is still a matter of scholarly argument. I would like to think he balked because of the slavery article and also because there was no Bill of Rights—no explicit statutes on the rights of American citizens to free speech and assembly and religious practice, and to speedy trial by jury of defendants in criminal charges; no prohibition against government search and seizure without judicial warrant; no guarantee of a free press; and so forth. Alexander Hamilton argued that those things were implicit in the Constitution and did not have to be spelled out, much as people now say the Equal Rights Amendment is unnecessary. But in the subsequent debates around the country the lack of a Bill of Rights was a powerful argument against ratification. Imagine where we would be if anti-Federalists such as Patrick Henry had not forced the issue. We would trust our rights and liberties to the reading of the Attorney General, who today believes that people who are defendants in criminal trials are probably guilty or they would not be defendants, and who has said that the American Civil Liberties Union is essentially a criminals' lobby. The first ten amendments were passed on to the states for ratification by the first elected Congress in 1791.

It is true of most of the sacred texts that a body of additional law usually works itself up around the primary material, and also achieves the force of prophecy. The Torah has its Talmud, and the Koran its *hadith*, and the New Testament its apostolic teachings. In like manner we have our sacred secular humanist amendments. Mythic or sacred time is endless, of course, and it was not until 1920, with the passage of the Nineteenth Amendment, that the women of the United States achieved suffrage. (I am told that this amendment has still not been ratified by the state of Georgia.)

Hermeneutics

I notice at this point a certain change of tone: my song of the miracle of Philadelphia has wobbled a bit; my voice has broken, and here I am speaking in the bitter caw of the critic. Yet there is a kind of inevitability to this. One cannot consider the Constitution of the United States without getting into an argument with it. It is the demand of the sacred text that its adherents not just believe in it but engage to understand its meanings, it values, its revelation. The continuing argument with the Constitution shows up every day in the newspapers, as different elements of society represent their versions of its truth. President Reagan argues with it, Attorney General Edwin Meese argues with it, and so, as a defenseless citizen from a different point of view, do I. And, of course, the federal judiciary has amended, interpreted, and derived law from it. From the days of the great John Marshall on down—way down—to the days of William Rehnquist, the courts have not just worshiped the Constitution; they have read it. Their readings are equivalent to the priestly commentaries that accrue to every sacred text, and the commentaries on the commentaries, and we have two hundred years of these as statute and opinion.

It is the nature of the sacred text, speaking from the past to the present and into the future in that scriptural voice that does not explain, embellish itself, provide the source of its ideas or the intentions from which it is written, but which is packed with wild history—the self-authenticating text that is pared of all emotions in the interest of clear and precise law-giving—it is the nature of such a text, paradoxically, to shimmer with ambiguity and to become finally enigmatic, as if it were the ultimate voice of Buddhist self-realization.

And so I find here in my reflections a recapitulation of the debate of American constitutional studies of the past two hundred years, in the same manner that ontogeny was once said to recapitulate phylogeny. Thus it was in the nineteenth century that historians such as George Bancroft celebrated the revolutionary nature of the Founding Fathers' work, praising them for having conceived of a republic of equal rights under law, constructed from the materials of the European Enlightenment but according to their own pragmatic Yankee design—a federalism of checks and balances that would withstand the worst buffetings of history, namely the Civil War, in the aftermath of which Bancroft happened to be writing.

Then in the early part of the twentieth century, when the worst excesses of American business were coming to light, one historian, Charles Beard, looked at old Treasury records and other documents and discovered enough to assert that the Fathers stood to gain personally from the way they put the thing together, at least their class did; that they were mostly wealthy men and lawyers; and that the celebrated system of checks and balances, instead of insuring a distribution of power and a democratic form of government, in fact could be seen as having been devised to control populist sentiment and prevent a true majoritarian politics from operating in American life at the expense of property rights. Madison had said as much, Beard claimed, in *Federalist* number 10, which he wrote to urge ratification. Beard's economic interpretation of the Constitution has ever since governed scholarly debate. At the end of the Depression a neo-Beardian, Merrill Jensen, looked again at the postrevolutionary period and came up with a thesis defending the Articles of Confederation as the true legal instrument of the Revolution, which, with modest amendments, could have effected the peace and order of the states with more democracy than a centralist government. In fact, he argued, there was no crisis under the Articles or danger of anarchy, except in the minds of the wealthy men who met in Philadelphia.

But countervailing studies appeared in the 1950s, the era of postwar conservatism, that showed Beard's research to be inadequate, asserting, for instance, that there were as many wealthy men of the framers' class who were against ratification as who were for it, or that men of power and influence tended to react according to the specific needs of their own states and localities, coastal or rural, rather than according to class.

And in the 1960s, the Kennedy years, a new argument appeared describing the Constitutional Convention above all as an exercise of democratic politics, a nationalist reform caucus that was genuinely patriotic, improvisational, and always aware that what it did must win popular approval if it was to become the law of the land.

In my citizen's self-instruction I embrace all of those interpretations. I believe all of them. I agree that something unprecedented and noble was created in Philadelphia; but that economic class self-interest was a large part of it; but that it was democratic and improvisational; but that it was, at the same time, something of a coup. I think all of those theories are true, simultaneously.

The Two Hundredth Year

And what of constitutional scholarship today, in the Age of Reagan?

Well, my emphasis on text, my use of textual analogy, responds to the work over the past few years of a new generation of legal scholars who have been arguing among themselves as to whether the Constitution can be seen usefully as a kind of literary text, sustaining intense interpretive reading—as a great poem, say—or better perhaps as a form of scripture. I have swiveled to embrace both of those critiques too, but adding, as a professional writer, that when I see the other professions become as obsessively attentive to text as mine is, I suspect it is a sign that we live in an age in which the meanings of words are dissolving, in which the culture of discourse itself seems threatened. That is my view of America under Reagan today: in literary critical terms, I would describe his administration as deconstructionist.

And so, by way of preservation, text consciousness may have arisen among us, law professors no less than novelists, as in medieval times monks began painstakingly copying the crumbling parchments to preserve them.

All told, it is as if the enigmatic constitutional text cannot be seen through, but, shimmering in ambiguity, dazzles back at each generation in its own times and struggles. It is as if the ambiguity is not in the text but in us, as we struggle in our natures—our consciences with our appetites, our sense of justice with our animal fears and self-interests—just as the Founding Fathers struggled so with their Constitution, providing us with a mirror of ourselves to go on shining, shining back at us through the ages, as the circumstances of our lives change, our costumes change, our general store is transformed into a mile-long twenty-four-hour shopping mall, our trundle carts transmogrify into rockets in space, our country paves over, and our young Republic becomes a plated armory of ideological warfare: a mirror for us to see who we are and who we would like to be, the sponsors of private armies of thugs and rapists and murderers, or the last best hope of mankind.

It may be that as a result of World War II and the past forty years of our history we are on the verge, as a nation, of some characterological change that neither the Federalists of the convention nor the anti-Federalists who opposed them could have foreseen or endorsed. We are evolving under *realpolitik* circumstances into a national military state—with a militarized economy larger than, and growing at the expense of, a consumer economy; a militarized scientific-intellectual establishment; and a bureaucracy of secret paramilitary intelligence agencies—that becomes increasingly self-governing and unlegislated. There may be no news in any of this. What may be news, however, is the extent to which the present administration has articulated a rationale for this state of being, so that the culture too, both secular and religious, can be seen as beginning to conform to the needs of a national security state. More than any previous administration this one apotheosizes not law but a carelessness or even contempt of law, as internationally it scorns the World Court and domestically it refuses to enforce federal civil-rights statutes or honor the decrees of judicial review, or gives into private hands the conduct of foreign policy outlawed by the Congress. And more than any previous administration this one discourses not in reason and argument but in demagogic pieties. Its lack of reverence for law and contempt for language seem to go hand in hand.

By contrast, I call attention to the great genius of the convention of 1787, which was its community of discourse. The law it designed found character from the means of its designing. Something arose from its deliberations, however contentious, and that was the empowering act of composition given to people who know what words mean and how they must be valued. Nobody told anybody else to love it or leave it; nobody told anybody else to go back where they came from; nobody suggested disagreement was disloyalty; and nobody pulled a gun. Ideas, difficult ideas, were articulated with language and disputed with language and took their final fate, to be passed or rejected, as language. The possibility of man-made law with the authority, the moral imperative, of God's law, inhered in the process of making it.

That is what we celebrate as citizens today. That is what we cherish and honor, a document that gives us the means by which we may fearlessly argue ourselves into clarity as a free and unified people. To me the miracle at Philadelphia was finally the idea of democratic polity, a foot in the door of the new house for all man and womankind. The relentless logic of a Constitution in the name of the people is that a national state exists for their sake, not the other way around. The undeviating logic of a Constitution in the name of the people is that the privilege of life under its domain is equitable, which is to say, universal. That you cannot have democracy only for yourself or your club or your class or your church or your clan or your color or your sex, for then the word doesn't mean what it says. That once you write the prophetic text for a true democracy—as our forefathers did in their draft and as our amending legislators and judiciary have continued to do in their editing of its moral self-contradictions and methodological inadequacies—that once this text is in voice, it cannot be said to be realized on earth until all the relations among the American people, legal relations, property relations, are made just.

And I reflect now, in conclusion, that this is what brought the people into the streets in Philadelphia two hundred years ago, the wheelwrights and coach builders and ribbon and fringe weavers:

the idea that the United States of America was unprecedented, and the faith that it would come to pass.

I'd like to think, in this year of the bicentennial celebration, that the prevailing image will be of those working people taking to the streets, those people owning only their wit and their skills, forming their processions: the wheelwrights and fringe and ribbon weavers; the railroad porters and coal miners; the steel workers, the ladies garment workers, the automobile and farm workers; the telephone operators, the air traffic controllers, the computer programmers, and, one hopes, the printers, stationers, and booksellers too.

Notes

A good annotated constitutional text at the secondary-school level is Bruce and Esther Findlay, *Your Rugged Constitution* (Stanford: Stanford University Press, 1952). Of the available dramatic reconstructions of the Constitutional Convention of 1787, I relied most heavily on Carl Van Doren, *The Great Rehearsal* (New York: Viking, 1948). All popular studies of the convention depend on the original scholarship of Max Farrand, whose *The Framing of the Constitution of the United States* (New Haven: Yale University Press, 1913) is a classic contribution.

My view of the sociopolitical ferment in America before and after the Revolution owes much to Howard Zinn's *A People's History of the United States* (New York: Harper & Row, 1980), a bracing antidote to complacent historiography, and to J. C. Furnas, *The Americans* (New York: Putnam's, 1969), a wonderfully compendious examination of daily life from the colonial period to the twentieth century. My summary of the scholarly debate from Bancroft and Beard on through the 1960s would have been difficult without *Essays on the Making of the Constitution*, ed. Leonard W. Levy (New York: Oxford University Press, 1969). This astute anthology presents the central ideas of the major constitutional historians in excerpt, thus relieving the lay person of extended and perhaps unseemly acts of scholarship.

Finally, although the following scholars may take exception to the uses I've made of their work, I credit my conversion to constitutional scripturalism to James Boyd White, "The Judicial Opinion and the Poem: Ways of Reading, Ways of Life," *Michigan Law Review* 82 (1984): 1669, and "Law as Language: Reading Law and Reading Literature," *Texas Law Review* 60 (1982): 415; Thomas C. Grey, "The Constitution as Scripture," *Stanford Law Review* 37 (1984): 1; and Sanford Levinson, "The Constitution in American Civil Religion," *Supreme Court Review*, ed. Philip B. Kurland and Gerhard Casper (Chicago: University of Chicago Press, 1979), pp. 123–51.

Contributors

THOMAS BENDER, Professor of History and Chair of the Department of History at New York University, is the author of *Community and Social Change in America, The New York Intellect: A History of Intellectual Life in New York City from 1750 to the Beginnings of Our Own Time,* and *Toward an Urban Vision: Ideas and Institutions in Nineteenth-Century America.*

LESLIE C. BERLOWITZ, Deputy Vice President for Academic Affairs and Director of the Humanities Council of New York University, is co-editor of *America in Theory.* She is at work on a study of the novels of Bernard Malamud.

JOHN BRADEMAS became thirteenth President of New York University in 1981. Before coming to NYU, he served as United States Representative from Indiana for twenty-two years, the last four as Majority Whip, the third-ranking leadership post in the House. During his service in Congress, he played a principal role in writing most major federal education legislation as well as measures in support of the arts and humanities. He is a graduate of Harvard University and of Oxford University, where he studied as a Rhodes Scholar and earned his doctorate. He is the author of *Washington, D.C. to Washington Square* and, with Lynne P. Brown, *The Politics of Education: Conflict and Consensus on Capitol Hill.*

McGEORGE BUNDY, Professor of History at New York University and former President of the Ford Foundation, served as Special Assistant to the President for National Security in the Kennedy and Johnson administrations. Professor Bundy's books include *On*

Active Service, The Strength of Government, Pattern of Responsibility, U.S. Interests and Global Natural Resources, and *Presidential Promises and Performance.*

JAMES CHACE, former editor of *Foreign Affairs,* is a member of the Editorial Board of the *New York Times Book Review,* the Council on Foreign Relations, and the International Institute for Strategic Studies. Mr. Chace is the author of *Endless War: How We Got Involved in Central America and What Should Be Done, Solvency: The Price of Survival, A World Elsewhere: The New American Foreign Policy,* and *The Rules of the Game.*

JOHN PATRICK DIGGINS, Professor of History at the University of California at Irvine, is the author of *The American Left in the Twentieth Century, Up from Communism: Conservative Odysseys in American Intellectual History,* and *The Lost Soul of American Politics: Virtue, Self-Interest, and the Foundations of Liberalism.*

E. L. DOCTOROW, the distinguished novelist and essayist, is Lewis and Loretta Glucksman Professor of American Letters at New York University. Professor Doctorow is the author of *Welcome to Hard Times, Big as Life, The Book of Daniel, Ragtime*—for which he received the National Book Critics Circle Award for Fiction—*Loon Lake,* and *Lives of the Poets.*

DENIS DONOGHUE, Henry James Professor of English and American Letters and Co-Chair of the Humanities Council at New York University, is a noted literary and cultural critic whose works include *The Sovereign Ghost, Ferocious Alphabets, The Arts Without Mystery,* and *We Irish.* Professor Donoghue is co-editor of *America in Theory.*

NORMAN DORSEN, Stokes Professor of Law and Director of the Hays Civil Liberties Program at New York University, is a former President of the American Civil Liberties Union and has written extensively on civil rights. His books include *Our Endangered Rights, Discrimination and Civil Rights,* and *Frontiers of Civil Liberties.*

DANIEL M. FOX, Vice President of Health Sciences at the State University of New York at Stony Brook, is the author of *The Discovery of Abundance: Simon N. Patten and the Transformation of Social Theory, Economists and Health Care: From Reform to Relativism,* and *Health Policies, Health Politics: The British and American Experience, 1911–1965.*

GERALD HOLTON, Mallinckrodt Professor of Physics and Professor of the History of Science at Harvard University, is the author of many works on the history of science, including *Science and Culture, The Scientific Imagination, The Advancement of Science and Its Burdens,* and *Science and the Modern Mind.*

MICHAEL B. KATZ, Professor of History and Director of the Urban Studies Program at the University of Pennsylvania, is the author of *Poverty and Policy in American History, The Social Organization of Early Industrial Capitalism, In the Shadow of the Poorhouse: A Social History of Welfare in America,* and *Reconstructing American Education.*

LOUIS MENAND, who teaches in the Department of English at Queens College of the City University of New York, is the author of *Discovering Modernism: T. S. Eliot and His Context.* He is co-editor of *America in Theory.*

NELL IRVIN PAINTER, Professor of History at Princeton University, is the author of *The Narrative of Hosea Hudson: His Life as a Negro Communist in the South, Exodusters: Black Migration to Kansas after Reconstruction,* and *Standing at Armageddon: The United States, 1877–1919.*

ROBERT L. PAYTON, Professor of Philanthropic Studies and Director of the Center on Philanthropy at Indiana University, is former President of the Exxon Education Foundation. Professor Payton has also served as United States Ambassador to the Republic of Cameroon, President of C. W. Post College of Long Island University, and President of Hofstra University.

J. R. POLE, Rhodes Professor of American History and Institutions and Fellow of St. Catherine's College, Oxford University, is the author of a number of works on American political history, including *The Pursuit of Equality in American History, The Gift of Government: Political Responsibility from the English Restoration to American Independence,* and *The American Constitution: For and Against.*

DEBORAH L. RHODE is Professor of Law and Director of the Institute for Research on Women and Gender at Stanford University. Professor Rhode, who served as law clerk to the Honorable Thurgood Marshall, Associate Justice of the United States Supreme Court, has published extensively on the legal profession, legal ethics, and gender discrimination. Among her recent publications are *The Legal Profession: Responsibility and Regulation* (with Geoffrey Hazard), *Justice and Gender,* and *Theoretical Perspectives on Sexual Difference* (forthcoming).

DAVID A. J. RICHARDS, Professor of Law at New York University, is the author of *A Theory of Reason for Action, Sex, Drugs, Death and the*

Law: An Essay on Human Rights and Overcriminalization, and *Toleration and the Constitution.*

JOHN E. SEXTON, Professor of Law and Dean of the School of Law at New York University, is an expert in law and religion. Dr. Sexton, who served as law clerk to Warren Burger, former Chief Justice of the United States Supreme Court, is the author of *How Free Are We? What the Constitution Says We Can and Cannot Do* and *Redefining the Supreme Court's Role: A Theory of Managing the Federal Judicial Process.*